D1539839

WRITING LIVES

This delightful collection brings together the older generation of
Virago's writers with their younger successors, who interview
them, creating a wide-ranging picture of twentieth-century
women's writing. Novelists, journalists, poets and historians recall
their childhoods and early years, and tell how the challenges and
demands of everyday life interacted with their literary endeavour.
Their creativity is not confined to writing, but spills over into the
essence of their lives, into personal relationships, family life and
politics. The voices in this book evoke a variety of cultures, classes
and backgrounds and include such writers as Maya Angelou,
Kathleen Dayus, Dorothy Hewett, Molly Keane, Rosamond
Lehmann, Paule Marshall, Naomi Mitchison, Grace Paley, Mary
Stott and Eudora Welty talking of why and when, how and where
they wrote.
Representing not only the range of writers published by Virago, but
the tremendous variety of women's writing in this century, these
memories fascinate and enlighten us in what they tell of the process
of creativity. They make a valuable testament, since for some of
these authors – including Phyllis Shand Allfrey and Dora Russell –
the interviews in this book are their last recorded
statements on their life and work.

WRITING LIVES

Conversations Between Women Writers

Edited by
Mary Chamberlain

PR
116
.W75
1988

Published by VIRAGO PRESS Limited 1988
Centro House, 20–23 Mandela Street, London NW1 0HQ

This collection and introduction copyright © Mary Chamberlain 1988

Copyright © in each contribution held by contributor 1988

All rights reserved

British Library Cataloguing in Publication Data

Writings lives: a celebration.
    1. Women authors—Interviews   2. English
    literature—Women authors—History
    and criticism   3. English literature—
    20th century—History and criticism
    I. Chamberlain, Mary
    820.9′9287   PR116

    ISBN 0-86068-708-2

Book designed by Sue Lacey

Typeset by Goodfellow & Egan of Cambridge

Printed in Great Britain by
St Edmundsbury Press Limited, Bury St Edmunds, Suffolk

21328772

Contents

Illustrations

Acknowledgements and thanks are due to the following for the use of photographs reproduced in this book.

Tim Richmond (Maya Angelou); Susan Mullally (Rosa Guy); Nick White (Pieta Monks); Laurie Andrew Photography (Marjorie Barnard); John Petherbridge (Zoë Fairbairns); Australia-Newcastle Herald Picture Service (Dora Birtles); Ballarat Courier Pty Ltd (Joyce Nicholson); Birmingham Post & Mail (Kathleen Dayus); Peter Aspé (Mary Chamberlain); Leslie Jean-Bart (Elizabeth Hardwick); Marianne Majerus (Helen McNeil); William Bowes (Sally Alexander); Dermot Donohue (Molly Keane); Steven Hyde (Polly Devlin); Albert Fenton (Mary Lavin); Carcanet & Arlen House (Eavan Boland); Don Pierce (Paule Marshall); Ellen Shub (Mary Helen Washington); Angela Catlin (Naomi Mitchison); Jane Monroe (Alison Hennegan); The Guardian (Grace Paley & Dora Russell); Ben Thompson (Cathy Porter); Christopher Cormack (Phyllis Shand Allfrey); Sally Greenfield (Mary Stott); Jill Krementz (Eudora Welty); London Weekend TV (Hermione Lee).

Editor's Introduction

*T*HIS ANTHOLOGY is, unashamedly, a celebration. It is a celebration of the Virago Press, and of women writers. On 13 June 1973 Virago received its articles of incorporation. That same year, it commissioned its first book which, in conjunction with Quartet Books, came out in September 1975. At the end of 1976, Virago began to publish independently of Quartet. By the end of that first year, 1977, it had published ten titles. Since then, it has published over five hundred. It was the child of a radical movement and still retains its radical impulse. But it has also become popular press, a commercial success, and a publishing legend.

The dream of Virago, and its success, is largely due to Carmen Callil whose brainchild it was, and to Ursula Owen and Harriet Spicer the original co-directors and workers. I first met Carmen in 1973, in her flat in Smith Street which, then, doubled as Virago's offices. I was a raw and untried author, an innocent in publishing and, indeed, writing. It is significant, and indicative, that Carmen took a risk on an unknown and untried writer rather than plump for a safe and established author.

By 1975, Virago was still run from home, but from a larger flat. Carmen, Ursula, and Harriet paid each other bare subsistence wages. In 1978 they were joined by Alexandra Pringle and Lennie Goodings, and in 1980 by Kate Griffin. Virago, now, employs eighteen women. It joined the Chatto & Windus, Bodley Head, Jonathan Cape group in 1982. In 1987 when Random House bought this group, Virago decided that it would be better, in a world of increasing publishing conglomerates, to become independent again, and the management bought the company back.

But the chronology of a press conveys neither its history nor its significance. The revolution that was Virago is, perhaps, too familiar now to be appreciated. First, it proved there was a market and helped to establish it. Virago commissioned new writers in fiction, politics, health, autobiography, history, popular culture and poetry. Not only was there a *significant demand for women's writing, but there were also hundreds of neglected women writers out of print for years. Most of those interviewed in this anthology owe a contemporary popularity to Virago's reprints – their renowned Modern Classics series. Almost all of those who have done the interviewing can thank Virago for publishing them at some stage in their career. When Virago began, there were many who still argued that women, as readers and writers, constituted neither a significant public nor talent. In the wake of Virago's success have come other feminist presses and imprints. There are now many major publishers which have their own special women's list.*

But within publishing, too, Virago innovated. It was among the first to issue the 'trade paperback' and one of the few to publish hardback and paperback simultaneously. Until then, a book would have to 'prove' itself in hardback before it qualified for a paperback edition, usually with a separate publisher. But with simultaneous publication, it became possible for the author to reap immediate paperback sales from a critical success.

Then there is that distinctive livery and design. Until the advent of the 'trade paperback', paperbacks laboured under the yoke of the 'cheap edition'. Virago changed that, too, and brought to the paperback edition a standard of style and design that raised it to the ranks of 'quality' editions. It brought to the paperback a new aestheticism, and to Virago a distinctive trade cover whose only parallel then, was with the launch of Penguin books in 1936. The green spine on the Virago stand is now a familiar feature in the local bookshop. Although the use of paintings for covers had been begun with Penguin, Virago's use of painting, retaining more of the image and using less familar artists, combined with an elegance of design, quickly came to dominate the field of book design.

The history of any publishing house is really located within its writers. Virago was the first mainstream feminist press, run by women, and publishing books by women. From the start it sought a readership beyond the ghetto of the committed. Many of its readers are feminist; as many are not; many are women, but many, also, are men. The point was never to preach to the converted, to find a channel for publication for the few. The point was always to create a consciousness in which the sheer scope and quality of women's writing could be recognized for what it was: good writing. Yet women who write have laboured, and still do, under peculiar conditions. Virago has helped change the critical climate under which women writers are received and has helped make the publishing environment more receptive.

But the domestic circumstances of most women writers wear away at their time and concentration; it requires a special dedication to produce a written work, creativity squeezed by and between the myriad distractions of home. Few women have a partner who will keep the world at bay and the children from the door. For many women, writing is their livelihood, for which there is so little time.

I wanted this anthology to be as much about why women write as how they write, about motivations and logistics. But it is an anthology of interviews or conversations. Each interview is its own product, made of the relationship between two writers of different generations and reflecting the preoccupations and silences of each.

We hear the voices and the memories of the authors. But memory lapses and lies, and its prompts and pauses expose the mind's murkier side. Creativity draws on memory, presents it in an aesthetic form. But memory recorded through speech is often a raw document. Its hesitancies, its repetitions expose the process of writing, as well as the writer. Memory's silences and syllogisms speak, cause pain and refusals. The rhythms of speech duplicate the rhythms of the mind. A life history teased out by another is a less prepared document than a thought-through autobiography. While it can ask different questions and make separate connections within the variables of an individual's life, it can also expose the writer's vulnerability.

The spoken word is forced into a literary strait-jacket not of its choosing and for which it was never intended. Some writers felt deeply unhappy about the medium, for the result was not how they read, or heard, themselves. A few, therefore, reworked their interview. Others simply could not face its publication.

The motivation to change must be at the heart of any writer. Writing exposes not only the self, but a self view of the world, and the energy it requires is too charged to be confined to a single act of creativity. Creativity rarely confines itself to writing, but spills over into the very circumstances of lives – into politics, or education, into a desire to make the writer's world, and that of others, more humane. This drive to expose, to change, can be global or familial. But it is a common theme and unites the varied testimonies collected here.

The writers presented in this anthology come from a variety of continents, cultures and classes, and show a diversity of skill and circumstance. I hope it is indicative not only of the diversity of Virago's publications, but of the range of writing talent and directions. Represented here is a selection of writers whose work spans this century, and whose lives reflect most of the social and domestic conditions and most of the political and cultural movements of the Western world in the twentieth century.

It was important that these memories be collected here before they be lost forever and with them an essential part of women's history and culture. Variety was a clear criterion for the choice, but time and space constrained the voices. Many of the writers whom we would like to have chosen were simply, and sadly, dead. Others felt they could add no more to a life lived through words and wished to be left peacefully to their ancient frailty. From those we chose, some like Dora Russell and Phyllis Shand Alfrey, have died since their interviews and these represent their last public utterances.

The choice was made principally by Carmen Callil, Ursula Owen and Alexandra Pringle at Virago who best know the representatives of their own press, and with their help I 'matched' the interviewers. Without their profound inside knowledge, and without their help, advice and support, this anthology could not have been compiled. But then, without them and the others who now work in Virago, Virago itself would never have been.

Mary Chamberlain
London, 1987

Postscript: Very special thanks are due to Anna Davin who, as a true friend, came to my aid by checking these proofs – thereby enabling me to pack and transport abroad my entire household. Anna sacrificed her very valuable time and space to come to my rescue. It is deeply and warmly appreciated.

WRITING
LIVES

Maya Angelou
talking with
Rosa Guy

MAYA ANGELOU *and* ROSA GUY *stand apart in this anthology. Close friends for over twenty-five years, they chose not to present
an interview but allow us a glimpse, through conversation, at the
intellectual, political and emotional depth of their relationship.*

*Rosa Guy, though born in Trinidad, grew up in Harlem. She started
factory work at fourteen. Realizing that she got the worst jobs because
she was Black, she became involved first with unions at her workplaces
and then in the larger struggle for Black freedom. She also started to
write, for the stage, and then novels. She was a founder member of the
Harlem Writers' Guild and is the author of* A Measure of Time *(Virago
1984) and a number of novels for young adults including* Friends, Ruby
and My Love, My Love *(Virago 1987). She lives in New York.*

2

Maya Angelou was born in 1928 in St. Louis, Missouri but grew up in Stamps, Arkansas and California. She has been a waitress, singer, dancer, Black activist, editor and mother. In her twenties she toured Europe and Africa with Porgy and Bess. *Moving to New York she joined the Harlem Writers' Guild and continued to earn her living as a night club singer and performer in Genet's* The Blacks. *She became involved in Black struggles in the 1960s and then spent several years in Ghana as editor of* African Review. *Maya Angelou has published several volumes of poetry including* And Still I Rise *(Virago 1987) and her five volume autobiography, published by Virago, has been widely acclaimed. She is now Reynolds Professor of American Studies at Wake Forest University in North Carolina.*

M.A. How did you decide to become a writer? You're Black, female and a Trinidadian . . .

R.G. I wanted to be an actress. But I didn't look exactly like Hilda Simms and that was the type they liked, very pale and very pretty hair . . .

M.A. Pretty hair? You mean hair like white folks?

R.G. Yeah. Like white folks. I decided to write my own play and put myself into it. I had my first play done off Broadway. From then on I considered myself a playwright. But the canvas proved too restrictive. I decided to try the short story. And then that too was restricted . . .

M.A. I want to go back to 'pretty hair'. It's of particular interest that you, whom I know personally to have been engaged in the projection of the concept of Black beauty long before the phrase 'black is beautiful' became popular, would use the phrase 'pretty hair' meaning straight hair, white folks' hair. That shows the profound power of the self destructive-image –

R.G. – that we are burdened with, even in the West Indies where I was born. We were taught that you didn't go round with a person who was 'pickey headed'. We have to fight through a lot of things, and the first is the self image that was given to us. We've had to struggle through a lot of things that other people generally don't. It's particularly true in the Western hemisphere. Isn't that why we both straighten our hair?

M.A. There is that contradiction in knowing that one is gorgeous and lovely, in good health and about the size one wants to be, and feels sexy and sensual, that one is attractive. There is that and at the same time there is the contradiction of it. And then to be Black and female as opposed to being white and male is a total contradiction. A double contradiction.

R.G. We were demeaned yet always had to aspire to freedom – the heights. Our ambition was nurtured by the Western society – the same society which said that you're female. You're Black. You can't climb here. That probably made us strong.

M.A. Using the canvas of contradiction, I'd like us to talk about deciding to be literary, a part of the literature which, in Western society, has been, and probably will be, dominated by white men. When people talk about American literature, they really mean Hemingway, Faulkner and Poe and when they do include women it's Emily Dickinson and Edna St Vincent Millay. To decide to take that on and say, 'I will speak and will be heard' – that takes a lot of guts.

4

R.G. Historically the Black American woman has been forced into this position. There had to be a certain period in the history of Black folks when the women had to say, 'Look, this is what's happening.' Literature is an emotional history of what is happening at a specific time, at a specific place. And so our literature is as meaningful as any. Perhaps even more because of a changing world. The world is so small . . . We are the tools of the progression of people's understanding. We're saying we are here, and we are . . .

The courage that it takes to break through so many different barriers is always intriguing. It takes a lot to decide you're not going to live a certain type of life. For instance, when you were a prostitute and you decided to make this break because of your son. I could understand that. What always impresses me is how did you come to the point where you decided?

M.A. The only two things I've ever loved in my life are dancing and writing. I have a belief that if you don't love something, you'll never be great at it. I made my living as a singer, but I never loved it. But I loved to dance as much as I loved writing, but by twenty-two my knees were gone and so there was no chance of ever achieving the best I had to give in that, and I never loved anything else but writing. To love it and have that sense of achievement when you almost got the sentence right.

R.G. Didn't you feel that sometimes you had to prove yourself? Feeling rejected by your mother, having to go through the traumas of being rejected and not being able to reach her, feeling that cold core that you couldn't reach. Did you feel bitter?

M.A. Bitterness is a different word. Anger. Bitterness is like cancer. It eats upon the host. But anger is like fire. It burns it all clean. I was very angry. I haven't stopped being angry at a number of things. I saw my mother once between the time I was three and thirteen. As far as I know, I got one letter, one package from her in those ten years with a little white doll. The very idea! I was young and all that, but I knew that this was an insult and I convinced myself that she was dead and somebody else who couldn't have been my mother had sent me this doll.

R.G. But those are the angers that people rarely live through. Children have a tendency to hold more against their parents than anybody else. Even when they feel that it's all been worked out, they remember.

M.A. You remember, you don't forget. But I think the reason I've been able to be successful, not just as a writer, but as a woman and as a

5

person is that at about twenty-two – Guy, my son, was already seven or six – for some incredible reason, I saw my mother separate from me. Absolutely separate. And I thought, I see, you're not really my mother, the mother I wanted and needed; you're a character. And I began to see her like a character I would have read about. Now that didn't mean that in lonely or bitter or painful moments I didn't still want her to be that big-bosomed, open-armed, steady, consistent person. But I'd say that 60 per cent of the time I saw her as a character. Then it grew to be 70 per cent. Then 80. And then my own resistance allowed me to accept her as the character.

R.G. I still go back to that resentment against people who have rejected us at a particular time. Somewhere in the mind it sticks . . .

M.A. We all bring almost unnameable information from childhood. We are unable to shuffle all that particular mortal coil. If we are lucky, we make transitions, and don't live in that time of pain and rejection and loneliness and desolation. But there will understandably be bits of it which adhere to us and will not be pulled off by love nor money. You know? And when you speak of my youth and aloneness, I'm obliged also to think of yours. Being a pre-teen, eight or nine years old, and coming to the United States from the security and awe and beauty and warmth of Trinidad. One of the most poignant pictures I have in my mind is you and your sister in summer dresses coming to New York on a boat –

R.G. – On the coldest day, January, of the year, and freezing on the deck –

M.A. – and having less than the couple of years with your Mom before she died . . .

R.G. Coming to a new country, losing one's mother, and living with an intolerant father, made the first years of my life even more precious; I have relived my youngest years in the West Indies as much as I lived my actual growing years in the United States. Then I got into my rebellious teens. When my father died, I was fourteen and alone – my sister and I were alone, in the United States. It's not easy to be alone even when you're a rebellious teen. If you get angry, there's no one to be angry with. You can't stay angry with someone who died – except to blame them for their own death . . . which I did . . . The struggle just to survive in New York had its telling effect on my sister (and I want to write about her) as well as on me. My sister had such a terrible time taking care of me. In later years she was really bitter against me. I had robbed her of her youth – through no fault of my own. It's strange that

6

when one rebels, one copes much better than someone who gives. My sister gave her youth to protect me and the rest of her life she was vulnerable. She never had a rebellious spirit. She didn't rebel against religion, against society, against anything. She was always begging. She begged me to be good. She begged others to love me, to understand me, to love her. That begging quality followed her into adulthood.

M.A. I don't know, because I look at my brother and myself. I was the one giving and I gave to him although he's older . . .

R.G. But you were angry with your mother. You had anger. My sister never had anger. She had sorrow. She felt abused. She was the orphan. It puts one in a special category; it has its moulding qualities.

M.A. I felt as an orphan –

R.G. – but you had parents. That's where your anger grows. You could get angry with them. When you have no one to get angry with, to react against, you fall in upon yourself . . . I think here is where we may have similarities. We both wanted love, and our lives were so unrestricted, we didn't have our families to say do this and do that, nor support through tragic experiences. A lot of anguish that I live with today come from those tragedies I experienced as a teenager. The pain is so brutal when you're hurt, just asking to be loved . . .

M.A. I know, you're really up for grabs. I know that in my case I was grabbed, and so were you.

R.G. I love deeply. I couldn't ever have a romance without falling madly in love. And each time the young man turned from me, I would suffer intolerably. I went through this process endlessly.

M.A. I know it is endless. We carry that love of the man into our adulthood and into our work.

R.G. There are different levels of love . . . But I always have to say 'I love you' because I have to love.

M.A. That's right. Those I love, my friends; I am in love with my friends. Now, that does not mean that we have sex. But the moment I begin to identify myself with someone . . . and I have the vulnerability of being physically attached I consider myself in danger. That is, there is the possibility that someone can control me. Now no sister friend or brother friend can control me because I'm not vulnerable to that extent.

R.G. To a certain extent all my friends control me – as long as they don't interfere with my work. Then I have a battle within myself. I have a

7

tendency to fall in love. I always hope that once that feeling goes, then a friendship can stay and it's very important.

M.A. I have been in love many times with men with whom I was sexually involved. And they became essential to my life. A break-up of a friendship is terrible. Devastating. But a break-up of a friendship with sex in it is absolutely obliterating. It tears me up – that absolute tearing apart of my body and my mind and my heart and my thoughts and I and romance have been thrown on the floor. I hang over the chairs. I weep . . . I'm very cautious, very, about sexual love . . . I remember your insistence upon your space to work and remember years ago you might have a gentleman friend at your house and you and your friend, lover, would go to bed and in the morning when I'd get up about six you would already have been working. We'd have coffee and I'd ask, 'What happened to your friend?' And you'd say, 'He had to go.' And the first year or so I used to say, 'Damn. All Rosa's lovers are surely early risers.' And finally it was revealed to me that they were awakened and told, 'I'm sorry, but you have to go. I have to work.' And sometimes there would be snow outside . . .

R.G. That's not quite fair! But I do get a restlessness in the morning when I get up and I'm working. Anyone around or very near to me can compute my restlessness. I become another person. I have to work . . .

M.A. When I was married – I've kept the habit now – at five o'clock in the morning there's no sleeping, there's no being with me. I cannot bear it. I don't have to see anybody, I don't have to talk, but try and stay in that ambience of investigation.

R.G. Sometimes people think that you're selfish or self centred. But it isn't that at all. I don't feel selfish.

M.A. Or is it that? And so what?

I want us to look at the question of need. I would like us to look at our own involvement with the immediate past, that is in our lifetime, and then the greater past out of which we came. The writers you read and I read as we were living –

R.G. Most of the writers with whom I was most impressed were the French and Russian writers of another period. The one American writer who stood out to me was Richard Wright – and Dreiser. I took to their naturalism. I was able to understand so much of the country through them. Certainly I understood Black America because of Richard Wright. But then, I had come up through the slums of Harlem and had seen so much of what he wrote about. My writing evolved like that, pulling into me everything in terms of what is happening, particularly to young people of the United States and in the hemisphere. I developed a hemispheric consciousness. I feel particularly well equipped to write about the hemisphere having been born in the West Indies and having suffered the injustices of the North American continent and travelled extremely in that region. When we formed the Harlem Writers' Guild together, John Killens used to say – something I thought very important – you must write as though you are God. I was! Pooling my experiences, my understanding, I was creating my world. My creation which I projected, to give more understanding to the world.

M.A. I started writing when I was mute. I always thought I could write because I loved to read so much. I loved the melody of Poe and I loved Paul Laurence Dunbar. I had memorized so much of Dunbar, Poe, Shakespeare, James Weldon Johnson, Longfellow. When my son was able to be quiet enough to listen, I taught him those poets. A few years ago he gave a reading of his poetry and he started the reading by saying 'First, let me recite to you some of the poets my mother raised me on . . .' In the contemporary world, I confess to having been impressed by Ann Petry. I had *The Street* in my hand, I used to carry it around . . .

In the early 1950s – the Garvey movement – I went to Harlem and saw Black Ethiopia. These were my people and they didn't have accents, but they were Ethiopians. I mean, they didn't have African accents. Those that I listened to spoke just like everybody else and that broadened my light a great deal, my own understanding of our oneness.

R.G. Yes, this oneness, I believe I bring to the literary scene. I was a little girl when I went to my first Garvey parade. My shoes were tight. I had walked for miles before anyone noticed my torment. I was in pain – crawling. Then someone picked me up and put me in a truck. Around that time I was in the midst of a political upheaval, not really understanding a thing about it. I just knew that we West Indians were all for Garvey. I thought we were the only ones conscious of Africa.

Years later when Alpheus Hunton, Lou Burnham and Lorraine Hansberry started *Freedom*, the newspaper in which Paul Robeson wrote, they portrayed Africa – a big black giant, in shackles, ready to break loose. I realized then that there was a large segment of Black America caught up in the African movement, in African history. Before that . . . I remember having a fight in grammar school. I had been

9

talking to a friend . . . an American girl . . . I had ended my remark by saying, 'Anyhow, we all come from Africa!' She answered, 'Oh no, I don't come from Africa.' Whereupon I informed her, 'Your ancestors did.' No, my ancestors did not, she said. 'My ancestors live in New York. Right on 118th Street.' 'No', I insisted, 'they all came from Africa.' She socked me. We ended by pulling each other's hair out in the street . . . There was such a division then. Most Americans didn't want –

M.A. – an African connection. But it must be remembered that in Garvey's heyday, there were not that many West Indians anywhere in the United States. His existence was used as a focal point for the West Indian community and they were able to stay together, but the Black American, without his charisma and his presence, went on into other things. But the tales of the Black American who didn't want to be connected with Africa can be recounted as the West Indians who didn't want to be connected either, who would say, 'I'm a British citizen' . . . The self loathing which is always part of oppression had its way with all of us.

R.G. At the Harlem Writers' Guild we were trying to teach African history in some of the schools to young people . . . and these Black kids would just fall on the floor and laugh. John Henry Clark would get furious and he'd have to tell them about themselves.

M.A. Well, all they had seen was Tarzan. I noticed it in Africa too. There were so many people I encountered who really thought of us all as Rochester. That's who they'd seen. Eddie Rochester, Mantan Moreland, Willie Best, Dorothy Dandridge's aunt, Hattie Daniels. Just the people who were in the movies. Who else did they have? So a hundred people met Dr Dubois, five hundred met Leo Hansberry. But the majority of people, their only connection with us were those movies . . . Then, as one gets a little wiser, a little more erudite, we begin to see the oneness of our struggle. And I think that view influenced both you and me, and those friends we had with whom we became involved in New York.

R.G. Because we were artists struggling to be known and having to fight against the stigma of being Black in the United States. What a struggle! Everything was a struggle.

M.A. Everything. I meant for the political. I'd rather for us to get up and try to lead demonstrations against the horrors that were taking place in Africa, and were taking place in the US . . . We became the radii which came in finally to touch that circle which was our oneness and our responsibility to everybody. We reached the point where we thought we were one with all oppressed people.

R.G. ... a historical development, really. There was also the whole question of activity on the Left. It was all broadening, reaching, and touching each other and broadening. And finally understanding the horrible oppression –

M.A. – in the world. You see, I had gone to a Communist school in the 1940s and had read Marx as an intellectual exercise, not knowing how much had actually gotten down into the old brain. I had had so little real connection with the Left that I must say that in 1956 I met Oscar Brown Jr, Frank London Brown, Big Clyde, Daddy O'Daley in Chicago. There were about eight Black men in Chicago who were political – clear, severe, funny. They knew how to laugh and they influenced both Abby Lincoln and me. We used to sit and talk as you and I talk. And we found no Black men to talk this political, with what was happening in the world and what was happening with Blacks, and shouldn't we call ourselves Black as opposed to negro. Abby and I had decided in California that we were Black. That is what we were and wanted to be called. Black. They put into words for me and for Abby thoughts we had had, but we had never heard articulated by live human beings and live Black men. So by the time in 1957 I got to New York again as a singer, I was singing folk songs, calypso and Black American blues. And I would have for my march-in music 'Lift Every Voice and Sing' in these swank places. I had a decent shape and wore very tight clothes, but I would sing these terrible folk songs about their killing me. My political horizon had been enlarged by so many things so that by the time I met John Killens I became totally politicized. All the people who I admired were thinking as well as I, and better. And articulating as well as I and much better.

R.G. I had been in the American Negro Theatre before. There was Sidney Poitier and Ruby Dee and Alice Childress and Clarice Taylor and Maxwell Glanville, Harry Belafonte, Isabelle Sanford. Just a group of people who really were interested in acting, not politics. They were all for drama. I went to Connecticut, to rescue my marriage. When I came back ANT was no longer in existence. I had no place to go. I kept looking around. I wanted to write. Someone told me about the Jefferson school and I went there. I met Phillip Bonosky there. He had a workshop. I started writing. But I wanted to be in Harlem so I left, and went to join a group called The Committee for the Negro in the

11

Arts. I also met Paul Robeson and Alpheus Hunton. Absolute giants. One could not help but be impressed. Minds were pried open by their keen insight, the manner in which they explained things. One had to join the struggle for the oppressed . . .

M.A. Speaking of giants, let us touch on Malcolm X and how we met him.

R.G. That was an exciting day! That was an exciting time. We had then made our views felt to the world. We had stopped Adlai Stevenson from speaking at the United Nations while protesting about the death of Lumumba. New York was seething. Everyone who had any consciousness was out in the streets. And we were a little upset that Brother Malcolm had not joined, and Madame Maya Angelou decided, well, we have to get this brother to join with us.

M.A. It was so exciting. When neither Malcolm X nor any of the Nation of Islam came to be with us, we were terribly put out and didn't understand. And so, you and I called him and asked for a meeting. And he told us to come to the restaurant the next day; so we went that morning and Malcolm X came in his dark suit and white shirt and tie. Very impressive and very gentlemanly to us – holding our seats while we sat down at the table. Of course, there were the three or four bodyguards who were in the background, and he said to us, 'You're wondering why . . .' I mean, he took over the meeting immediately and said, 'You're wondering why our people did not participate in the demonstration at the United Nations.' And we both said yes. I mean, we were, one would have to see us in those days because we were pretty bold and –

R.G. – very dedicated. As I remember it, although he sympathized with us, their struggle was an entirely different struggle.

M.A. He said the Nation of Islam does not demonstrate. 'We do not have anything to do with asking whites, the blue-eyed devils, for anything,' and so forth. Now, he was really, I thought at the time, talking at cross purposes. I didn't see why he didn't think it was one struggle, but what he did say was so amazing to me because he said he had been called by the *New York Times* and all these different magazines to ask what did he think. That since the Nation of Islam didn't participate, didn't he condemn us? And he said no, he didn't condemn any Black person who did anything, but the Nation of Islam wouldn't. Then he said, 'But I tell you this' – it was like Jesus speaking to Peter and the Disciples – he said, 'Before this time tomorrow, every

12

Black leader they can find will condemn you.' We couldn't believe it. We had met him like mid-morning. It was a bright day and by the time the evening paper came out there was a statement from Roy Wilkins, and almost everybody except A. Philip Randolph. Everybody said that there was implication that these were Communists, these were outsiders who had come in . . .

R.G. And even some of our very close friends were condemning –

M.A. – us as outsiders who are trouble-makers. And that wasn't the way to do it.

R.G. It was really a fantastic demonstration. Also it was a turning point, I feel, even though Malcolm X did not come with us. Malcolm was a fantastic person, I believe, because he was in the process of growth.

M.A. Yes, exactly.

R.G. And he just kept on growing and growing and he never stopped growing. And he changed.

M.A. He certainly changed. And it was wonderful to see it and to be a part of the time in which one could see that kind of growth, and to know it is possible, is encouraging as well. I look at some of the men of the time and think of how they grew . . .

R.G. Would you say they grew because of us? We sort of forced it on them. Because everyone was sitting back . . .

M.A. Yes, us, but us in a very large way because while we happened to be in New York and close to media, there were young men and women at the time who were doing some pretty brave things in other parts of the country.

R.G. Not at that time. Not at that particular time. After. Because one of the things that we saw very clearly at that point: everybody was upset by the death of Patrice Lumumba. Young people in Central America were protesting. Students in Africa, in Europe, in China, but not one in the US. After our demonstration there was a ground swell of students in the United States coming out in support.

M.A. That's true. I hadn't thought about that. The Civil Rights Movement in this country was very active and very inspirational, but was really focused on American civil rights.

R.G. After we demonstrated a group of young students came in from Boston. I remember that particularly. *Freedomways* was being launched. Its reception was given at the home of DuBois. I met the Boston group outside and they said 'You are Rosa Guy!' To them I was

13

a heroine. Really. I mean, they could have put me on their shoulders.

M.A. They almost did that with us in Harlem everytime we go.

R.G. Do you remember this fellow who always had this little cap? He'd say 'You two. You should never be separated. You should never be separated.' And there we were on the street corner shouting and carrying on and drawing a crowd.

M.A. And, really, always talking about Africa. Always . . . There was a qualitative growth in Martin Luther King. To me, having just to see him grow from the American Civil Rights Movement, the passive resistance, the non-violent resistance, and to see him grow into one going to Africa, meeting with Nkrumah, returning, broadening his sight to include all oppressed people (which is why he was killed, of course), so that his poor people's march said, 'I want Black people, poor white, native American, Mexican American, Asian American; I want everybody who is poor, downtrodden and oppressed, come. We will sit in Washington.' I believe this is why Malcolm was killed. When Malcolm said, 'I no longer believe that by nature a person is born evil. I have seen blue-eyed, blond-haired men who I can call brother with a straight face and an open heart.' The minute he said that, he had to be done. If he had kept narrow, he would have remained, you know?

R.G. It was all right to be a Black nationalist and to talk about the blue-eyed devils. It was all right to talk about the establishment, and what should be done to it, or about aspects of life that dealt with Black/white hatred. But the moment that Blacks and whites seemed united, they were always condemned, called Communist or some vicious anti-Americans and were not allowed to parade. They were not granted permits. I've known groups of Blacks and whites at that time trying to obtain permission, licence to parade. They were refused. But the Black nationalists who were violent against whites, for whatever reason, or those who were trying to exploit the newly emerging African nations, were never refused. That was when I realized the establishment feared unity between Blacks and whites. So long as we fought alone, we were ineffective.

M.A. It's fascinating. But these are the things we have seen.

R.G. After that period we were into the Vietnam War. Fantastic whites were joining anti-war movements, anti-oppression movements. But the Kent State massacre. Suddenly it changed and there was once again a complete separation. The whites really didn't believe that they would be killed like we were being trampled on, had been trampled on. And the minute they realized that, they became a little bit more fearful. And the movements all sort of started diminishing.

M.A.   I think that the movements also became more and more particular, more and more exclusive. They began to involve other aspects of the American society with which they didn't agree. So one already got ecology and the struggle for better air, and better earth preservations. And this is coming out of the Civil Rights Movement. There's the anti-war movement which seemed to a number of non-Blacks to be a safer struggle. I'm sorry to say, the women's movement seemed to be a safer struggle. The free student movement seemed to be a safer struggle. If they were all white, if they were not involved with the Blacks, they thought they wouldn't be killed. And they were right.

R.G.   They had to have lost interest in Blacks.

M.A.   They were all right as long as they were not engaged with Blacks . . .

Some of the most distressing subjects which I encounter on university campuses are one, the subject of the schism between Black men and Black women and two, that Black young people have no commitment, no awareness of the struggle and their places in the struggle, and the inheritance which is theirs naturally of triumph, of defeat, of the glory of struggling for equality and fairness which they have inherited by right from the people who went before them. And I wonder, let us take the last subject first, what do you think of young people, young Black people in particular, of today?

R.G.   This generation of young is a generation cut off from their past. They have no role models, no direction and are taking their cues from the movies, the television – that dream world. They to a great extent reject their past history, believing that they have arrived. That is not true, of course. But today there seems a lack of leadership on just about every level – black and white. Strange ideas and ideologies abound. One doesn't know what is going to happen. I'm concerned . . .

M.A.   I find it of effective use to repeat to young people a story which has been in our lore since the nineteenth century, about the Black person who decided because he had a job and a title and a wife who looked like he wanted her to look, and a house with a two-car garage, and all that, that he was beyond the long reach of prejudice and discrimination. Only to find, of course, that if you are Black, you are still, to so

15

many people, that ex-slave, no matter what you wear, no matter what job you have, no matter how clearly you speak or how profoundly you think. And, when I tell that to young Blacks, more often than not, they look at each other disbelievingly. And it's so heartbreaking to me that I also see a generation who will live out that bitter statement, 'He who does not learn from his history is doomed to repeat it.' And I think that, oh, if you could just learn, you might not have to repeat *all* the experiences. But I'm afraid that many will.

There are some young Black women, however, that I particularly want to talk about, younger than I in any case, young Black women who are writing, who are inspirational to me. For example, a group of young women in Atlanta have a magazine called *Sage*. I'm impressed with Gloria Naylor's continuing to work. I'm impressed certainly with Alice Walker. I was hopeful and am still hopeful of Alyse Sutherland who wrote a book many years ago called *Let The Lion Eat Straw*. A wonderful book. Lucille Clifton and Carolyn Rogers and those younger Black women who have not become well known. That they continue to struggle and write is inspirational. Do you think so?

R.G. Yes. There is something that disturbs me, and that is the thinking of the middle class. One of the phenomena in this country is the widening, the deepening, gulf between the haves and have-nots which I find in the devastation of inner-cities throughout the country. There is no concern about the struggle – or lack of it – going on in the inner cities throughout the country. Yet this is where the majority of our next generation of Blacks is emerging. With the progressive use of drugs in the inner cities there is a new, live-for-the-moment, don't-give-a-damn-about-dying, attitude that is being concretized in the streets and being exploited by the drug barons. It's an attitude which needs concern.

When Sonny Bonds, the drug dealer and murderer, was jailed, young Blacks looked up to him as a modern-day Robin Hood. A hero. Making it big. The inner cities might have some of the best-dressed people in the world. The biggest cars. They are single-minded about let's make it. That's what society is about. The American dream as expressed in *Dallas, The Colbys* etc. Too many children are coming into the world and being exposed to only this environment – drugs and the American dream. Crimes are committed in its name. And the middle-class Blacks also condemn them. We are all victimized by the excesses, which is rapidly becoming the norm. But what happens when the Black middle class forget the historical roots of this development?

16

Who then can readjust the imbalances? It's frightening. Young writers coming up must address themselves to this problem. There must be a way to turn the rapid deterioration around. Billions are being spent in world destruction while our Black communities are dying. We need our middle class, our young writers to understand, to raise a hue and cry over this. To at least start a dialogue. There are many good, sincere young writers coming up. Many well-meaning. Gloria Naylor I find to be one of the most fascinating, Lucille Clifton. But the cries and screams from the inner cities must be louder. Must be heard. We can no longer allow ourselves introspection about the days that were, we have to ready ourselves for the battle of days that are coming which are so . . .

M.A. Absolutely new!

R.G. New and terrible, and it needs young minds to address themselves to it. To face the problems.

M.A. I know that many of us of another generation, established writers and so, are looked at almost as if we are relics. But if a near contemporary of theirs . . .

R.G. They do need someone who will speak to them. Shout at them.

M.A. I mean of their type to speak to them. I'm thinking of somebody about twenty-five who is angry, has a burning need to speak for that group.

R.G. Yes, and for everything that it represents and what it will represent because I think that the tragedy is too imminent.

M.A. Now, I'll tell you what is happening. A number of young people are being satisfied with 'rapping'. And so they take this cheapest way out of saying something about the street. And quite often I'm asked, is this poetry? And I say no. That is rapping. There may be poetic lyric, that kind of rhyme structure, AB, AB, ABC; AB, AB, ABC. But most of it, of 100 per cent, 15 per cent may be considered to have poetic imagery in it. Too many young Blacks, as far as I can see it, and young whites for that matter, have been told that if you just tell what you think, that is great writing. Well, that is not so, as we know. Some, in fact, very established Black writers were frigging irresponsible in the 1960s when they told any Black person that if you're Black you can write poetry. Now that is such a lie. The truth is that if you're Black in the US, or any country for that matter, you are living in a poetic existence. In that there is struggle and loss and pain and tears and humiliation and all that. But writing poetry is a different matter. And

17

so a number of young people, I think, today have inherited some of that casual indifference. And so instead of going on to sit down and really tell it –

R.G.   – they become hero-worshippers. They are willing to opt for trying to become big names, and they're not concerned with the quality of struggle, of craftsmanship and struggle. And as we were talking about a while ago, where we have joined the struggle of the world, they have become so fully American. They have no concern, no understanding in actual terms of how their future, or our future is linked with –

M.A.   – Nicaragua –

R.G.   – And South Africa –

M.A.   – the Middle East . . .

I want to go back to the world of Black women, the world of Black women writers. I think first I'd like us to talk about the propensity to build friendship and the need for friendship among Black women. I want us to talk about it because I'm serious about encouraging young Black women not to lose this thing we have had historically, and might be the singular most important aspect of our survival.

R.G.   Do you see a pulling away or a changing from the patterns?

M.A.   I did see it in the Sixties. And it frightened me a great deal because a number of men told a number of women that in order to prove how really loyal and supportive they were they should be like servants to them. They should walk three steps behind them. They couldn't have these binding relationships, these friendships which we have had during slavery, since slavery. During and after slavery, Black women who would have children would always have auntie so-and-so, or cousin so-and-so, or sister so-and-so with whom they could leave the children and go to work. And that was always those friendships which were not only supportive but, I believe, helped us together so that we could be as good mothers as we could be, and as good lovers, and as good wives as we could be. And so, in the Sixties when I saw that waning I became very concerned about where we were going. Now, what I seem to see is a coming back together, a re-establishment of those bonds. But it's not healthy. Quite often young Black women come together to – not to support themselves, but to bemoan their outcast state and to attack Black men, to say Black men are nothing. And to reinforce their own loneliness and aloneness. Not to get joy out of being with a woman friend or sister friend. And it worries me.

18

R.G. I don't know what to say about that, I really don't. I look at the young women I meet in Europe, in the US and educated women in the West Indies. Many of them are alone. Many are involved in professions. Some because this is what they have. It is not because they are not looking for a relationship with Black men, but they seem not to be able to establish the relationship with Black men. I suppose that there are not quite as many, never have been as many men as there are women. There are, of course, more women getting educated and men hate that. Wars take men away. Drugs take the men away –

M.A. – and prison takes the men away.

R.G Women find themselves alone. That's the reason that in the inner cities, particularly, there are so many single women, single parents, mothers. In the middle class, many hard working young women are without men. Now, I don't find that they are pulling apart from other women. Rather they have women as friends. Groups of women meet, talk, plan strategy in terms of work. They are very healthy in that respect, which doesn't prevent them from being lonely. What do I say to them? I say, well, if there is a possibility, if loneliness is there and you need a male companion, then I don't think one necessarily has to stay with Black men. Just broaden yourself out and meet white men, or Asian men –

M.A. – Hispanic –

R.G. – Or Hispanic, and have a real international or inter-racial sort of relationship.

M.A. I agree with that, but I think the need we have for friendship is so deep, it is part of race memory, if you will, and yet, in a temporary world with sit-coms where everything is resolved in twenty-seven minutes, a number of young women, I think, satisfy themselves with superficial acquaintances, and I think of you and me talking together, having lived through twenty-five plus years of friendship – loss on both parts, and gainings, and love affairs that we've had, and marriages and children threatened and children found – and all these things that we have lived through, speaks of the power of a profound friendship. Not just that superficial 'we work together, let's stop off at a bar and have a drink.' I really want young women to develop those kinds of bonds which allow people to know that they can count on somebody who will give them the best advice, the best shoulder to lean on, and somebody who expects the most from her.

R.G. One person goes out and gives of herself and in return receives. If one goes out selfishly, one does not. I think that this is certainly true. I think that in this area one can be quite a lot of help if one is generous and broad. I find that I have fantastic friends. My friends span Continents –

M.A. – and races, and sexes.

R.G. Yes. There are very few places I can go that I don't have a friend, that I can't knock on the door and say, 'Look, I'm here, I'm out of money. What do I do?' And they'd say, 'What do you mean "what do you do?" You come in here.'

M.A. You come in first, and then we will think of what next to do.

R.G. And I find it's one of the most gratifying things. But then, too, my door is always open. Everything that I have belongs to my friends. I love my friends, male and female.

M.A. A number of young women I've met cannot conceive of having men friends, brother friends. And they don't realize how out-of-the-balance their lives are without a brother friend. And so I would like to encourage young women to reach out. In some cases, they have to do the instruction, because a number of men do not know anything about having a woman sister friend, because they're thinking, 'Are you expecting me to go to bed with you?'

R.G. Or marry you?

M.A. So that's why I think that a young woman must reach out and, knowing that if she likes somebody who she's not physically attracted to, but she is at one with them, and a generosity of spirit, and she can train him into becoming a brother friend . . . Everything worth having is going to cost the earth.

R.G. Yes, and on this level I say that you are certainly one of the people who can give better instructions in this because of your generosity and your understanding, and you do not mind the rejections, the primary rejection, the secondary rejection, and you will go again. And this, young women cannot stand. They cannot stand rejection. Because you say to a young man, 'I love you.' Right away, he thinks, she's trying to trap me, and he starts to run. His whole posture is the posture of someone who is very precious, who feels his preciousness, and is in demand, therefore vulnerable. That's something that young women find very, very hard. Young women band together. They say they'd rather be free. They have occasional affairs, and then it's over.

M.A. Yes, and they may be left with a child.

20

R.G. I think it's a tragedy. Here again, I'm a romantic. I love the relationship between man and woman. I like the idea of having a close male friend and of being able to be stroked.

M.A. I believe that Black women can find sex on any corner, and maybe romance in maybe every few blocks. But to find a brother friend who is not intimidated by the strength we have developed over these years of surviving and keeping the race alive, not intimidated by this, it's of such value that I would encourage every young woman to try to make a friend. I would encourage them because for a balanced life, if there is a husband or a lover who is also a friend, wonderful. But if the person is alone, maybe a single parent, or no parent at all, just alone struggling to make a living and struggling for her identity, I encourage the development of friendship, profound friendship between that particular woman and two, maybe three, other women and friendship with at least one man which does not include sex. And if you don't have that, I don't know how you can consider that you are safe in an unsafe world. I mean safe inside yourself. Nobody to give you advice and support and to thump you, and really tell you you are wrong. Somebody you appreciate and respect who will also tell you you are right when you are right. I think that for young women out there there is this mean and unsafe world, they are desperately in need.

R.G. And I think that there are many souls out there just struggling in the society for money and for position and power or something like that, hoping to get friends that way and feeling that's the only way to get friends. And some of them, because they're so busy struggling, they have nothing to give.

M.A. It is more convenient, more commodious, to fall in love and marry the boy next door, or people in your own culture, because you don't have the problem of having to translate or apologize to anybody. That is best. *But* if you find no one, no one comes knocking at your door, I say again to Black women, widen, broaden your views and realize that there are those people who would rather see you martyred by loneliness, solitude and abandonment than to see you happy. And I have only one life to live and be *present*, make a contribution to life, not mope about, feeling sorry for oneself because one is alone. If there is a chance for a balance in life, some love, some laughter, some security, some growth – then take it.

R.G. The important thing is having someone in your corner when you need them. The important thing is having someone who loves you and whom you love. With all that we have to go through in work and the

21

struggle, the need for somebody to be there, is always present. And I would never say to any young woman, 'Look, you're a Black girl so you have to be with a Black guy.' No, just be with somebody who is with you. I'm very upset by Black men being unreasonably angry about Black women who will marry or make deep friendships with white men, when they are not willing to give of themselves at all. They stand in the sidelines and they criticize . . .

M.A. There is a terrible incident which devastated me for a long time. This was in the early Seventies. *Caged Bird* had just come out. I was living in New York. *The Post* had profiled me, I was the woman of the week. There was also that day a release in *Newsweek*, with Robert Gross's wonderful review of my book, there were like three things in New York on that day. So I was so excited. I walked from my apartment over to Terry's Pub. I ordered a Martini, knowing full well that I am no able Martini-drinker. And there were five major Black male journalists. And they sent me a drink. So I had the drink, and I sent them a drink. Then the bartender gave me a third Martini which I needed like one more hole in my head. Then this group sent me another, a fourth Martini. I sent them a final drink. By this time I was really looped, so I walked over. Five good-looking Black men of my age group and each one was married to a white woman, and not one had actually come over to say, 'Hello, Maya, congratulations.' So I went over and I said, 'Let me tell you something. I have created myself. I have taught myself so much. I have learned to speak a number of languages, I'm a good cook and a good housekeeper. I love to laugh, I enjoy sex, and I'm usually cheerful, and I'm hardworking. I've done all this to attract you, and not one of you is attracted by me or to me.' And my booze and the truth of it made me weepy so I started to cry. I asked them, 'What more do I have to do?' They all hung their heads. They were terribly embarrassed. I was too drunk to be embarrassed at the time. A Puerto Rican friend, married man friend, came by and asked me in Spanish how I was and did I want to go home. He said, 'You need a brother.' And I said, 'Yes, I do.' And he took me up. And I looked back at these five men who had bonded themselves together as if I had been an attacker, when in truth I was really almost literally begging for recognition, if not for love at the moment. That was 1970. We are now in 1987. Not one of those men from that day to this has given me a friendly hello.

R.G. They're frightened. They feel somehow as though you wanted to trap them. You try so hard and you do everything that you know how . . . It's never enough . . .

M.A. Let's talk about hopeful expectations in 1987. Personal.

R.G. Well, I have three books under contract that I certainly should like finished. And I don't know exactly where I am going to sit down to write, whether I'm going to the West Indies or Europe, or the US, but wherever I am I would like very, very much to finish and promote them. I have a family that I'd like to get together. You know, I have grandchildren around that haven't been as close to me as I would like them or close to each other, and I would like to be useful in that sense as a grandmother. And being the continual romantic, I would like very much to consolidate a fantastic romance.

M.A. I think that just sounds the nit's tits to me. That sounds the best thing possible. I mean, to be able to get the work done, to have that adhesive and cohesive force in the family, and to have a love affair.

R.G. That's not asking for much, is it?

M.A. It seems not to me. When I think of my expectations or my desires of 1987, they are pretty much the same thing. I ask for health. I'd like to have health so that I can achieve the work that I have either contracted legally, or contracted inside my mind, and to be present as a family member, and to have some splendid love affair that will not ask too much . . . And yet, I want to make lots of money. I don't ever want to be without money. I think that's the most chicken shit thing in the world, to be without money.

R.G. I don't know that we can ever be really satisfied, but one hopes that in 1987 we do really come as near to achieving what we want. And I do hope that we can help influence the young . . .

M.A. That is the need, in fact. The desperate need. So many young Black women are not spoken to by white women. Are not spoken to by Black men. Are not spoken to by white men. And if we don't speak to them, there will be no voice reaching their ears or their hearts.

Natalya Baranskaya

talking with
Pieta Monks

ʻCOME tomorrow after lunch. I'm afraid I can only spare you a couple of hours. You see, the day after is the anniversary of my husband's death and I am going to visit his grave. I have to pack.'

Natalya Baranskaya's voice on the telephone was clear and firm, surprisingly so for someone in her mid-seventies. But then, she is a surprising woman in many ways: she started writing at the age of fifty-five on retiring from her job in the Moscow Pushkin Museum. Six years later, in 1969, she acquired prominence in the Soviet Union and the West with the publication of her short novel A Week Like Any Other. This described honestly and compassionately the twin pressures on a typical Muscovite woman of her career and her home, pressures from her colleagues and, most of all, from her husband.

Natalya Baranskaya herself never remarried after the death of her husband in 1943 on the Western front. Her personal experience as a single woman is a recurring theme in her fiction, revealing both the strength and the vulnerability of such women. When we met in her Moscow flat on a grey, rainy day she impressed me as someone who is both representative of modern Soviet women, in her independence and self-confidence, and typical of the women of her generation who have lived through revolution, civil war, war of intervention and a world war. Together with her optimism for the future there is a deeper sadness and anguish for the past, for the horrors seen and felt in the last world war.

She talked unfalteringly in her precise, classical Russian as we drank hot, sweet tea in the bare flat, already cleared for her departure.

I WAS BORN on 31 December 1908, on the eve of the First World War.

My parents were revolutionaries, engaged in underground work, printing leaflets, etc. . . . My mother knew Lenin, she worked with him on Iskra. She was from Siberia, but when she finished high school she left for St Petersburg, to carry out her plan for her life. She signed up for midwife and nursing courses. Of course her parents, especially her mother, protested, but my mother had a very strong character, and she had a passionate desire to get involved in the student groups in Petersburg – they were so vital at that time, they got involved in everything: read books, thought about the revolution, about social transformations, about social revolution. They were very ideological and all filled with ideas of change, gripped by them. My mother needed this, emotionally and mentally. She was a very brave woman and a very beautiful one.

My father was completely different, he had a sensitive, artistic nature and if he had not immersed himself in the revolution he might have been a writer or an artist. I was a love-child. My mother and father never married.

At one time both my father and my mother were in jail (this was before the revolution, of course). Then my mother was released, but in order to get my father released from his sentence of hard labour we had to find a merchant who put up five thousand roubles. Then they let him out on the condition that he emigrated. He went to Switzerland, where we joined him, and then we moved to Germany, where we stayed until the outbreak of war. My father could not return to Russia – he would have been arrested immediately – so my mother and I went, via Denmark. We stayed a few days in Copenhagen, and then we came to Moscow where, with a few absences, I have remained ever since. My father never came back to live with us. He found another woman and made a new life with her.

At the time of the revolution I was about six or seven. I remember street demonstrations and then that terrible hunger, when there was not even a bite of bread to eat. My impressions of my childhood, which was a very interesting one, are bright and strong, but fragmented – probably most childhood memories have these qualities.

I grew up in a period when Russian women first started working outside the home on a massive scale. It wasn't that they thirsted after freedom, but just that they were needed – there weren't enough male workers to fulfil the needs of the country. Like many young people of that time I was consumed by the need to transform society, I was full of ideas about what I would do, what and where I should study, what I would work at and where I should live and work. There seemed to be endless possibilities then and I wanted to do everything. It never for a moment crossed my mind that after I got married and had children I should stay at home and look after them. And I think the young girls today also never think in those terms; they are accustomed to thinking in terms of a career, in terms of going into higher education after they have finished school. They don't realize the difference a child makes. Until a woman has a baby she can do what she wants; even if she is married, she can structure her life the way she wants it; but when a child appears, or maybe two (everybody nowadays says that two children are better than one, and some women want even more), her whole life changes.

Village women, of course, are quite different: they are still used to the old family ways, to large families, to the women being mainly engaged in domestic work. Also they are still quite religious and would not think of terminating a pregnancy.

I didn't start writing until after I started drawing my pension. I worked in a literary museum before that and for the last eight years before I retired I worked in the Pushkin Museum, which I liked very much. I love Pushkin, which is perhaps why in 1977 I wrote a book vindicating his wife – the first book ever to do so. After Pushkin's death she had been subject to terrible, vicious attacks from people which have continued almost to the present time. Anna Akhmatova, for example, hated her, thought of her as an empty-headed, stupid, spiteful, flirtatious, good-for-nothing woman, to blame for his death. But according to Pushkin's letters to her, which are charming and delightful, she was nothing like that at all. He not only loved her deeply but she was also his best friend to whom he could tell everything. It is true that she was not a poetess like Anna Akhmatova or Marina Tsvetaeva, but if she had been they would probably not have been able to live together. She was a modest, even shy, woman, beautiful but unsure of herself. The fact that she went a lot to the ballet and to balls meant nothing – it was the accepted aristocratic way of life. It was just unfortunate that Nikolai I liked her so much that he ordered her to appear and dance at all his court balls, and to make sure of this he made Pushkin a Gentleman of the Emperor's Bedchamber: this title was very demeaning to Pushkin – he was a glorified footman. Furthermore, in order to attend all these balls she had to have a lot of dresses, and her accusers have added up the cost of buying all these dresses and claimed that she ruined herself and her husband. But they forget that she had a rich aunt who loved to make her look pretty and willingly gave her money for this. They also forget that Pushkin was an avid gambler and used to pile up quite substantial debts at the gambling table.

When I worked at the Pushkin Museum I would listen to my colleagues when they took groups of visitors round describing Pushkin's wife in the usual way as a woman who lived only for parties and balls and I would say to them afterwards, 'But listen, in her six years of marriage she gave birth to four children and had a further pregnancy which ended in a miscarriage. How could she have spent all her time dancing?'

Before my novel *A Week Like Any Other* was published there had been nothing written, either as fiction or fact, about how hard life was for our women, who legally have equal rights with men. There had been nothing written about the difficulties of running two jobs at once – one outside, one inside the home – especially if the woman is a wife and a mother. In our literature women always managed to do everything. I remember that I once read something in the journal *Znamya* like this. I can't remember the name of the author but I do remember that the story infuriated me so much that when I had finished it I hurled it to the floor. It was about a woman – I can even remember her name, Polina – who was married to an army man. She worked outside the home, and had been awarded medals for her excellence; she also had three children, whom she looked after and read to at night. Her home was so tidy and clean that it sparkled. Perhaps I could have swallowed all this, but in addition to everything else she sewed and knitted all her children's, her own and her husband's clothes. After I had recovered from my rage I started to work things out: there are only twenty-four hours a day and it turned out that it was simply a physical impossibility for her to do all these things.

People just closed their eyes to reality. Supposed literary models were set down for women to base their lives on, but the writers did not describe how women should accomplish the impossible. Women tore themselves to pieces trying to do everything, and still do. They're constantly under stress, they cry suddenly, collapse. Their relationships with their husbands are ruined. The children fall ill because there is not sufficient supervision in the kindergartens and the groups are too big.

A Week Like Any Other was accepted at once for publication. Tvardovsky was then editor of the journal *New World* and he slipped it in ahead of Trifonov's *The Exchange*, so Trifonov had to wait for the next edition before his story was published. My story immediately created a great stir. There was a queue for it; it was passed from hand to hand. And I received a tremendous number of letters about it from women who thanked me for saying that a woman's life was so difficult; they said just the fact that somebody recognized this now made their lives a little easier, the fact that somebody saw how they battled on and on without normally getting any recognition for what they do. The letters were wonderful and touching.

One said: 'I waited a long time for the journal but at last my turn came. I can only read when I'm travelling in the tube, I have no other spare time. But it's difficult to read your story in the tube because it makes me cry all the time.'

Another one said: 'You know everything about me, as if you lived in the same flat as me. You even know that I cry in the bathroom.'

And a third said: 'I couldn't get your story for a long time. Everything you write is just the way things are, just the way things are.' And then she went on to tell me about her own life.

Of course my story was written primarily for women readers, but men read it as well. I myself knew a married couple who were both extremely talented, both engaged in research, and they had two children. The husband read my story and then he suddenly said to his wife: 'Why didn't you tell me before how hard things were for you? Now that I understand I'll really help you properly.' Why he couldn't understand how hard things were for her before I don't know; still, I was pleased that at times my story produced direct and immediate results, although I wouldn't like to say how long-lasting this particular one was.

But that was all a long time ago. Has anything changed since then? Well, change happens slowly, but certain measures have been taken. One of the women in *A Week Like Any Other* says when she is filling in a questionnaire that has been sent round to all the workforce: 'I think that perhaps this questionnaire will change things. Maybe they'll give us more sick pay.' At that time they would give you three days' pay when you were off work with a sick child, now they give you ten. Then, after having a baby, your job was kept open for you for a year, now it's one and a half years, although they still don't pay you for this leave. I would like to see women get a percentage of their salary during this time.

I have always written short stories, they probably suit my style and capabilities, but now I want to write something longer, I want to write the truth about the war.

Soviet writers, men, have written movingly about the experience of men during the last world war, about their sufferings, their horror, the blood, the fire and the fear. I want to write about women during the war, and not about women who fought at the front either, but women who stayed behind with the children. I myself was evacuated to the Altay with two small children and although perhaps I don't know all the horrors of war, I know some of its difficulties.

I have written more than half of this novel: it is about the lives of seven women during the war, and their lives are interwoven with my own thoughts, and stories within stories and little polemical asides. It's very hard for me to write about that time, and I'm not sure that this is working out. To relive that time of despair, of partings, of fears, of waiting and, the most terrible of all, to remember receiving news of my husband's death. He died on 12 August in 1943, in the battle for Kurskaya Duga, near Bransk. And that is where he is buried – his comrades were able to dig him a grave in the middle of fighting. He was much loved by his comrades; he was brave and kind. I go and visit his grave from time to time, but increasingly rarely.

So I was left alone with two small children but, of course, I was not the only one. Perhaps it is difficult for people in the West to understand a situation where, in one small village, there is no household that is not in mourning for at least one person, perhaps two or three: husbands, fathers, sons, even daughters. I think that those of us who have experienced it must tell those who have not about the full extent of the horror of war. We had such terrible hardships, such long periods of waiting: we waited for help, for the second front, we waited for letters from our husbands and we waited for the end of the war. I want to write about all this in my book. I want to write about a friend of mine, a very nice woman of my age, a peasant from the Orlovsky region. She also lost her husband during the war and was left with three children in an area occupied by the Germans. On a freezing night, when the temperature was well below zero, she and her children were flung out of their house. The Germans wouldn't even let her take a blanket to wrap her youngest child in. She was left in the open in the middle of night with three children, with nothing to eat, suddenly deprived of all her possessions – her home, her livestock, her cow. In the space of a minute she and her children were turned into homeless wretches.

Women will always fear war more than men because they are mothers. A woman will always have a baby, her own or her children's, in her arms, she will always be tormented by fear for her children, the fear that one day she might be a witness to their own deaths. For some of our women this fear was acted out in the last war, and has remained a nightmare to haunt them. When my husband was taking part in the liberation of

Vyazma he wrote to me about what he had seen: 'With my own eyes I saw children that had been thrown into wells. The Germans had flung babies and small children into wells.' How can one explain this reduction of man to a beast? By the war.

If I can express one tenth of my feelings about the war and my experiences during the war in my novel, then I will have succeeded, then people must understand what our war was, and they will understand how it lives on in our emotions. It is not only in our memories and hearts, either, that the last war lives on. There are still today many, many crippled survivors of the last world war, men without arms or legs, or both, hidden away somewhere in a hospital or asylum, so completely crippled that nothing remains of the former man. And there are many, many people who were turned insane by their experiences during the last world war.

Russian people lack the capacity to hate. Sometimes I am surprised that our people show no feeling of personal vindictiveness towards, let us say, the Germans. But we can't seem to hate people, we care too much for peace, we want it too much. It seems incredible to me that in the West you are afraid that *we* might attack *you*. We would never ever start a war, and the fact that people say that we would upsets me enormously. After all we have gone through why should we want another war? We certainly don't need any more territory, we've got so much that hasn't even been worked yet. What we lack is workers. Why on earth should we want a war when we are still recovering from the effects of the last one? I think it must be American propaganda, but they are such a long way away from us, I don't know what they want from us, or why they hate us so much. I think they are afraid, and have been for a long time, but not of a nuclear war. And I am afraid of them: they seem, as a nation, to lack restraint, they have there the sort of freedom that allows anybody who wants to to go out and buy a gun, and once you have a gun there is a great temptation to use it. They have bandits and terrorism. We don't have any of that. They act spontaneously, in the heat of the moment, and they have not experienced war on their own territory for such a very long time, perhaps they have forgotten what war is like. We haven't. We are a disciplined nation, some people might think too disciplined, but that is our system. And, of course, we have our criminals, but not to the same extent as in the USA. We can still walk our streets at night. We are law-abiding. And we know what war is.

War is chaos. It is not the well-ordered, thought-out and planned event that some writers describe it as. Nowadays shooting happens from all sides, mines explode and kill those who laid them and those they were laid for, war is revealed for the terrible, tragic, anarchic absurdity it is.

I don't think that men are any more responsible for wars than women. In our country men and women take an almost equal part in social and political life, they equally form the values and habits of our society. There are all sorts of reasons for war in which women may also be involved. In fact, you in England have a prime example of a woman who is much more belligerent than most men . . . Margaret Thatcher must have a lump of iron or concrete where her heart should be.

I think that wars first started when people learnt to use long-distance weapons, started flinging stones and using the bow and arrow; with these people raised themselves above the level of animals, they were able to kill from a distance and reduce the risk to themselves.

Ever since I wrote *A Week Like Any Other* women in the West have decided that I'm a feminist. I'm really not. If some women gain a kind of freedom it will always be at the cost of others. Here it is the grand-mothers who are being rushed into retiring early from a job that they may very well like in order to help their daughters, who have children but no time to look after them because they have a full-time job. And then there are those women who have no mothers to help them, or just can't cope, or who don't care. Their children are on the street from the time they leave school to late at night, completely unsupervised. And if a mother doesn't care, then the children will grow up not caring either. You can teach a child to learn at school, but he is taught to feel at home. In a family where the mother tries to get everything done as quickly as possible, so that she can sit down in front of the television, and the father is stuck in front of the television from the moment he enters the door (at best; at worst the father hardly appears at all, he spends his time in other places), in such families the children are bound to grow up wild and aimless.

Our women have very strong characters, which is probably not only the result of female emancipation but also of the very hard life that most of them have had. Our men are rather weak. Perhaps here the problem is that they have ceased to be the head of the family, they no longer feel the responsibility of feeding and clothing their family. Their wives receive as much, perhaps more money than they do. They feel aimless and take to drink. Drunkenness is very widespread and one cannot blame it all on an inheritance from the past, it is also to do with a lack of education and proper upbringing.

In life today there are very few things left of the traditional masculine life. A man has nothing to do when he finishes work, there's nothing to chop or mend. Formerly, in any small town a man would have to mend

34

the fence, fix the gate and countless other physical tasks. In Moscow today if he is a good man he will watch television or play with the children, perhaps even help his wife with the household tasks, but most men will say: 'Let her do it. What's it got to do with me? She's got equal rights now, so she can do everything herself.' Whereas the woman thinks: 'We've got equal rights now, we both go out to work, why doesn't he go into the kitchen and make the meatballs?'

But she is fighting against the age-old tradition that it is women who do the cooking and cleaning. In some rare cases a man will agree to help with the cleaning – he might hoover, he might do some shopping – but it is unlikely in the extreme that he will wash the clothes or do the cooking.

Lately men have started to find the occasional bit of cooking interesting, but this is only when they feel like it, on a whim. A man will want all the special ingredients ready, a nice cut of meat, and he will put an apron on and enjoy himself, leaving a tremendous mess behind him; but there is no way that he will do it on a regular basis.

Probably one cannot expect any more than this occasional help from men. Men and women are different. A man is stronger, he is given muscles and he wants to use them, but instead he is told to wash the dishes. He would much rather chop up cupboards. To tell the truth, I would as well.

Traditional Russian women, who possess the qualities of patience, generosity, self-sacrifice and resignation, still exist. But a new kind of woman has now appeared as well, a modern woman who has lost her femininity and tenderness, who has become dry and businesslike. Who thinks there is no point in having children: they will only disarrange her well-ordered life. Well, I think it's natural to have children, but just to have them isn't enough. We must have time to bring our children up, otherwise we shouldn't be surprised when they turn out rude and incapable of the frank, honest, long-lasting relationships that are necessary for marriage. Of course, some women who have a vocation will work, as they have always worked. But there are other women who work because otherwise there isn't enough money: if their husbands earned more they might prefer to stay at home and look after the children. On the other hand, for some women work has become an agreeable habit, a bit like going to a club: it gives them an excuse to get dressed up, to paint their eyelashes. They like to get out of the house and meet different people.

However, I, as a writer, like staying at home. There I have the feeling of being completely free: my imagination takes me to so many places – it flies and I fly with it. I am happiest of all when I am working, when I am writing.

*P*IETA MONKS *was born in 1946, left school at 15; at 21 she did French, Italian and secretarial studies, became an airhostess for 16 months then lived on a kibbutz for two years. In 1970 she studied Russian at Sussex University, obtained two scholarships to Moscow for a year each, and has travelled extensively in USSR. She now works as freelance translator/interpreter and also teaches Russian. She has translated a collection of Natalya Baranskaya's stories, including* A Week Like Any Other, *to be published by Virago in 1989.*

Marjorie Barnard

talking with
Zoë Fairbairns

THE AUSTRALIAN writer Marjorie Barnard was born in Sydney, New South Wales, in 1897 and lives now near Gosford, a suburb of Sydney, with her companion Vee Murdoch and three cats, Aida, Christopher and Stars. She is author of history books, books of literary criticism and short stories, but is best known as a novelist, one half of the literary partnership known as M. Barnard Eldershaw. Marjorie Barnard and Flora Eldershaw together wrote *A House Is Built* (1928), *Green Memory* (1931), *The Glasshouse* (1936), *Plague With Laurel* (1937) and *Tomorrow and Tomorrow and Tomorrow*, the censored version of which was first published in 1947, but which was first published in full by Virago in 1983. It was shortly before the Virago publication that I met her at her home in May 1983.

She was sitting up in bed when we arrived, an enormously pretty woman of eighty-five in a fresh pink nightie, with long creamy-white hair. I had been brought to meet her by John Cody of the Australasian Publishing Company. He was obviously a welcome and familiar visitor. He handed over a gift – a bottle of whisky – amidst much mutual chaffing about certain people's capacity for drink. Marjorie settled the bottle beside her in the bed like a teddy-bear and jokingly dismissed us: the whisky would do very nicely, she would see us later.

We waited in the sitting room while she got dressed and Vee helped her do her hair, coiling it into a thick plait.

The interview had a number of false starts, mainly because Marjorie and Vee were concerned that while I was asking questions I wasn't eating enough of the oysters, the salad or the gourmet cheeses they had provided, or drinking enough of the whisky and wine. (I was, actually.) At one point, Vee got up from her own meal, came over and buttered a biscuit for me, adding a cheese coated in many-coloured seeds. 'The next one you do yourself,' she said firmly. Their hospitality was as warm and witty as the act they put on of being

38

Marjorie Barnard gave this interview in 1983. She died in 1987, at the age of eighty nine.

I asked Marjorie how – and why – she had first started to write.

'I used to tell myself stories, from a very early age, and invent things. I didn't learn to read until I was seven. There was an idea at the time that children's brains were still developing and they shouldn't learn to read till they were seven. I was allowed to learn the alphabet as a seventh birthday present. I used to read Dickens. I never read children's books.

'My father took absolutely no notice of my writing. My mother, who loved me dearly, thought if that was what I wanted to do, then she wanted me to be successful. But they weren't writers. I don't know where it came from. My great grandmother, I think, my mother's grandmother, was very interested in writing . . . but she died before I was born. There was an English teacher at school who encouraged me a lot – Pearl Barnes – she thought I had something to give; and then at university there was a man who used to read my things and talk them over with me and encourage me, and I thought, yes, I can write.'

As well as this encouragement, Marjorie obtained a first-class Honours degree in History while at Sydney University and won the university medal for history. She also met Flora Eldershaw, later to be her collaborator on the novels. Meanwhile, her history professor, who inspired her thinking mind, wanted her to be awarded a scholarship to Oxford, saying, 'Oxford would be proud of you.' But she was under age and her father forbade her to go and refused to pay her passage, so the scholarship was not awarded. She stayed at home, working as a librarian at the Sydney Technical College, looking after her parents, and – in such 'spare time' as these occupations left her – writing.

I wanted to know how the partnership with Flora Eldershaw had worked: how it was possible to write five novels with a friend and stay friends. Two of the novels (*The Glasshouse* and *Tomorrow and Tomorrow and Tomorrow*) contained novels-within-the-novel; had one author done the inner novel, the other the outer one? What did they do about jealousy, disagreement, ownership of ideas and conflict?

'There was no conflict,' Marjorie told me. 'I can't say where the first idea for a book came from because we both put in things. You begin by talking about it. There's no "your idea" and "my idea", it's completely shared. There was never any trouble between my collaborator and myself, we arranged everything before we put pen to paper. I did most of the writing, Flora put in plenty of ideas, it was a genuine collaboration. I would never have got there but for her, so I assure you it was genuine.

'We never lived together, but we talked the writing over, went for long walks, thought about it, and it matured slowly. She had a good critical mind and we very often changed things . . .'

What sort of things, I wondered.

'I overwrote . . . but it was always very happy, there were never any disputes. We always thought about it. It matters, you see, it matters.'

Although Marjorie's non-fiction books – such as her *History of Australia* – which she alone was commissioned to write, were published under her own name, the novels were published as the work of 'M. Barnard Eldershaw'. I wondered whether, in using this curious, cumbersome, sexless pseudonym, the two women had been trying to hide the fact that they were a partnership. 'No, there was no hiding,' Marjorie said. '"M. Barnard Eldershaw" was a good combination.' It was even used for *Tomorrow and Tomorrow and Tomorrow*, which Flora Eldershaw had not liked very much, and which Vee insisted was more Marjorie's work than Flora's (and Marjorie did not deny this). 'The name had been warmed up,' Marjorie explained.

We discussed other aspects of *Tomorrow and Tomorrow and Tomorrow*. It is a futuristic novel about the past, a historical novel about the future; which is to say, first published in 1947, it is set in the twenty-fourth century and concerns a man called Knarf writing a historical novel about internal political struggles in Australia in the 1920s and 1930s, leading to the Second World War. Its subject matter, then, is politics, but it has no clear 'line'.

'I am not a political person,' said Marjorie.'I didn't join the Labour Party, nor did I join the Conservative Party. I didn't join any party. I had left-wing sympathies, but in a general way. I never wrote politically. *Tomorrow and Tomorrow and Tomorrow* isn't a political book, it's a moral book. It wasn't a political book . . . unless it was behind my back!'

The Australian critic Drusilla Modjeska has said of the book: 'it condemns capitalism, holds no faith in parliamentary democracy and raises serious doubts about socialism.' Would Marjorie agree with that?

'Yes, but with a few reservations.' She laughed.

'What reservations?' I asked.

'That's a bit difficult, because it's part of me. It's hard to respond to a comment like that because it's part of me. And I'd have to explain an awful lot of things . . .'

'I wish you would.'

'I don't know that you'd be so pleased.'

'What led you to write it?'

'It was an idea that had been with me for a long time. I can't remember when it began but it became part of me. That is the book that did.'

I referred her to a passage in the book where the novelist character is describing the events of the 1930s leading to war, 'the whole slow conflagration, so incredible that no-one believed what they knew to be true.' I wondered if she saw parallels between that, and similar attitudes in the present.

'Yes, I do feel it's true of now . . .'

'Do you think there's anything novelists can do about people refusing to believe what they know to be true?'

'It's hiding, isn't it?' she said. 'If a thing's too painful, you don't believe it. I think novelists can believe it, help other people believe it. They can try, at least. People believe what they want to believe.'

The great climax – or anticlimax – of the book comes when the highly-centralized government of twenty-fourth-century Australia seeks to persuade the people to hand over total power: democratically to decide to abandon democracy. Various pros and cons are argued; it seems like a tense moment; but when the votes on the issue are counted, it emerges that the majority of the people are indifferent. It's a shocking moment, all the more so for being utterly believable.

'It was how I felt,' said Marjorie. 'I knew it would happen. It *is* shocking. It shocked me!'

Another thing that shocked her was the decision of the real-life Australian government censor to make cuts in this, her favourite of her own novels. 'I was mad. Furious. I could have bitten the censor. Every mention of Russia was cut out, it was sort of automatic. Political.' The censor also removed references to such matters as the progress of the war, pacifism, civil unrest and – ironically – government control and manipulation of information, finding them a bit much even for a post-war audience. There seemed to be some disagreement as to why, the war being over, the publishers (Georgian House) submitted the book to the censors in the first place.

Marjorie said: 'I wouldn't have rushed to the censors. But the publishers wanted to be safe. It was either publish it censored or not publish it at all. And I wanted to get it into print. It had already been turned down by another publisher. They told me they were terribly interested in the story itself without all the – what they called "additives" – the politics! They followed the story rather than the comment. No one knew quite what it *was*! They wrote the nicest rejection letter . . .'

Publishers seemed to be a sore point. I asked whether, when she had worked with editors, she had allowed changes to be made in her work.

'No,' she said firmly. 'They've been forced on me. But I thought a lot and then I wrote and that was final.'

'But sometimes you have been forced by editors to change things?'

'Oh yes, well, editors have their little ways. You know.'

'Have you had other books rejected by publishers?'

'Yes, I did have one. It's still in the box in the spare room. Virago turned it down. It just wasn't a good book.'

'You accept that it wasn't a good book?'

'No,' she said, after a bit more thought.

Again and again the conversation returned to the happiness and productiveness of the partnership with Flora Eldershaw, who died in 1957. Marjorie Barnard also spoke warmly of her friendship with Nettie Palmer, poet, critic and literary adviser to many Australian writers in the thirties.

'She was a dear friend of mine. She wasn't a great writer herself but she worked very hard for other writers. She always welcomed writers and she helped over publication, all sorts of things like that. Her husband was a writer, very well thought of. She didn't exactly help me in any practical way, but she read the books in manuscript and she helped in that way. She was one of my best readers. And a friend, a close friend.'

Speaking of the novelist Miles Franklin (author of *My Brilliant Career*) Marjorie was more ambivalent.

'She was a curious person. She had an extraordinary sort of vanity, and . . . it's hard to describe Miles, she was so complex. She had a lot of vanity. I didn't always agree with her . . . not that I disagreed, but I didn't agree. She had political views which she used in her writing, and I don't think writing is political. She was never wrong, which was rather difficult. It was a somewhat difficult friendship. It never broke up. She was very generous in some ways, and very ungenerous in others. A complex person.'

Finally, I asked her how she felt about writing. If she were going to write any of her books again now, would she make them different?

'They'd be quite different,' she said. 'I suppose because I'm older . . . but when they're written, they're written. I was a very eager writer. It's all died out now.'

'What were you eager for? Publication?'

'It was important to get published. But I was eager for the writing itself. It was something I had to do. I didn't always enjoy it. It was painful in a way. But it was something that I had an impetus to do. It's all died out now. I'm too old. I can't work on it. It's a long time since I wrote a book.

'Sometimes I get flashes. But I'm so tired.'

*Z*OË FAIRBAIRNS *is the author of* Benefits *(Virago 1979) and* Stand We At Last *(Virago 1983),* Here Today *(Methuen 1984, winner of the 1985 Fawcett Book Prize) and* Closing *(Methuen 1987). She has contributed stories to anthologies including* Tales I Tell My Mother, More Tales I Tell My Mother *(Journeyman Press), and* Despatches from the Frontiers of the Female Mind *(Women's Press).*

Dora Birtles

talking with Joyce Nicholson

'WE'RE BEING exhumed before we die,' said Dora, with a throaty chuckle. Virago had republished *North-West by North* and plans were being made for *The Overlanders* to be refilmed and republished. In addition, poems written by her and her husband Bert Birtles were being published in a new edition of *Hermes*, the Sydney University literary paper of the 1920s in which they had first appeared. 'They've rediscovered us. They're even writing a doctoral thesis on us. We were both expelled from the University, you know . . .'

Dora Birtles was born in Wickham, New South Wales, in 1903. She was the fifth child. Her father was mayor of the municipality, 'but we were nothing really because my father's business was transport and in those days, that was horses.' She went to the local school at Wickham and got a bursary to the high school at the age of ten. From there she won a teacher's scholarship and an Exhibition to the University of Sydney, and it was there that she met her husband Bert.

'I had to do a philosophy essay and it had to be handed in the next day. I was at the library when the doors opened. There was another student there and the librarian took him first. He asked for the four books which were on the required reading list. I said, "Oh, that's not fair. He can't read four at once." I mean, it was outrageous. So she said, "He was here first", looking very scornful. And so he said – I must have scowled – "If you sit at the same table you might read one." So I followed him to his table, in the hope that I might read one. And we began to talk. And I wrote in my diary "I met a young man here tonight."

'I thought he was married, I don't know why, perhaps because he was studying after work. I didn't know that he kept an eye out for me. I had the most horrendous birth mark and it embarrassed me. I hated myself. (My elder sister said, "The less you see of your face, Dora, the better!") But he kept an eye out for me and met me one evening by chance and

46

stopped me. I met him two or three times, and he spouted poetry. I must have looked awfully young . . . But one evening we went by train to some place and walked and walked – and missed the last train. It hadn't occurred to me to go somewhere where I could telephone, so we spent the night outside. A most uncomfortable, dreadful night. Nothing happened except that he stood on an anthill and in the night a leech attacked me! By the time we got back to the women's college, outside, near a big azalea bush, was my Aunt Jane. "Aunt Jane?" I said. "Yes," she said, "your mother's inside with the Principal." They had rung her up and she had come down on the paper train, which leaves at two in the morning! They told me never to see him again and rusticated me for two years. I wouldn't be rusticated! There was a rule that your Honours had to be consecutive. I said I wouldn't go down for two years unless I could do my Honours degree and they said "yes". That was the only stand I made. It wasn't foresight. It was pride, pride.

'But meanwhile I found two friends of mine and we took a couple of rooms and Bert came to the flat.' It was at this time that their love affair began. It was unusual for a well-educated woman of her generation to be so open about what was then considered 'immoral behaviour' and it typified Dora's life of writing, film making, activism and travelling. 'I was very happy, you can't imagine how happy I was. I was extraordinarily happy those times when he came to see me but I was always very conscious of the neighbours knowing what time Bert left. I wrote a poem about it, it was four lines:

> Pierrot, Pierrot, it's time to go
> That clock on the wall is terribly slow.
> Pierrette, Pierrette, don't fidget and fret
> There's ages and ages of time left yet.

'It was very reckless of me to send it to *Hermes* (the university literary magazine), and I was as proud as punch when I got this letter from the editor that my poem had been selected. But Bert published a poem in the same issue. It was called "Beauty", about being in bed. Mine was a mere nothing by comparison. So he was expelled from the university because of the poem and never finished his university degree. He was a poor boy, educating himself, so he was earning a living all the time I knew him.

'We had to get married right away. I was under age and my father threatened to put Bert in jail because I was under twenty-one. I got married but my mother had to bring down my father's written consent. So it was a very sad little wedding.' After the wedding, Dora trained as a teacher and then went to teach at a girls' school while she continued her

48

university studies. 'It was the toughest school in Sydney, but it was close enough to the university for me to be able to run down from 3.30 to the lecture at four o'clock. Now that was two kilometres, easily. And I would run it in about ten minutes. It's a long way but if I was fast it was because I played hockey. And in the end I got the highest distinction, the top BA in Oriental History, and Professor Saddler offered me a Readership. I realized to be a Reader was a terrific honour, but I refused it. I thought I had to pay out my five-year Department of Education bond.

'Bert gave up his job to write poetry and come to Newcastle. It was a very unhappy time. Well, you see, the climate was depression, I mean, bad depression. He was totally miserable writing poetry because the poetry didn't come and then we had quite a serious bust up. He wasn't working and I was teaching, so I was keeping him. I had just worked out my bond. Things weren't so beautiful as they had been. I had a very brief affair with a man. He took me to his home. He had a most prestigious job. He had been married and had a son. He introduced me to his son and his former wife, to his mother and took me to his golf club. All the proper things. I didn't ever want to leave him, but he hadn't said, "Dora, will you marry me?" He hadn't said that and I felt that Bert was out of work and alone. He needed me more.

'Then Bert got a job on the paper, which he loved. He loved it.'

This should have led to happiness. But Dora was not like most young women of her day. For one thing, she did not have any children. Bert did not want any. She continued teaching, and when her bond was completed she was able to save money. But her restlessness increased. She longed to go overseas.

'Everybody then wanted to go to England. According to my mother, my father had said that if I gave up Bert he would send me to England. But by now it was the Depression. We all wanted to go to England. That was the goal. And I said – I'd been thinking about it, you see – 'The best way is to have a boat.' I read Slocum. And I had read other navigators. I knew all about the navigators, I'd done them in my history. And my brothers had boats. So I said the best thing is to have a boat and sail it. It cost you nothing, except your food and you've got to eat anyway. And you've got your floating home, and you can travel. Bert didn't like sailing but it appealed to some friends. I wanted to go – to leave this very nice house. It was my act of rebellion. But Bert found the boat.'

She decided to sail with two old friends, Irene Saxby who had been at school and university with her, and Joyce Beeby who had recently married Hedley Metcalfe. They were joined by Henry Nicholson, a navigator, and another man, Nick, who soon left. But the tensions between Henry and Hedley over command and navigation surfaced even before they set sail. Other tensions were to follow:

'I had no sensual aims. I ran over most of those Barrier islands trying not to be left alone with Nick. I seemed to be running all the time. I'd only met him once and I didn't want an affair on board. But I wanted to know what sort of a man he was. And I said to him, when we were left alone for a few minutes, "How do you think you'll like travelling with women?" Just an ordinary, straightforward question. And he suddenly looked at me, and that look was intensely pathetic. He'd been without women all that way out. And there was such a look of desperate need that I kissed him, quite lightly, nothing, just as you kiss when you meet your friend, on the lips, but it was nothing. But at that moment I looked up over his shoulder and there was Rene coming down the hatch! That hurt Rene, but you couldn't explain to her.

'Then there was the question of money and provisions. The Metcalfes sold the engine and got us a little engine which never went. They sold it for an undisclosed sum. And we had to pay so much towards the boat, but they paid less. We had bought all sorts of stores, but she hadn't packed them. She had just ordered lavishly and put everything on the floor. There was no tea, or sugar, or anything. We didn't have a conference beforehand.'

As the journey proceeded, the conflict about money continued. 'There was no common purse, there was no accounting, and everyone bought what they felt like.' In a journey destined to be one of hardship and setbacks and desperately needing a good relationship among its participants, conflict was revealed from the first day. Their difficulties and tensions increased. By the time they reached Dutch Macassar, Dora had decided she could not continue beyond Singapore and so had Henry Nicholson. The remainder of the voyage was worse than anticipated and what was expected to take a month took three. They were becalmed, drifted backwards at times, and ran out of food. Nine months after they left Newcastle, they sailed into Singapore, where the party broke up immediately, each one going his or her own way, the three women never to meet again. The final parting between Dora and Joyce was one more disillusionment. One day Dora met Joyce and Hedley by chance in their car in a Singapore street. She hurried to speak to them.

'They didn't even turn off their engine. I couldn't get over the fact that they didn't even turn off the engine. That hurt. I was sad after that trip and wanted to go to Japan and China. I'd lectured – I'd stayed at the YWCA in Singapore. It was cheap and it was reputable. I'd given a couple of lectures for the YWCA and they had given me an introduction to Nell Hinder. She was a member of the Shanghai Municipal Council. So when I got there, she took me round. She introduced me to the underground, who brought out illegal papers. She showed me this terrible poverty . . .'

From China she finally set sail to England.

'When I got to London my sister came over – my elder sister. We took a car and we went for three months or more, through Vienna, Spain, Italy, France. This was in 1933. Then we came back. Vera, my sister, was interested in fashion, I was interested in churches and history. I was living on money I had and I went to a fashion show in Vienna with her. So I wrote a funny article about it, and sent it to the *Newcastle Sun*. I got a cable from the editor: "Write one a week." So I wrote one a week and got myself on to the Fleet Street list, by accident, because you couldn't get a job in England. The Welsh miners were singing in the streets, the poverty was bad. But I was on Fleet Street and I went to all these pansy dos, perfumed air, very rich clients – and the press.

'I got fed up with that. I wasn't getting enough money. Mother had sent me her old rabbitskin coat to keep me warm. There I was in Mum's old bunny, walking from the flat in Bloomsbury to the fashion show venues! Then a friend introduced me to this man who kept a sort of holiday place where people came to stay. And he lent me this caravan. It had been a horse-drawn caravan. Mosley had used it to tour England. I had to paint it because it was very dirty; there was an old lorry drawn up beside it, which I used to bath in. I went down in rent from twelve and six to ten bob.

'So I wrote *North-West by North*, chapter by chapter there, one chapter a week from the diaries which Bert had very kindly typed and sent over to me. I couldn't have done without those diaries. That's where the detail is. They're actually better than the book. I wrote the book originally because when I got to England I was still smarting.

'I had marvellous reviews. The *New Statesman, The Times* . . . In fact, the night I threw the leaflets in the House of Commons was the same day as when I'd been reviewed in *The Times* and *The Times Literary Supplement*.

'You see, I'd heard about the International Women's League against War and Fascism and I offered my services. They gave me a job addressing envelopes – you had to be very careful to get them right. There was a very big difference between a Baronet and a Knight! I became involved and one night we were to go to the House of Commons. I'd been told to hold the papers, the leaflets, very tightly and throw them as far as I could so they scattered. I was told to wait until another girl led us, and then I was to follow and throw the leaflets. My instructions were "Wait for her, and be sure you rush right in front and throw them forward." It was timed to be done at ten to catch the first edition. I waited at the door for over an hour but she lost her nerve. So I decided. I would put on my coat as if I was leaving and instead of turning up the stairs I would turn down, rush to the front and throw. I did just that. I did it like the way you rush in hockey. I suddenly turned, I rushed down the steps, threw and shouted "Women want peace!"

'Consternation! Upheaval! I went up the stairs to get out. Of course, I was apprehended. Two policemen escorted me. We went down and down and down, mobs of people suddenly round me. We went right underneath. You've got no idea how cold and stony and old the Houses of Westminster are. Cold and stony. I didn't know how long I'd have to be there. Hours passed. They said, "You will be confined till the rising of the House." It was a very long sitting. Then they let me go with a caution that I should report to the State Attorney General the next day. It would have been too much publicity, otherwise. And the review was in *The Times* the same day I threw the leaflets, by coincidence. The anti-Fascist people were important to me. There was a big conference coming off in Paris, and I visited Paris . . .

'In the meantime, Bert had published a journal in which there were poems by me and others. And I got a job at Dartington Hall, a progressive school, as housemistress. The children were so unruly that they'd given the previous one a nervous breakdown so I got the job! But Bert wrote to me to go with him to Greece, and so, after a term, I left to go with him. We were a year in Greece and I wrote lots of stories.'

These included *Three Days in Averoff*. It was during their stay in Greece that Bert wrote *Exiles in the Aegean*, a series of interviews with Greek poets and political exiles who had been allowed to return to Greece. It amuses both Dora and Bert that a book by a man who was expelled from the university because of his morals is now on the recommended reading list for students of modern Greek. After further travelling, two factors caused the Birtles to return to Australia. One was the threat of war. The other was Dora's wish to have a family: 'I finally talked him into it.' In 1939 Jarra was born and in 1943 another son, Kanga.

The political message of motherhood was not lost on Dora and in 1944 she wrote a strong article advocating greater relief for war-time mothers . . .

> . . . only last week the leader of the UAP Mr Hughes cried 'shame on childless couples' and exalted us to have more children. He spoke of patriotism . . . I have looked forward to this baby very much. I had to battle for a house to live in. I had a full time job looking after my home. There was no available kindergarten. I had been back from hospital for a few days when I realized that as things are at present I had sentenced myself to at least five years hard labour and the social conditions of penal servitude . . . I am not asking the politicians to wave a magic wand three times to do the impossible. The thing is to give wartime mothers a little relief and not to be too long about it . . . Spend a little money on kindergartens and nurseries, raise the loan to mothers. See there is a baby clinic to go to at the weekend, especially for new babies. Arrange aftercare hostels for mothers . . .

Dora continued writing and followed *North-West by North* with *Lovely, Lousy London* a novel which drew from her experiences of living in London in a bug-ridden attic.

'I struggled to finish that book. I had one child, and the other almost due. It won the Prior Memorial Prize in 1945. I had rushed the final version in on the morning of the competition . . . and I won! But the prize wasn't awarded, and I'll tell you why. There were three judges – and one, H. M. Greene, had a special quarrel with Bert. Greene didn't like the ending of *Lovely, Lousy London* and he wouldn't give it a hundred pounds – it was the 'esteem' of this Prior Memorial prize, not the money. So it wasn't awarded because of that – and there was nothing else to touch it. I had two children. It was a bitter blow. Then Cape refused to publish it.'

Dora was so disappointed by this that she did not try to find another publisher but turned instead to film. Dora had met Harry Watt in England through her anti-fascist activities. When he was looking for stories to make a film in Australia, he discussed his ideas with her. The result was the film *The Overlanders*, of which Dora then wrote the book. In 1947 *Pioneer Shack*, a book she had started many years previously, was published.

'That was written when I was teaching at Newcastle High. My first year, I made them write poetry. I can still remember one little girl who wrote about the moon. She wrote: "I'm sure the man in the moon/cannot feel an oppression/for all the silver that he's in/he's in his own possession." It was charming. The second year I made them write a short story. The third year, I was very fond of this class, and I said, "Come on, let's write a novel." So I said I'd start one too. So I'd read them a chapter a week, last period on Friday afternoon when you couldn't get anything else out of them. So they got interested. On board the boat I'd written a lot of *Pioneer Shack* and I had all sorts of portraits of girls, real girls, and it has a lot about the house in which Bert and I were forced to live that my father owned and to whom I paid rent. It was an old pub. That house is important. That was the period of my writing, before we got our own house, of course.'

Pioneer Shack was followed by another children's book, *Bonza The Bull*. Between the birth of her children and 1955 Dora's principal concern was with her growing family.

'But in that time I wrote articles. I used to do it on a Thursday, then it was published on the Sunday. On the same page, the feature page, was a short story, like Somerset Maugham short stories. And I did those short, short stories on ordinary suburban life.'

Throughout this time Dora continued to be politically active. For many years she was president of the Australian-Yugoslav Association, passionately pro Tito, and in 1951 she and Bert visited Yugoslavia where they co-operated on a book, although Gollancz rejected it for publication.

'In 1955 I went back to teaching. Kanga was about twelve, the eldest one was just at university. I liked my teaching and I liked my girls, but I had an English mistress with no degree whatsoever. She was a career climber. I was teaching with my heart and soul, and she had no soul. I, with my literary assets, was the lowest paid temporary teacher. She came in and interrupted a lesson I was giving. I was reading something which I used to get the girls to cry at the end of. And quite suddenly I thought to myself, "I think I'll go."

'I went off to Afghanistan with Constance Paul, who I worked with on the film. Did everything for her, driving the car, everything. She only took me as a swagman. I carried everything for her. But I was sick of being just a housewife and not getting enough money. It meant leaving Bert, but he was very good about it. I was fifty-six . . .

'I'd learnt a lot from Bert. He always interviewed people on both sides, and I learnt that. I selected Afghanistan because it tied in with Marco

Polo and Buddhism and all the things that I'd really been interested in, Oriental history and all that. I wanted to go up to the borders with Russia. So I went, with two men from the Hindu Kush Cambridge expedition, the headmistress of a girls' school in Pakistan who had a girl with her who spoke Urdu (Urdu is understood in Afghanistan) and a driver. We went on the old Buddhist trail from India to China – that road which is now being so desperately fought over. It was then unknown territory. A four-wheel drive vehicle like ours could just barely negotiate it, sometimes not! And you saw the travelling peasants, they come down from the mountains as winter comes, down to Kabul. Russia was just beginning to give Afghanistan things like kerosene lamps, tin dishes, primitive stoves, things that peasants needed, you see.

'We went as far as the Blue Lake that is almost on the border with Russia, and the track was almost impossible, with mountains on either side, steep rivers to cross, men on horseback with pistols at their side – they were Afghans. We climbed up very high. It was freezing cold. The Cambridge people had lots of white chocolate and if I hadn't had their white chocolate I would never have survived. I should have taken food. I had thought that food would be available, you can always get food. But food was not available. And it was frighteningly cold.

'On the way back we came up a steep hill and we were resting on a corner to look at the valley. Some peasants were coming round a corner, and they came round too sharply. They clung to the buses like flies and one man who was hanging on at the side caught himself on the cliff face. The bus pulled up. There was a big altercation. We were arrested by the police – and the man was seriously ill. Suddenly a truck driver with plenty of sense said the injured man should have hospital attention. He was speaking his language – I didn't understand a word, but I knew what he was saying, so I agreed with him emphatically and told the police. And do you know, they put the man in with me, and we went on in our car with this wounded man in the back with me. I gave him an Aspro I happened to have. We drove into this village. They were very frightened that we should be killed, the driver was frightened. They all came flocking up. He must have said we'd been good to him. I attended to the man as best I could, but he was dead. I'd never seen anyone dead before. So we had to go back to his village. We thought we'd be stoned and killed. We weren't to blame, but we thought that. But they accepted the body and we got away quickly.

'We were stopped on the way by the police. They were everywhere. It was a police-organized state. And I suddenly saw the man's shoes. They were expensive shoes . . . Then we travelled the whole night in fear. We were stopped by the police and kept two hours in a cold police station while they phoned through to Kabul.'

The film was never made, but the travelling continued. Three trips to New Guinea, and three to China, the last in 1968.

'After the Afghanistan trip I went back to university, New South Wales, and I did drama. I got a High Distinction – I must have been about sixty-four! And I represented the university on a trip to China – the first one for students. I had qualified for it legitimately. There were a lot from all over Australia and New Zealand, more men than women. We went to Japan first, and stayed in the very best. I stayed with a woman who lived out there. All the millionaires took the girls and boys to their homes, but I fell to the lot of the academic woman who was very poor. Because of *The Overlanders* I had an introduction to the film world. I went to the home of a film-maker, and he prostrated himself. I felt so humiliated, because he was a very famous film-maker . . . Then I went last year again, to Inner Mongolia, on a travel tour . . .'

One of the reasons Dora was able to travel so extensively as she grew older was that in the 1960s her father died and for the first time she was not short of money. Yet it seems sad that someone with so much imagination, writing ability and success wrote so little after the 1940s. Dora attributed this to her disillusionment about the way she was treated over the 1945 Prior Memorial Prize, the rejection of *Lovely, Lousy London* by Cape and the similar rejection by Gollancz of the book on Yugoslavia. But Dora is essentially a doer, a talker, an activist, a lover of travel and of people. Her rebellious spirit still keeps her pale blue gimlet eyes on the people around her, and she enjoys to the full, with great glee and a pixyish sense of humour, the resurrection of her career.

*J*OYCE NICHOLSON *was born in Melbourne in 1919 and educated at the University of Melbourne. She has four children. She has written over twenty-five books including* Freedom for Priscilla, The Convict's Daughter, What Society Does to Girls, The Heartache of Motherhood *and* Why Women Lose at Bridge. *Her activities in the women's movement include early involvement in the Women's Electoral Lobby and founding Sisters Publishing Ltd. Until recently she was managing director of D. W. Thorpe Pty Ltd, publishers of trade journals and reference books, notably the* Australian Bookseller and Publisher.

56

Kathleen
Dayus

talking with
Mary Chamberlain

KATHLEEN DAYUS *was born in 1903, the youngest of thirteen children of whom six survived. She grew up in Camden Drive, in the slums of Birmingham's jewellery quarter. Her father was often out of work and the family survived for long stretches on parish relief.* * *After school, Kathleen and her brother would beg for food outside the local factory. At eighteen and pregnant she entered into marriage to escape. But with a child, few would offer her lodgings and she and her husband were forced back to live with her parents. In 1931, two days after their fifth child was born, her husband died. She sold firewood to supplement parish relief until the Relieving Officer threatened to sue. With the threat of a prison sentence, no money, and a young family crammed into the attic of her mother's house, Kathleen turned in desperation to Dr Barnardo's and surrendered her children into their care until she found work and a home. Although both were found within a few weeks, she recovered her family only after an eight-year battle. But by then she had left the slums for good and had built up a small but successful enamelling business.*

While the memories of activists or labour leaders have taken a respectable place in the history of socialism, not so those who struggled without a political framework. Kathleen Dayus, her family, her community, appeared beyond and immune from the wider struggles of the labour movement. Mostly unemployed, condemned by capitalism and forgotten by trade unionism, they emerged from pauperism for brief, sporadic forays into the world of labour. Deviousness became a way of life. By any accounts it was a 'lumpen' community, within which the women, apparently submerged beneath the vagaries of Capital, the Poor

---

*Parish relief was assistance given, under the old Poor Law, to the local poor and destitute. The Relieving Officer judged the claims. Those receiving relief were classed as paupers. It was a system feared and hated by the English working class.

Law and often their husbands, negotiated the truce between life and death. Exploitation bred insecurity and conservatism, an apolitical existence where surviving each day was the only viable goal. It was a life lived on nerves, turning some, like her mother, to hardness and ulti-mately drink, and others to a determination to get out. Such life histories are not comfortable stories; they are rarely told.

When Kathleen Dayus was seventy-nine she published Her People, *the first volume of her autobiography. It won the J. R. Ackerley Award for Biography. Three years later its sequel* Where There's Life *was published. Written without nostalgia, sentimentality or self-pity, but with humour, simplicity and colour both books spell the rhetoric of raw experience. They are statements about power and powerlessness. Sometimes, simple statements are also needed.*

I met Kathleen in her home in Birmingham where her daughter and son-in-law live with her. She was waiting for me by her garden gate and took me warmly and instantly into her home and her life. I asked her how Her People *came to be published.*

This introduction is an amended version of my review of Kathleen Dayus's *Where There's Life*, published in February 1986 in *New Socialist*. I am grateful to *New Socialist* for their permission to republish part of it here.

I WENT to my daughter's and we were sitting round the fire talking about the old Christmas days and all the children, grandchildren, were there and they said, 'Tell us about your old days, Nan.' So I said, 'Oh no, t'aint the place or the time now,' I said, 'but one of these days I will.'

I give it a thought, and when I got home after Christmas I lay in bed and I thought yes, and I got an exercise book out and I started writing bits, and as I wrote bits and pieces my past came back clearer and each night I added to it as it came back to me, and that's how I went on . . .

I was eighteen. I was eighteen in the February and got married in the April. I was two months pregnant when I got married. I thought, if I get married it will be a chance for me husband to get me out and start life afresh. We had a furnished room and then I had to have the bab and the woman up above said the baby was crying, they couldn't get no sleep. I had to clear out and get another place. I told me Dad, I used to tell me Dad all me troubles. He said, 'All right, me wench,' those were his words, 'all right, me wench, you'll pack your traps up and come back home.' Those were his very words. I thought, well, it's only for a short time, till I can get another place.

Then I had another baby. I kept having children after children, I couldn't get rooms with children, they didn't want children in rooms. I had to stop there. Of course, if I had known about presentatives [*sic*] and all that then I probably wouldn't have had them.

I didn't know anything about anything, these precautions, because I was brought up ignorant. A French letter to me was something in writing. When I had my baby I thought it come out your navel. That's how ignorant we were brought up. We were never taught the facts of life and sex was a dirty word.

When I went in this factory, I used to listen to the women, to what they were going to say, so I could learn something. I wasn't very big then, fourteen, fifteen, and this woman had got hair growing there, you know? Of course, it frightened me, and I went home, and I didn't want to grow a horse's tail, I got the scissors and cut it all off. Me sister come and caught me. Of course, I'd nicked meself, ain't I? It was all bleeding, and I told her. So she said, 'What you done?' 'Oh,' she said, 'that's nothing, it's only what you see every month.' I said, 'It ain't that,' I said, 'I've cut meself,' and I told her what I heard. 'Oh you daft thing,' her said, 'I've got a big bunch here,' and her pulls her frock up and shows me. Some of the things you can laugh at now, but you couldn't then. It was serious. It was life and I think the title of that book, *Where There's Life*, I think is a very good title, that. I never thought of it. I didn't think of any title. Virago thought of the title for the first book, *Her People*.

My husband was out of work. There was no work for anyone then, with the Depression years, 1926 and 1932. Of course one time I was that depressed I nearly committed suicide. I didn't know what to do. I went out scrubbing and cleaning and I had to leave the two other children in bed and then come back and get them up ready for school.

Then my husband died. He was thirty-one when he died. He died on my wedding day, anniversary day, 25 April 1931. Ten years to the day. And Mary was two days old. I didn't have a widow's pension because he hadn't got enough stamps. That was the laws then. Got to have so many stamps. I was only living in the attic, living and sleeping in the attic and there was six of us.

I went to the parish, and demanded something for the children, I got nothing for me cheek, not for a fortnight after. Then what I got wasn't enough. Of course, I went mad then, lost my temper, and told them what to do with it. It all come out. I got a bit of me mother's blood in me. It was in me. I wouldn't stand for no nonsense, oh no. But I knew it got me nowhere so I just checked meself. I don't think it does, losing your temper. You live on your nerves on parish. You think you'd go and steal for the children and all that, but I used to think, if I do that, what's going to become of the children if I'm put in prison?

I could see all the little children all running about with snotty noses and no boots on their feet and I thought, oh my God, I'll never let my children come to that. But I could see it coming to it because Katie and Johnny went begging outside the same factory as I did, and I didn't want that for them. No, I didn't.

I wanted to get out myself, you see, but I couldn't do it with the children, that's why I let them go for a few weeks [to Dr Barnardo's], thinking I could, you know, have them back if I could get another house. Because I left when I put the children in the Homes. I left and I was determined to build meself up. They wouldn't have gone in the Homes if I'd have had a better mother. But she was drunk and went off and neglected them when I was out at work.

They said that when I got a house that I could have them home. Six weeks after I'd taken them in I told them I'd got a place for them. They said, 'Oh no, they've been taken to Barkingside, Ilford, Essex.' Never told me anything. Never notified me or anything. I wouldn't have cared so much if I'd neglected them and they'd been taken off me but I didn't. They wouldn't let them come back because I hadn't got a proper home for them. I'd only got lodgings. I was in lodgings for years until I got a house and then they came and visited it and then I had them home. It took me eight years to do what I intended to do.

They were very very strict. Very very strict. Not like today. Cruelly strict. Of course I tried to get Mary, the youngest, because Mary was two days old when her Dad died, there was only a few months when she went into the home and I went off with me sister Liza to go and get them back and she suggested I should steal her back, you know, and I did try and of course got into trouble. They stopped me pass.

And I didn't . . . I couldn't . . . they wouldn't let me visit them, not till Katie was taken ill and they sent for me because she was so ill, and I went to see her. That was the only time I seen her. And I enquired about Jean and Mary and they said that they were boarded out. They never even give me the address.

They wanted them to go to Australia, and I wouldn't – John went to, on board a ship, the *Ganges*, when he was sixteen, and I couldn't get him back then because the war had started. But the girls, Jean and Mary, were at King's Lynn, boarded out; Kathleen was kept there at Dr Barnardo's, Barkingside, till she came out.

I had one thing in my mind. I wanted them home with me, but I wanted them home before the eight years was up because I lost the love of them. I missed them all that time. I missed them running about and talking to them and saying little things and correcting them . . . but I knew there where I lived in Camden Drive it wasn't a place I could bring them up properly, and I think meself I got a bit of me dad's ways in me.

That's why when I wrote the book in bed, I used to write bits and it was sad and I used to think, 'I won't write it,' and then I thought, 'Oh why shouldn't I write it.' Let the children read it when anything happens to me, realize what I did go through. I've never told them. I couldn't tell them, I couldn't sit down and tell them unless they asked, and they never asked, and I couldn't tell them, you know, everything. I'd think, it's too hard, it would upset them to tell them so I thought, well I'll write it down and let them read it, see for themselves. I couldn't have told them.

I wrote it for the children, my children, to read and the grandchildren and great-grandchildren, to let them see what went on in that generation to what the generations are today, and thought, well, if anything happens to me they can read it and they'll understand. And when they read that first book, the manuscript, they started to cry; Jean said, 'We never thought you'd gone through that, Mum.'

I did the right thing. I regretted it at the time when I went to Moseley and tried to get them back and they'd already left, I regretted it then and for weeks I worried about it but after, now I come to think, I done the right thing because they were clean, they had something to eat, they were brought up properly, they had an education, things I could never give them in the position I was. I'm not ashamed. That's why I wasn't ashamed to write it and put it down in the book. When it got a bit sad, the sad bits, I thought oh, I'd better put it down now. And I had to cry meself to sleep sometimes, because I used to think of me Dad and me sisters and brothers and – I never cried over Mum. No. Although she got killed in the air raids. No. Because she was – she was very cruel. She was hard. Very hard. I mean, if she had been more kinder my life might have been bit different.

M.C. Did you ever imagine you would write a book about those days?

K.D. No. No. Before I ever started the book, I went down the Drive for the first time after years of leaving it. It looked different to me then, because all the buildings was knocked down and I walked down that Drive, down that little hill, and I could see Mother's house where I lived and had me children and I could imagine all the neighbours there, you know, and I could imagine the kids coming up to go to school and I was amongst them and I stood there and I thought, 'How awful!

What days they were then.' And I walked down that day and I looked at it and I remembered the ghosts, I could imagine them, the people there, how they were in the brew house, and maiding tubs, and fetching the washing in off the line to pawn and I thought, 'Oh, how dreadful.'

When I looked down the Drive and I see the cobbles and the school and I had a funny feeling, you know, it was awful, I went right into the past. It's like something guided me down that place. I didn't mean to go down there and then I thought of Mother, me Dad and me sisters and brothers and all the kids that I went to school with . . .

It was painful when I wrote the book. I thought about it, and I thought, well, at the time it wasn't painful because it was life, it was what I had to do and what I had to go through, yet it didn't seem painful, you know what I mean? It was what I had to do, one of them things. I suppose there's thousands of people the same and they just go on with living, you had to survive and that's it.

When I wrote I thought of them, you see. I could never forget Mum. Never. I can see her now. As I was writing I could see all those people that I wrote about. I could see and describe them, and Mother especially, because she was a tartar, and me Granny. Mum was six foot tall. Very strong. Very bombastic. All the neighbours used to be frightened of Mum. Her hadn't used to walk. Her used to stride, you know, Dad's cap on her, back to front.

Poor old Dad. He used to suffer and when he died in the workhouse, Mother never shed a tear. And I loved me Dad. Yeah, I loved me Dad. He loved me, too . . . He was ever so good to me. He'd often slip me sixpence or a shilling, you know, to get some food for the children and he'd say, 'Don't tell your Mum now.' Daren't tell your Mum. Used to bring me up a bit crafty, see . . .

Me Dad I think was a bit above Mother because he was – he knew how to converse with people, he could talk, and everybody admired him and respected him and I mean, as old as he was, he always raised his billycock to people and spoke to them and he had a nice speaking voice, Dad did and he used to correct us at times, if we used to 'yeou ain't gooing there' and all that. 'Now, now.' He taught me a lot Dad did. I think somehow my Dad must have had something in him, like to inspire me, because he was a scholar. I mean, he was a good scholar, he could write and he could read. He never read books, he always had the paper. But Mother was very hard, very hard. She was more like a gypsy. She was dark-skinned, dark hair, big woman.

M.C. Was your family politically active or aware?

K.D. No, never talked about politics. Well, I didn't understand politics, anyway, not in that sense. It was living from day to day, and come day go I didn't care.

You know, it all came back to me, and then I started writing the book. When I was in bed, quiet, there when it's quiet because my daughter and her husband have the television on and you can't concentrate and write then. So I wait till I go to bed. Of course, I don't sleep much, I sleep about two or three o'clock in the morning but I get a chance then to write and I don't get up till about ten and when I'm quiet it all comes back to me and since I've wrote the second book I've thought more and some more's come back of the later years . . .

It just came to me as I was writing a bit, you see, as a little girl going to school, and what I did, and then as I got older and older and gradually, and I put it down, scribbled it down.

And it took me, might have been three years, four years, before I finished it, because I did it when I thought about it, perhaps sit for an hour or two hours, writing, in my scrap book. Then one day – oh, it had been in the drawer two or three years – Christina, my granddaughter, said to me, 'When are you going to let me have that book you wrote?' So I said, 'Oh, I'll let you have it one day.' So I thought, well, she might as well see it.

So I gave it to her and she read it and she gave it to her schoolteacher. He passed it on and Mr Rudd caught hold of it, the historian, and he rang me up, and I was surprised because I didn't think, you know, nothing more about it. I'd forgot it really. So he said, 'You've written a documentary on your childhood, haven't you?' and I said, 'Yes.' So he said, 'Well, could I come and see you?' he said, 'I'd like to see you about it.' So he came and when he came he said, 'You shouldn't put this away in the drawer,' he says. He says, 'It's history.' He said, 'People should read this, what went on in those days.' So he said, 'Would you like me to get it published for you?' And I said, 'Oh, yes, if you would like.' And I was thrilled, you know? Of course, Mr Rudd had it and he put it together for me and put the commas and full stops and what have you, because I'm not that clever . . . He said, 'Well, I'll do me best.' He asked two or three publishers and Virago said they'd publish it and then the *Birmingham Mail*, Clem Lewis and Nora Lewis came from *Birmingham Post and Mail*, they interviewed me and there was a lot of write-ups in the Birmingham papers and Wolverhampton papers when it came out, when it was published.

I was thrilled. Because nothing ever happened to me like that in my life before. No.

I did a lot of interviewing when the book come out, BBC and West Midlands, and television. When television came, I felt a bit nervous at first because it was something new for me but after a while I was all right.

But being an author, I don't think it's caught up yet, to tell you the truth. It was a thrill when I had it televised. They went back to Camden Drive and the place where Granny lived, and the funeral, and me sisters and brothers all in the old house, and it was very very good, what they put over, Central TV. I featured in the documentary in parts, showing them where we used to live and that. That was on for an hour and I had loads of friends and people, people I'd never heard of before, knew me. It was quite thrilling to meet them all.

Oh, they all come and congratulated me, wanted a book. Oh, there was crowds of them at Lewis's. I signed over three hundred books one morning and they knew me, a lot of them knew me. And yet I don't, I don't know, I don't feel as if I'm a somebody and all the girls at the club, me bowling club, all had a book each and congratulated me, and they are all waiting for the next one.

M.C. Before you had written the book, had you read any autobiographies, or books like this one?

K.D. No, no. I don't bother about reading, myself. I read, I've read, history books. The kings and queens, and Henry VIII and all those sort. I like history. I get those from the library but I don't bother about any other kind of books. They don't appeal to me, other books, you know.

M.D. What do you do with your days now at home?

K.D. I go bowling and on a Monday I go to one of me clubs, play a bit of bingo and have tea and cakes and in between that we book down for day's outings. Tuesday, I go off to me bowling club, Wednesday I go to another club, Thursday I go bowling, Friday I sometimes go down to Jean and stop the weekend. And then some of these clubs, you know, we have a little bingo, a little whist drive, ten pence or twenty pence and that pays for our little day's outings.

I was eighty-two last February. I feel it at times. But I do me work. Bit of washing, dusting, and cleaning, cooking. Help me daughter. And I write in the evening, night time. They all ask me down at the club now, 'When's this other book coming out?'

*M*ARY CHAMBERLAIN *was born in London in 1947 and studied politics at the University of Edinburgh and the London School of Economics. She was, briefly, a research officer in the Foreign and Commonwealth Office and then taught in East Anglia, and from 1977 to 1987 at the London College of Printing. She is the author of* Fenwomen *(Virago's first book, 1975) and* Old Wives' Tales *(Virago 1981), and a forthcoming book on women in Lambeth. She now lives, temporarily, in Barbados with her husband and three daughters.*

Elizabeth Hardwick

talking with
Helen McNeil

ELIZABETH HARDWICK *was born in 1916 in Lexington, Kentucky, the eighth of eleven children. After receiving her B.A. from the University of Kentucky, she left the South and went to New York, where she studied towards a Ph.D. in English at Columbia University. Instead of finishing her degree, she turned to writing, beginning with stories, numerous reviews for the left-wing intellectual journal* Partisan Review *and her first, autobiographical novel* The Ghostly Lover *(1945).*

In 1949 Hardwick married the poet Robert Lowell, whom she had met in 1948 at Yaddo, the writers' colony. After an important year in Europe and residence in Boston, their daughter Harriet Lowell was born in 1957. Lowell is referred to by his nickname 'Cal' in the interview. Her second novel, The Simple Truth *(1955), deals with middle-class psychological misreadings of the complex truths connected with a murder trial.*

Always a writer concerned with political justice and intellectual freedom, Elizabeth Hardwick was one of the founders in 1963 of the New York Review of Books, *of which she is now Contributing Editor. For the* NYRB *she has written dozens of long, speculative reviews, a critical genre which she and the journal virtually invented. The* NYRB's *consistent attention to past and present Eastern European and Russian writers (particularly dissidents) owes much to Hardwick. As the* NYRB *became the focus of American intellectual opposition to the Vietnam War, Hardwick and Lowell became public figures, participating in (among other actions) the 1966 March on Washington. Hardwick was separated from Lowell in 1970 and then divorced, although a reconciliation was in progress at the time of Lowell's death in 1977.*

After her separation, Hardwick entered a period of prolific writing which still continues. For some years Elizabeth Hardwick has been a central figure of New York literary life and a powerful arbiter of taste. For several years she has also taught at Barnard College in New York City, influencing a younger generation of women writers. Elizabeth Hardwick helped edit and revise this interview.

Hardwick has collected some of her literary and political essays in A View of My Own *(1962) and* Bartleby in Manhattan *(1983). In* Seduction and Betrayal *(1974), a classic of feminist criticism, she praises the consciousness of women writers and characters while taking a notably unsentimental view of 'patriarchal baggage' – wives, widows and mistresses who have permitted themselves to be absorbed into the lives of great men. Hardwick's memoir–novel* Sleepless Nights *(1979) addresses the necessary subjectivity of memory by interestingly directing memory outward, towards other people, rather than inward. Her numerous short stories have not yet been collected, and an incomplete memoir of life with Lowell has been destroyed.*

I met Elizabeth Hardwick in the elegant West Side New York apartment where she has lived and written since she and Lowell moved to New York from Boston in 1960. A massive twenty-foot high bookcase and paintings dominate the two-storey-high living room where we sat and talked over cups of fierce black coffee.

H.M. In *Sleepless Nights* you talked about growing up in Kentucky.

E.H. I read a great deal as a child but it was not very serious reading, although I did read the Bible a lot just before being a teenager; that gripped me for a time. We were a large family, actually I am one of eleven children, of which seven were girls. We lived in town, Lexington, a beautiful place, dominated by two views, tobacco and race horses.

H.M. Where were you in the family?

E.H. More or less towards the bottom, eighth. And most were going to college, so I learnt a great deal from them. Every year that passed I read more and more and went downtown to the library.

H.M. But you weren't a journal keeper?

E.H. No, no. Actually I decided I would start to write some years after I went to the University of Kentucky. Then I went to Columbia University, partly in order to come to New York, but also because I wanted to do graduate work. One summer I went home and made up my mind that I wouldn't get a Ph.D. because it was getting to the rather nerve-wrung part. Also, it did dawn on me that as a woman I wasn't going to get a job in New York . . . I just took that for granted. I thought I would try to write, and that's when I started to do it. I was about twenty-four, I think.

72

H.M. Was there a Southern influence?

E.H. Well, the strange thing was that the Forties was a very vivid period in Southern writing – Katherine Anne Porter, Eudora Welty and, naturally, Faulkner. *The Southern Review* was an important magazine. But I never had the idea of wishing to be a Southern writer. I loved Southern literature but that was not my thing, so to speak. I was much more interested in left-wing politics.

H.M. And you started writing for the *Partisan Review* at that point.

E.H. No, that came after I published some stories. I published stories here and there, sometimes in literary magazines, and then I published *The Ghostly Lover* [1945]. It was after that that I met Philip Rahv [editor of the *Partisan Review*] and I started doing reviews. The *Partisan Review* group became enormously important to me. It changed my writing, and it changed my attitudes. However, as with all groups you can't enter it without already having that kind of sensibility. So I was rather anti-Southern, or at least I didn't really want to be the Southern girl in New York . . .

H.M. Ghostly Lover sounds a bit like Eudora Welty's *The Demon Lover*. Were you thinking of Welty?

E.H. No. I gave a very bad review to Welty's *Delta Wedding*. When I look back on some of my early reviews and their terrible presumptions – and they weren't very well written either. No, I was not influenced by Welty. And I don't have that kind of gift anyway for the rural and the small-town thing.

H.M. Were you at all connected then with any of the poets in the group that Eileen Simpson has written about in *Poets in their Youth*?

E.H. Well, I am afraid, certainly one of them [i.e. Robert Lowell]. And yes, all of them. I knew John [Berryman], I knew Eileen [Berryman], I knew Delmore [Schwartz]. I knew all those people, of course. I knew John as a young man around *Partisan Review*. He was married to Eileen then. He was a great friend of Cal's and in his young days most dashing and intense and affectionate.

H.M. At this point in the late Forties when you were at Yaddo and then met Lowell, did you see yourself as a particular *kind* of writer?

E.H. I don't know . . . From time to time I still didn't quite know what I was doing. It became hard for me to write fiction, perhaps, after writing the little reviews you start out with as a young writer. I am very glad I did reviews because as I persevered with them I put as much into them as I could put into any kind of writing. But I think it did make it harder to write fiction. I think other members of the group felt that too, though fiction writers felt it more. Mary McCarthy remembered the *P.R.* people saying, 'What do you think you are doing, trying to write a novel?'

H.M. Did the *Partisan Review* provide your literary models?

E.H. The great loves that the magazine helped revive were Henry James and also Melville and Kafka and Dostoevsky. Well, you can't exactly make those enormous giants your models. But what was happening in *avant garde* literary culture of America was a passion for foreign literature. *Partisan Review* was instrumental in ending American parochialism.

H.M. There's the famous line in Lowell's poem 'Man and Wife' about how your 'invective scorched the traditional South' one evening at the Rahvs'. Were talk and argument very important to you in the *Partisan Review* group?

E.H. Oh yes, enormously. As I look back, things have changed a bit, people have become – what shall I say? – a little bit more bourgeois. It's not cool to go on that way, talking and arguing far into the night.

H.M. And you relished the role you played in these debates.

E.H. I don't know that I played much of a role when you're talking about Rahv and Dwight Macdonald. There weren't very many women in the group. As I look back, there were wives and they tended to be intimidated. I remember they just sat there. I once said to Mary [McCarthy] that I look back with a good deal of shame on how I never addressed a word to those wives. But it was in some sense a kind of battle. It was difficult insofar as women who were not writers were concerned.

H.M. Did you find yourself the only participating woman?

E.H. No, there was Mary and others. Originally there had been Eleanor Clark but she wasn't there much any longer when I knew these people. But there weren't many women. Diana Trilling came but she didn't say very much at that period. Her silence later abated, as we all know.

H.M. So many literary memoirs describe a group of young men sitting and talking late into the night, hammering out their ideas. It seems a male mode of literary bonding, as it were. I am interested that you may have seen yourself as the exceptional woman and therefore not perhaps typical of womanhood. Perhaps that kind of self-definition made you able to wade in.

E.H. It was one's interests and passions about ideas that counted.

H.M. Did you find that you changed roles or that each of you in the group had a symbolic role that you were defending?

E.H. I don't think so. I learned a great deal from the people around *Partisan Review*. I learned even more from Cal. We all had a sense of engagement in whatever was happening at the time, both politically and culturally.

H.M. In *Sleepless Nights* you describe other people who came from the South: these characters seem to be fulfilling their fates, acting out something written for them. In most cases that fate was a life that from the outside looked like failure.

E.H. I think that all writers feel that they are failures in some sense. And maybe they see everyone as something of a failure. I can't really imagine that any creative artist wakes up and feels, 'How good I am!' and 'Look how far I have come!' because you know yourself to be up against your limitations. If anything it seems to me to get harder as you get older. You address yourself to some invisible audience for whom you would like to feel that you have done your best. I don't think it gets easier as you get older and I find it remains difficult to be up against the limits of your knowledge, your intelligence, your talent all the time. Just adding to the gross print of the world is a presumption . . .

H.M. But you have been involved twice in major American cultural efforts to create an audience, once with *Partisan Review* and again in *New York Review of Books*, and I think in both those cases you succeeded.

E.H. Yes. It was not due to me, but the two publications represent something valuable for America and for American culture, or so I believe.

H.M. Your second novel, *The Simple Truth*, came out in 1955.

E.H. That's right, it is ten years after *The Ghostly Lover*. I did publish some stories which I have never collected – I don't know that I ever will. That seems rather a long gap – I did essays and things but somehow I just couldn't get back to fiction.

H.M. *The Simple Truth* seemed to me to mark the beginning of one of the qualities I like most about your prose style. It has a number of epigrams. In *Seduction and Betrayal* I noted down about a dozen epigrams – for example, when you described how Branwell Brontë supposedly went to the National Gallery in London, saw truly great

75

art, and gave up his own artistic ambitions. You remarked, 'This is hard to credit, since the example of the great is seldom a deterrent to the mediocre.' Or you remark that Nora in Ibsen's *The Doll's House* 'has the amiability and endurance that are clues to moral courage'.

E.H. Well, that came from writing essays, you learn how to say things in a precise way.

H.M. You have been writing more criticism than fictional prose over the last twenty years. I wonder whether you may have a view about character as something without gaps – a view of character as moral example, perhaps – and whether modern fiction might not allow for such a unified view of character.

E.H. I'm not sure we believe any longer that there is such a thing as character in the old sense. Instead of character we have 'improvisation'.

H.M. Do you feel that the essays in *Seduced and Abandoned* are also ethical commentaries?

E.H. I suppose they are. I think I do read certain works of literature in a rather personal way. Of course I don't look on them as real live people. I know they are constructs out of the mind of the author but, particularly I think in *Seduction and Betrayal*, I did that. Maybe when I am writing critical pieces, I look at the literature as if they are real and when I write fiction I look at people as if they were fictional, not real.

H.M. In *Seduction and Betrayal* you seem to criticize style *per se*.

E.H. For an excess of style you have to be not only dramatic in yourself, but also be in a dramatic situation. I think most people really don't have style and don't see themselves as a figure, even unconsciously so. That amorphous lack of definition is, I think, true of most of us. But certain people did have style. It is a burden, I think, to certain of our writers now . . . Maybe I should say it is a burden to *me* that certain of our male writers now are consumed by their image – or at least it appears that way.

H.M. Like Mailer?

E.H. Yes, that one. There's always Mailer. I don't suppose concern with image makes writing good or bad, but it's strange how determining it can be. A very brilliant writer like Philip Roth, who is also a very intelligent man, wrote three books about having written an earlier book, *Portnoy's Complaint,* a masterpiece. An oddity certainly. I can't think of any women writers who are so concerned with the details of their being a writer and having written such and such.

76

H.M. I don't think that temptation is given to women . . .

E.H. We are not allowed to throw ourselves around in that way. You must have an audience for it before you can do it. It is a two-way street, acting out your fame.

H.M. Parts of *Seduction and Betrayal* read like a certain kind of autobiography written as criticism, as if it were about your own relation to Lowell . . .

E.H. It might be, I don't know; I wasn't really conscious of that. You are not the first person to say that. Actually I started writing these essays because of an invitation to give three lectures at Princeton; one was on Ibsen. Then I began to write more, but somehow in the Ibsen essays there is a good deal of heartwrung passion.

H.M. Ian Hamilton's biography of Lowell says that you were very deeply involved in revising the manuscript of his collection *Life Studies* [1959]. Were you?

E.H. Not really. I wouldn't say that. Cal began to write *Life Studies* as prose. I was certainly rather annoyed when he began turning all this wonderful prose – which it was, because everything Cal wrote was magical – into poems. I think overall my greatest influence on Cal may have been in the area of politics. My political interests were somewhat different from his. Some of that might have gotten into *Life Studies*. I don't think I had anything noticeable to do with the rather violent shift in his style away from a highly formed metrical verse. I think it was more the times, actually. I was very sympathetic to this change, and astonished by such poems as 'Waking in the Blue' and 'Home after Four Months Away'. At certain times I felt that he had gone too far and also that the poems were too prosey, but I didn't feel that in the end.

H.M. Did you regularly read and comment on Lowell's manuscripts?

E.H. Well, he asked for that from everyone and so you couldn't be there and not be read to from what he had done during the day. Of course I did comment but other people did too. That was simply the consequence of the rather wound-up and concentrated and dedicated kind of life he led. You always had to talk about what he had written. Poets, I think, do that more than prose writers; it is a little harder to bring out long prose passages. Cal read his work to all his friends. It is something that was done with me every night and I am afraid I did comment.

H.M. What was your role in setting up the *New York Review of Books*?

77

E.H. Cal and I were friendly with Jason and Barbara Epstein and we knew Robert Silvers. I had written an article in *Harper's Magazine*, where Robert Silvers was an editor, about something called 'the decline of book reviewing' . . . The opening came when there was a newspaper strike in New York which went on for several months. Jason was in publishing – he knew there were books coming up and he knew about the possibility of getting advertising money. There were about five of us – Robert Silvers, Barbara and Jason Epstein, and Cal and me. I think the reason we survived was that we knew the writers and we were able to get them to write. Our first issues were a kind of missionary work; almost everybody we asked produced something. So it was very impressive. That was in Spring '63; we got a large number of letters, so we decided to go on, although there was a gap in publication until September or October. Barbara Epstein and I edited the second issue. Bob Silvers and Barbara have been the editors since then. I have never been a real editor of the paper.

H.M. Your title is Contributing Editor, isn't it?

E.H. Or Advisory Editor. Any credit that might accrue from the quality of the *New York Review* is really due to them, but I have always been connected with the paper.

H.M. Were you involved in the decision to make the *New York Review* a political magazine?

E.H. That was not a decision. We were Sixties people, not in the sense of being hippies, far from it, but that was a political time. We meant it to be a kind of intellectual newspaper. However, the wisdom lay in not just starting another magazine but offering some kind of service, which was the reviewing service. I don't think we would have survived without that or without the mixture of politics and art. We offered reviews of many different kinds of books and by many writers, and at greater length.

H.M. One of the most impressive contributions of the *New York Review* is that it has created a new essay form available to the common reader.

E.H. The common reader . . . whoever the common reader is, the *New York Review of Books* is willing to tax his or her concentration.

H.M. I thought your essay on Simone Weil in the *Bartleby in Manhattan* collection was a tremendously moving tribute to a woman who lived 'to honour the sufferings of the lowest'. Have you had a long-term interest in Weil?

E.H. Yes, I have. My interest in Weil goes back to 1945 when Mary

McCarthy translated Weil's essay 'The Iliad: A Poem of Force', appearing in Dwight MacDonald's magazine, *Politics;* I was so struck by that, I never got over it. You treasured your copy of that essay. It was out of print for a long time. Another essential member of our group, was Hannah Arendt. Hannah was not one of the silent women, she was incredibly formidable and opiniated. Of all the women here in New York I think Hannah has left the greatest impression on those who knew her. Renate Adler, who was much younger, knew Hannah, and learned a lot from her. And of course, there is Mary McCarthy. I never knew Mary to defer to anyone as she did to Hannah . . . She realis ed she had encountered a unique, irreplaceable being. I think Hannah was truly one of the great passions of Mary's life. For myself, *The Origins of Totalitarianism* floored me with the vastness of the learning, the intellectual confidence and deftness to bring her scholarship and arguments into an original focus. Hannah was one of the great lights that passed through our city.

H.M. I wondered whether the commitment of the *New York Review of Books* to opposing the Vietnam War might have some origins in Hannah Arendt's lessons?

E.H. I think everybody opposed the Vietnam War, even the people fighting it, even the people in Washington. They were kind of stuck with it. It was so appalling to be sending bombs and condoms and whisky and soldiers halfway round the world. Really, I think that even the people in Washington felt repelled by this enormously sickening, destructive thing they were caught up in. I remember the first demonstration in Central Park right over here. Of course we went. It was amazing, the number of people, but it wasn't only the numbers, it was *who* was there. Every place we turned there was someone we knew. When we went down to Washington for the first 'Teach-in', the administration had some people speaking for them and then there were people speaking against the war. That was the beginning of the articulate protest which then built up all the time. Nobody was for the war. I think there are more people for it *now*, like Reagan, than there were then. This is the turn of the screw.

H.M. Were you on the famous March on Washington in 1966?

E.H. Oh yes. All we did was go down to Washington and on marches; it was a lot of fun, I must say.

H.M. Through the Sixties you were writing quite a lot for the *New York Review*, then came trouble with Lowell and your marriage breaking up.

E.H. That was the early Seventies.

H.M. How do you feel now about Lowell's collections, *History, For Lizzie and Harriet* and *The Dolphin*, where a lot of your personal life and feelings went directly into his poems?

E.H. It was *The Dolphin* that used my letters directly. I didn't like it, I was horrified when I saw it. I also didn't think the letter poems were good poems. I once said to Gore Vidal that if they were better poems I wouldn't mind, and he replied, 'Oh yes you would! You might mind more!' Some of them were bad. They were unrendered although otherwise there were wonderful things in the book. I think the best poems in the book are those about Caroline [Blackwood]. I told Cal that later. But otherwise, as far as using your life for literary purposes is concerned, that was what he was doing throughout his writing, starting with *Life Studies*. I didn't particularly like his calling that volume *For Lizzie and Harriet*, though. I thought it was rather silly. It seemed a little intimate, but perhaps that's all right. That was what Cal did, he used himself in every way possible and so, since one sort of had to tag along in a line or two in any case, you just sort of got used to it. I take literature as personally as other people do, but somehow I don't resent, except for the letters, this personal element. I must say I can read Cal's poems – well, that wouldn't be true of all of *The Dolphin* – say, I can read *most* of Cal's poems just as if they were written by someone else. When you have spent your life reading and sometimes you see a little phrase about yourself, you fester for a day or so and then try to forget. You can't correct everything . . .

H.M. I brought that up for a couple of reasons. In *Seduction and Betrayal*, when you talk about Lady Byron, Jane Carlyle, Countess Tolstoy, etc., you use a very telling phrase, 'patriarchal baggage', to describe these women who lived through their husbands. It seemed to me that by the act of writing *Seduction and Betrayal* you were saying that that was not what *you* were.

E.H. No, I was not that way. To take one example of baggage, I particularly like Pasternak. His prose – memoir and stories – of which there isn't a great deal, at least not in English, has been a kind of inspiration to me. I have learned a lot from Pasternak. So when his mistress's book came out I was really horrified and that started me writing that essay. It is so obsequious and at the same time so self-dramatizing about Our Love. I felt that was the worst thing that could have happened to a woman, to feel that you were being validated by a famous person and by his talent which, of course, you can never have. That belongs to him or to her, alone. In my own case I can say that it is a puzzle to me that I wrote more after I was separated. I don't know whether I would attribute that to having more time, but I don't think so. I suppose there may have been some change. I do think that what happens in your life – and this may be more true of women than of men – does give you a kind of spur so that you must do whatever you can do. Whether that spur is financial or whether it appears as a loss or a sense of personal destiny doesn't matter. I *have* written more since then, and I don't know just exactly how to analyse that.

H.M. In *Seduction and Betrayal* you were strikingly generous about situations which must have had a sort of burning parallel to painful events in your life. For example, you were able to understand Sylvia Plath's rage and unresolved hatred without needing to indulge in it yourself.

E.H. The rage is one thing and life is another. Sylvia Plath found the images and structures for rage, the emotion itself is of no literary value.

H.M. In *The Simple Truth* and in your essays you criticize women with high intelligence but few aims. At the same time you show tremendous respect for the combination of intelligence and drive which character- ized – for example – the Brontë sisters.

E.H. There is a tendency to feel sentimental when you look back in history and you read that this writer's wife or sister was so intelligent and so full of energy. I don't think everybody should be a writer or a painter or a musician – it just doesn't work that way. I think it is wrong to feel, foolish to feel, that Jane Carlyle would have been a great novelist. There is no reason for us to think that. It is just a mercy of heaven that we have her wonderful letters. It is a kind of Sixties notion that everybody is supposed to be an artist. It is very difficult to be an artist – there is such a thing as talent, for one thing, which isn't so widespread. Also there's character. So I feel that we look at these things wrongly.

H.M. Who are your friends now?

E.H. I have always had friendships with writers ever since I began to write. Not all of my women friends have been writers but I don't have any really close friends at the moment who don't work on a rather high level at something. It isn't that I don't want other kinds of friends but it just doesn't happen that way. I suppose you do kind of drift apart, life is somewhat narrow. My closest friend is Barbara Epstein; she's like a sister. Among my other close friends, there's Mary McCarthy; Susan

Sontag is a close friend. I must speak about her. She has mostly addressed herself to large talents and subjects. So often you can get swept up in the second-rate – with what people temporarily consider to be the first-rate – one sees the mediocrity and expends one's energy trying to make some kind of adjustment of taste. It's a sort of arrogant thing to do. And perhaps wasteful, being corrective.

H.M. Are you speaking of when you were a young reviewer?

E.H. I am speaking of now. Even though I feel that what is most important for me to do is write about things I feel are valuable for one reason or another. As you get older you want to devote yourself to things that are valuable.

H.M. I want to ask you about your relationship with your daughter.

E.H. I have had nothing but pleasure from my daughter. Someone asked me how I felt about my daughter and I said I felt the way Stendhal felt about his mother: a passion almost criminal.

H.M. I wonder whether the nineteenth-century model of the great man's life may finally be on the way out because women writers' relation to their children and family is so different.

E.H. I know. It is very, very strange that all of these social combinations shift so much. Attitudes can take dramatic shifts within a year. Almost every year there is a slight shift in attitude between men and women. Do you know what I mean? Literature is under pressure to keep up with society. It takes three or four years to write a novel. Meanwhile this shifting is taking place. Most books are retrograde in what their intention was.

H.M. Do you see yourself continuing to work pretty much the way you have been working, or do you have a particular project?

E.H. I hope so. You have to work, you have to earn a living and you have to work – that's what you do. One good thing about being a writer is that you can go on as long as your mind lasts and you are not sick and you have built up a little audience or a large audience for yourself. I know I stress what a hard life it is, with the constant awareness of your limitations. On the other hand I must say I have been thinking recently that I am very happy I have this little career built up over all these years, starting when I was twenty-three, of course it is a great consolation to me and a great joy and a kind of a privilege too. The labour of it. You feel every bit of reward is earned.

*H*ELEN McNEIL *is a American writer and critic who teaches in the School of English and American Studies at the University of East Anglia, where she is mainly concerned with poetry, feminist literary theory and aspects of representation. Her critical study* Emily Dickinson *was published by Virago in 1986, and she writes articles, reviews, and broadcasts regularly. She is married and has two children.*

Dorothy Hewett

talking with
Drusilla Modjeska

*D*OROTHY HEWETT, *born in 1923 and raised on the flat expanses of the western Australian wheat plains when Perth was a small provincial town and there was no bridge across Sydney's harbour, is best known as a poet and one of Australia's few radical playwrights. Influenced by Brecht and German Expressionism, her writing draws on symbolism, paradox and archetype in plays that are fast, daring and iconoclastic. She learned from Christina Stead, Eleanor Dark and Eve Langley whom she read at university in 1941 and after, that it was possible to be formally experimental and socially confrontational, even in Australia and even as a woman.*

There have been many women poets in Australia, and novelists, editors and journalists, and there have been many actresses, but few women have survived the tough environment of Australian theatre as writers, and fewer still a tradition of writing and production that has, until recently, been doggedly naturalistic. For a long time Dorothy Hewett was regarded as eccentric for her style and dangerous for her sexual honesty; or worse, damned with the faint praise that slides into silence. But with contemporary feminism and more experimentation in Australian theatre, her writing is better understood and her crucial part in those changes appreciated.

Dorothy Hewett started writing as a student at the University of Western Australia. She moved to Sydney in 1949, already a member of the Communist Party. She lived in the inner city, in those days still a proletarian domain, working in a notorious spinning mill, an experience which found its way into her first major publication and only novel, Bobbin Up, published in 1959 (Virago 1985). The 1959 edition sold out quickly amid controversy and nervous interest, the first of many shock waves from her writing.

Dorothy Hewett left the Communist Party when the Soviet Union occupied Czechoslovakia in 1968, but her doubts had started more than

*ten years earlier with the invasion of Hungary and Krushchev's 'secret
speech' denouncing Stalinism. In the shadow of these events she found it
impossible to reconcile the party's literary expectations and her own
complicity in them with her feminism and a taste for modernism and
literary experimentation. By the end of the Sixties her writing showed no
trace of socialist realism. She was back in Perth, teaching at the
University and reading the German Expressionists.*

Her first play, This Old Man Comes Rolling Home, *was produced in
1965. Since then she has written sixteen plays, including* The Chapel
Perilous *(1971),* The Tatty Hollow Story *(1970),* The Man From
Mukinupin *(1979) and* Fields of Heaven *(1982).*

*Dorothy Hewett is now living in Sydney again, in a very different inner
city, with her second husband, Merv Lilley. She has five grown-up
children. She is writing for film, but poetry and drama remain her
favoured forms although at the moment she is absorbed in the autobiography she is writing for Virago.*

D.M. Dorothy, you have survived nearly twenty years in Australian
theatre, and you have always said that it is a hard place to work. Why
has it been so hard for a woman playwright?

D.H. Until relatively recently the Australian theatre for both men and
women has been basically naturalistic and writing in any other mode
has been considered rather weird. So that has been difficult for me.
Even Patrick White has never been taken seriously in theatre. This
situation is changing, but although one tries very hard not to be
paranoid, which is often difficult, there is still a feeling that my sort of
writing is not quite the thing for a woman to be doing, particularly not
a woman of my age. It should be the province of young men. And then
there are the male structures and dominant attitudes in theatre. For
example, in rehearsals directors are much more prepared to accept
men defending what they've written. If women defend what they've
written they are considered difficult, whereas men can be quite
aggressive and everyone thinks this is perfectly natural. And I remember quite early on being absolutely astonished at some of the things
that were said to me in theatre foyers. One male director said to me,
you're a ball-crusher and you write about ball-crushing women, and
later a member of the theatre board of the Australian Council, and
quite an influential member too, said, when are you going to stop
writing those bloody dreadful plays of yours and go back to poetry

which you can write? These sorts of remarks seem rather ephemeral now, but at the time they were incredibly confronting because they were made by people who were very well known in the profession and from whom you might have expected some sort of support.

I don't think that attitude is as bad now, though there are remnants of it around still. But I do think this sort of thing has stopped women from writing for theatre because theatre is a communal activity. You can't just have a room of your own and write in bits and pieces on the side from family life. You have to be there. You also have a very brutal confrontation with the audience, much more brutal than in any other kind of writing. You're sitting out there on the first night. All this is very difficult for women; all that life which is so much a part of the theatre, opening nights and the strain of it, and the talk in the foyers and everyone knowing everybody.

D.M. Part of the hostility must have come from your confrontation with sexuality, as well as from your rejection of naturalism.

D.H. Oh, yes, it was taboo. Australia has been particularly narrow on the question of sexuality and I think at first the feminist movement found it quite difficult to deal with female and male sexuality because in a way it threatens other concepts of women's freedom. But to me it's always been a very intrinsic part of feminism and also of being a woman and a writer, because I suppose I am still naïve and idealistic enough to believe that love is a very central part of our lives and that our sexuality is part of that ability to love other human beings. For me it was necessary to come to terms both with questions of freedom for women to develop and be themselves and also the question, as I'm heterosexual, of how to relate to a person of a sex whose role in our society has been, to say the least, oppressive.

D.M. Sometimes in your writing you cast women and writers in a similar role, as the silent critic or the not-so-silent critic. But you also insist that although they are very often outsiders, at a tangent to society, they are victims and are not without responsibility for what happens.

D.H. It's no good going off and saying I don't want to have anything to do with men, with the family, I'll create my own feminist ghetto. You have to have this double role. That's the paradox, that's what life is all about. On the one hand you have to create for yourself some sort of separation, some sort of role as critic. On the other hand you have to be right there in the middle of it, there's no way out. You have to be the eternal naïf, the god's fool, if you like, the clown, the one who plays many roles, the one who remains open to experience. It's a very vulnerable position.

D.M. Is this appreciation of paradox and fragmentation part of your attraction to modernist, symbolic forms of writing?

D.H. I think I have always been drawn towards what is most difficult, thinking if I could only overcome in my own way the problems of being a poet and a playwright and still come to terms with a fragmented life, then I would have got somewhere. Using that impressionistic symbolic style of writing, that highly imaginative poetic style is like grasping the nettle danger because it's more difficult to structure than anything else. Thinking about it critically, I think I had to find a way of dealing with subjects which were suspect, if not taboo, that would be forthright and yet have a mythical content. I became enormously interested in basic myths like the story of Psyche and her monster-husband that Beauty and the Beast comes from, and the story of Rapunzel. I often take these myths especially in poetry, but in plays too, and twist them to a modernist viewpoint and a different vision – for lack of a better word, a female vision.

D.M. Was that how you approached *The Chapel Perilous*, your first play to confront all this head on?

D.H. I wanted to tell the whole life-story of a woman and it seemed absolutely impossible to get it into two acts. So I had to find a method, like a shorthand, to compress time and events so that they still made sense. At the time I was teaching Brecht and Durrenmatt and Frisch whom I'd always been interested in, and also the Elizabethans, Shakespeare and Ben Jonson. So I kept going to them for ways of doing this. And outside my study window was the New Fortune stage, a huge great platform for that kind of epic theatre. I remember going down onto that stage and walking around saying the lines. I was trying to cure myself of naturalism because so much of what I had done before, while not exactly naturalistic, was very influenced by Ibsen and by the American theatre from the Thirties – Clifford Odets and Lillian Hellman, people like that. It was walking around that theatre and going back to those Elizabethans and German Expressionists that got me out of it.

D.M. You grew up and started writing in Western Australia, which you have described as particularly parochial. How have those formative experiences affected your writing? There's another dichotomy in your work. There are the rivers that run dry and the women trapped in

90

dusty country towns; but there is also the magnificent beauty, the space and largeness of that landscape which tugs at the mind.

D.H. I still have an enormous affinity to the landscape I was brought up in. I lived from the age of two to almost twelve in the country, quite an isolated life, having correspondence lessons. The only other child I saw much of was my younger sister. We were very free compared to most children because we didn't have fixed times when we had to do school work. There were three thousand acres to wander around in and it gave us a very great sense of space and freedom. It is very bare, that area, and yet it has its own arid beauty. I think it's Randolph Stow who says it's the sort of place where characters have to be larger than life, like border ballads, because everything is so big and the cry of a crow is magnified until it becomes archetypal, something like that.

D.M. And that centrality of landscape goes with you when you write about the city, which you do as much, if not more than, the bush.

D.H. Well, I like to create mythological landscapes, landscapes that are larger than life, which have signposts standing out in them for all kinds of things, symbolic things in the lives of characters or in my own life. I always start a play from the landscape and unless I've got that right I really can't write. Unless I know exactly where those characters are and I can see the set both in real terms and in symbolic terms, I can't start people talking or moving around. So the landscape has always been central and this may be because of that great open space where there was very little to look at. You were a very small figure in it.

D.M. So where does the other side come from, the alienation and the isolation?

D.H. This comes much more from the experience of shifting to the town and going to school there from the age of about twelve on. It's probably why I dislike country towns, because Perth at that stage was really not much more than an overgrown country town. I found it very narrow and parochial. I was looking at a picture the other day of the intake of first year students at the Western Australian University in all disciplines. I was struck first of all by how very few of us there were, only about fifteen rows, and secondly by the fact that there were only one and a half rows of women. In that day and age if you went to university at all as a girl you were the intellectual elite because so few went or were in a position to go or had parents who thought it was important for you to go. My parents did, so both my sister and I went to university. I became a writer and she became a doctor, which was pretty unusual, but then we were just a two-girl family. But even though we were the intellectual elite of a very small parochial society, it also set us apart because we were considered bluestockings and this was very suspect. If you were so well educated no one would marry you!

D.M. How did you deal with that?

D.H. From a very early age I wanted to be a bohemian. I don't know where I got the idea from, but I thought being a bohemian was about all it was possible to be and still do the things I wanted to do. It seems a very old-fashioned term, now, bohemian.

D.M. 'Alice at the University/smoking Camels/in pale blue slacks/and a college sweater.'*

D.H. Yes! They were very pathetic revolts when one looks back, just pathetic, but in that community they were quite shocking.

D.M. How did you come to leave Perth?

D.H. My original dream was to go overseas, but then the war came and I joined the Communist Party and it was your bounden duty to stay and work in Australia. You became a sort of Australian patriot, I guess. Then in 1949 I met a man who was a Communist from Sydney, a boilermaker, and we fell quite desperately in love. I was already married to a radical lawyer who was also in the Communist Party and we had a child who was then about one and a half. The Western Australian Branch of the Communist Party was so incensed by my relationship with this man that my existence on the *Workers' Star*, where I was working, became untenable. The only thing to do seemed to be to leave and go to Sydney. Then my husband refused to allow me to have the child and of course in those days the absconding wife and mother was the lowest form of human life, and I would never have got him. So, not without terrible wrenchings, I left for Sydney with Les Flood.

We were in Sydney for about a week when the coal strike hit and everybody was locked out. It was an incredible period for someone who had been so easily brought up and had always had sufficient money to live on, even if only just enough sometimes. This poverty was something I had never come in contact with before. We had virtually nothing and we used to go and work in the Redfern branch of the Party where there was a soup kitchen. Things were very bad in Sydney. It was a freezing cold winter and we used to take wood round to people.

Alice in Wormland, Paperback Press, Sydney 1987.

92

The strike was enormously unpopular amongst the working class, they were suffering so desperately. I think it's now generally realized that it was a tactical error, and of course it failed. But it lasted quite a long time, and that was my blooding in the working class.

D.M. How did your difficulties with the Party start?

D.H. The idea in the Left at that time was that class politics were all important and if you brought up any other kind of politics like sexual politics, it was a red herring. It was also thought that working-class men of necessity had the right attitudes towards women and therefore any criticism was bound to be wrong. But I had moved from the middle class and it became fairly obvious to me that a great deal of male chauvinism existed within the Communist Party and that maybe working-class men were worse than middle-class men in this respect. Like Marx said, the working-class woman is the slave of the slave and the slave at the bottom of the pile naturally gets the wrong end of the stick. It seemed to me that all this needed looking at and I continually found myself at loggerheads with the Party, asking the wrong questions. I can remember asking why the Party Secretary's wife wasn't active in politics and being told that her job was to look after Lance and keep him active by being a domestic treasure. I was very scornful and was criticized for daring to voice this sort of idea at all. So there was this paradox going on, these awful attitudes to women and yet the sort of women who were attracted into the Communist Party were strong, passionate and revolutionary. But on the other hand it was possible within the Party for women to act with more force than in any other political area I can think of in Australia at that time. And there were certain people, if not many, the intellectuals in the party mostly, who were very enlightened even sexually which you wouldn't have found to the same extent in other parties. There was always conflict over these issues, but most of it was hidden most of the time. And then of course there was a very uneasy relationship between writers, intellectuals and the Party. When I first came to Sydney I never mentioned that I'd written anything. I suppose that I'd almost accepted that it was more important to be a political activist than to be a writer. There was always a terrible struggle to get time to write. It was considered self-indulgent and egotistical to want this time, to want to write.

D.M. This must have added to your conflicts over socialist realism because if it was so hard to get time from activism you must have felt under additional pressure to write the right kind of things.

D.H. For eight years I virtually didn't write anything except a bit of reportage. I was unable to write. I was unable to express what I felt in the terms of the dogma of the time. I think I was frightened that once I sat down to write it would all come spilling out and that it'd all be wrong and I would not be helping the cause which I believed in. It was only after I started asking questions about the actual dogmas themselves and about socialist realism that I started to write. I began to write *Bobbin Up* around the time of the Hungarian uprising and the Twentieth Congress. All those events freed me to write, I really think it is as simple as that. I suddenly realized that there were things happening which I had not understood. It was no longer the simple black-and-white world I'd been trying to convince myself of. It was very complex and contradictory and I had better start trying to make some sense of it otherwise I would go down into the maelstrom.

D.M. But you didn't leave the Party until 1968.

D.H. It was a long slow period and I struggled against leaving for a long time, for years. Part of my disenchantment was a trip to East Berlin to a congress of anti-fascist writers in 1965 and then to Moscow. The experiences I had in East Berlin were devastating on general questions of political freedom, and I came into contact with East German writers, hearing bits of their side of the story. Moscow had improved since I was there on another delegation when I was twenty-nine, all starry-eyed, but it was still terribly repressive. But I came back to the university branch of the Party in Perth which I had been in with my second husband Merv Lilley since the early Sixties. When we first found out about the Sinyavsky-Daniel affair, the two Russian writers jailed for having written what were considered anti-Soviet novels, we organized a petition of protest from left-wing and Communist writers in Australia. Many refused to take part in this, but quite a number did. And then the Russians marched into Czechoslovakia and although by this time the Communist Party of Australia was asking very serious questions itself about the policies of the Soviet Union, I felt I had to leave because there were still so many people in the Party who really believed that Sinyavsky and Daniel should be jailed and perhaps shot and who really believed that the Russians had marched into Czechoslovakia to put down counter-revolution. And because of all that had happened I couldn't believe any more that they meant what they said. With those Russian tanks it was the end as far as I was concerned.

D.M. You rejected the cultural programmes of the Communist Party and you moved seriously into drama which seems like a big break with

94

the past. But it must have confronted you with new versions of old problems. It didn't solve the problem of aesthetic strategy, maybe accentuated it. On the one hand there is the momentum of your own work, its integrities, the experimentation and the aesthetic choices it involves, and on the other hand the realities of box office, making a living, reaching the people you want to speak to, making a statement in a particular social and political environment.

D.H. I didn't really confront this problem, although I was very conscious of it, until after I wrote a play called *Pandora's Cross* which had such a terrible hammering from all the critics that it closed after two weeks, virtually closing the Paris theatre with it. And for a while I even thought – for the first time – that I wouldn't write for theatre again, it was just too painful. Then out of the blue I was given a commission to write *The Man From Mukinupin*. For the first time I sat down and thought to myself, all right, there's obviously some difficulty with how I am communicating with audiences and critics. Why is this? Does this mean I have to adopt other strategies? Partly because the commission was for a ceremonial occasion, the 150th anniversary of Western Australia, I thought I should write comedy with some sort of carnival atmosphere. So I went and read all Shakespeare's romantic comedies and thought about musical comedy generally. There were serious things I wanted to say in that play but I deliberately set out to capture the audience by using devices like crossed lovers, happy endings, doubling up, all those absolutely comic devices, as well as dance music, songs. Rather to my astonishment it worked. But I think it also worked because it came at a watershed in Australian theatre when people were beginning to be more open in what they would accept. Although it appeared on the surface a fairly traditional romantic comedy, there were strands in it which are not traditional at all, like the massacre of the Aborigines, the figure of the Aboriginal girl, the use of archetypal voices, the dark side of the town. Yes, I think it's a very real problem because I very often think that a lot of those considerations which are politically important can be quite conservatizing. You can get caught on that.

D.M. I'm interested that you tackled all this in theatre and not in the novel. You say you've thought of other novels, but you haven't written one since *Bobbin Up*. What happened?

D.H. I started another novel called *The Lurk Men* which was about working as an advertising copywriter in Sydney and I got about five chapters of that done and then I stopped dead. It was around this time

95

that I had gone back to Western Australia. I had always wanted to write plays but it seemed hopeless. Then I met an old friend who said, what happened to all those plays you were going to write? So I started to write plays again but writing drama is enormously difficult, particularly the sort of drama I wanted to write. So I began to think, okay if I'm going to be writing all these things, how am I going to do it? I write short stories, I write poetry. I've written a novel and I want to write drama, I write articles. I'm going to end up a jill of all trades and mistress of none. If I'm going to get control of drama it's going to take me all my life and by this time I was in my forties. If I'm going to catch up there's no way I'm going to be able to write novels as well, I've only got a certain amount of time and I've got all these children and I'm working at the university, how in God's name am I going to do all this? So I made a deliberate decision. I stopped writing short stories and the first time I've returned to prose, to fictional prose let's call it, is with this autobiography I'm writing and I'm enjoying it enormously, much to my surprise.

D.M. One thinks at once of your poem, 'Creely in Sydney':

> I can't write autobiography   because there is no me
> *Me* is not a stable reality/the collective
> *Me* in a changing world   no propped up statue
> in the square for pigeons to shit on turning green.

D.H. At first I was very nervous of this 'I' and I found it very difficult just to write that word 'I'. Then I began to think, which is a truism, that once you write 'I' you've created a character anyway and that no one can write who they are because no one really knows. As soon as I came to terms with that, it became much easier, although at times I still find it difficult because there seems to be nothing to protect me. It's more like poetry. But maybe there is one bonus in growing old, maybe one does get a slightly more structured view of the self because you've got more to look back on and therefore you can start making patterns more easily.

D.M. And finally, how hard has it been to make a living from writing?

D.H. It was impossible until I first got a grant from the Literature Board. In 1974 when the first three-year grants came out under the Whitlam Labour government, much to my astonishment I got one. Before that I had always had to have other jobs, even when the kids were little. I had the amazing luck to get two three-year grants one after the other which made it possible to shift back to Sydney which I had wanted to do for a long time and which was important if I was going to keep working in the theatre. It was too isolated in Western Australia and I had worked that lode anyway. So I came back here with the chance to write without having to worry about money. It was the most astonishing liberation of the spirit and physical energy that I have ever experienced. It came almost too late, I felt, because I was fifty and it had taken all that time, but it was amazing that it happened at all. And I'm still enjoying it.

*D*RUSILLA MODJESKA, *born in 1946, grew up in England. She left for Papua New Guinea and Australia in 1968 and now lives in Sydney. She has written* Exiles At Home: Australian Women Writers 1925–45 *(Sirius 1981) and, with Marjorie Pizer,* The Poems of Lesbia Harford *(Sirius 1985). She is currently writing a novel/history based on the life of her mother.*

Yvonne Kapp

talking with
Sally Alexander

I FIRST *became acquainted with Yvonne Kapp through her biography of Eleanor Marx, published in two volumes in 1972 and 1976 respectively when the author was in her late sixties and early seventies.** Eleanor Marx *is a magnificent book, a tour de force, a work of careful scholarship and literary skill which makes a distinctive contribution to the histories of Marxism, anarchism and labour in the nineteenth century. Eleanor herself, her beliefs, wants, fears, her family, friends and comrades, are brought vividly to life. In the 1970s I was absorbed in the Women's Liberation Movement (WLM). In small groups we campaigned, consciousness-raised and studied. In my study group we read volumes one, two and three of Capital, Lenin, Mao and Freud – in order, we hoped, to give new vitality to class struggle and the politics of sexual difference. Sex and class were the two insistent preoccupations of socialists in the early WLM. No wonder then that Eleanor's life and politics should fascinate us. Her socialism – a blend of passionate enthusiasm for oppressed peoples, Marxism and a fervent belief in freedom (she yearned and failed to become an actress, declaring once that the artistic life is 'the only free life a woman can lead') – seemed to anticipate the complexities of our own.*

And the circumstances of Eleanor's personal life – from her father's claim that 'Tussy is me', through her despair over housework and the struggle to earn a living, to her ultimately tragic love for Edward Aveling – were bound to intrigue the generation of feminists who voiced the slogan 'the personal is political'.

Reading Eleanor Marx *then, for a feminist of my generation, was to enter a dialogue with two other political generations: Eleanor's, but also, if more obliquely, the author's. Yvonne's Communism, interest in*

*Yvonne Kapp, *Eleanor Marx*: Volume I, *Family Life 1855–1883*; Volume II, *The Crowded Years 1884–1898*, Lawrence & Wishart 1972, 1976; 2 vols., Virago 1979.

Marxist theory and determination to raise the events of Eleanor's life above the level of a melodrama shaped the biography. Had one of us written it the emphasis might have been different; less perhaps on the power of the father and more on her emotional ambivalence and self-denials. Those differences were what interested me when I first read the book, and continue to do so. Yvonne, I think, is more exasperated than interested in the differences between us. She wonders at our preoccupation with antagonism between the sexes. Having played down Eleanor's feminism, and emphasized (eloquently and with dignity) what Eleanor gained from her relationship with Aveling, 'Why do all you girls hate men?' she once asked me, 'What dreadful things have men done to you?' . . .

Standing in Yvonne's elegant living room (everything about Yvonne is elegant, from her literary vocabulary to the delicious cake she offers with afternoon tea), gazing out on to her leafy garden in Highgate, I searched for a reply, 'Oh no, no, no, Yvonne. Not all of us do hate men . . . only some of us, and only some of the time . . .', reaching as I hoped for firmer ground: 'Socialist feminists don't hate men. The sexual division of labour is the problem, the undervaluing of femininity, of everything that women do and have done.' I sank weakly into silence.

The different emphasis didn't simply indicate different political forma-tions, but also emotional contours. If, since Mary Wollstonecraft, feminists have struggled to combine work and political being with love and motherhood, then the particular ways in which these seeming incompatibilities have moulded women's and men's lives is the very stuff of history.

Socialism in England, at least since the 1890s, was born partly out of compassion for the poor. Through the early twentieth century the well-educated, the propertied and the wealthy lived worlds away from the working classes. Autobiographies of those many socialist and labour women and men who came from privileged backgrounds are full of the shocked discovery of poverty: the evidence of deprivation and hardship that unemployment and poverty – capitalism's twin evils – bring. Over and over again one reads: I went to the slums, and I saw, and what I saw changed me. I became a socialist. The language is Biblical and so is the experience of conversion. If those with a social conscience submitted themselves to the service of socialism, then faith in the moral and ethical superiority of their service sustained them. Both Yvonne's generation of educated women and men, and my own, are heirs to this tradition of socialist service. We also both rejected Fabian gradualism – ours was a revolutionary socialism. But there are vital differences. My generation, *born in the 1940s, grew up to accept education, health and economic subsistence as their right. We grew up with the self-confidence to demand changes in the immediate and most intimate conditions of our own lives – not just in the lives of others. How different from Yvonne's generation, who had come to maturity in the shadow of the Great War, when to be alive at all seemed mere chance. In the 1930s unemployment, poverty and fascism swamped the claims of feminism, whereas each political generation since the Sixties has been preoccupied with liberation, personal identity and sexuality. In the 1930s the Soviet Union floodlit the consciousness of many Western Socialists with the promise of proletarian government, economic planning and the austere paternalism of Joseph Stalin. Indeed, there is no ideal socialist commonwealth, except in the imagination.*

When I went to meet Yvonne – writer and Communist – it was with the curiosity of an historian of socialism as well as feminism, keen to discover the ways in which these different social forces might emerge in one woman's long and active life. I was not disappointed.

I have always been a writer

Eleanor was not begun until the 1960s, Yvonne having 'discovered' her 'between the lines' of the correspondence of Frederick Engels with the Lafargues (Eleanor's sister and brother-in-law) which Yvonne was translating in the 1950s for Lawrence & Wishart. Nothing was written or known, it seemed, about this interesting person who kept cropping up in the letters. So Yvonne seized the first opportunity she could – which, given the demands and contingencies of the life of a freelance writer, took a while to arrive in the unexpected form of a small inheritance – to devote herself to research and to write the biography of Eleanor.

In a sense all her life had been a preparation for such a task, in particular the central activity – writing. The desire to write seems to have been born out of isolation as a child and galvanized by a combination of rebellion and economic need:

'I have always been a writer. I wrote verse at the age of seven, comic poetry. I did write an awful lot of verse. All through adolescence. I had a short story published when I was about twelve or thirteen somewhere.'

I was curious as to why she had started writing so young:

'It's very difficult to say. I don't exactly know. I think it may have been influenced by the fact that I was a tubercular child and so I had to spend long months lying on my back and just reading and reading and not going to school.'

103

Yvonne's pursuit of writing, indeed of education and a career at all, was born out of intense personal struggle with her parents:

'I didn't like my parents very much . . . and as I grew up we didn't get on at all. They wanted me to live a completely conventional life. My father was a merchant. And they just thought I would come out; get married to some nice, presumably well-off young Jewish businessman, or something of this sort. Instead of which, having been to a finishing school in Switzerland and a ghastly family outside Paris I was determined to go to a university and got myself into King's College, London. Just after the First World War they took people coming out of the forces who had not got the qualifications for university entrance. I had an interview with the head of the English Department and he let me come in on a special course.' Yvonne believed the course, was in journalism, and London University did offer a Diploma in Journalism in the 1920s which Vera Brittain claimed was the 'next best thing to a degree as preparation for a career in journalism' (*Women's Work in Modern England*, 1928).

'This upset my mother very much. My father was really rather proud of me. He thought it was a good idea. It did cut me off from the social swim my parents wanted me to be in.

'I had a lovely time. I edited the college magazine and I enjoyed myself no end. Eventually there was a real bust-up and I ran away. We had rows all the time. My father would say, "Daughters don't behave like that," and I would say, "Well, I'm a daughter and I do behave like that and if you don't like it I will leave home." And eventually I did. I literally ran away. I just went out of their flat in St John's Wood and ran down the road.' This was in 1921 when Yvonne was eighteen.

'I was eleven years old when the First World War started. Anyone who grew up during the First World War belonged not only to a different generation but to a different epoch. My parents were literally Victorians . . . That war made more of an abyss between one generation and another than anything that's happened since. The world changed in those years. Ideas were different. I can remember at thirteen saying to my father that I couldn't possibly believe in God, which shocked him dreadfully. It could not be possible that there was a God because how could each side claim that God was on their side? And these appalling deaths. People who never lived through that would hardly know what it was like – the casualty lists. I read the newspapers. And all the girls at school (Queen's College, Harley Street) had brothers in the army. And people were always being sent for, their brothers being killed. Their fathers being killed. It was all around you.'

Having left home Yvonne stayed with a girlfriend and launched herself into a career as a journalist. Her first job was on the *Evening Standard* which paid £4 a week ' – riches in those days'. Audacity and good fortune secured her the job:

'I had been a great admirer of Alec Waugh's book called *The Loom of Youth* which was one of the very earliest books critical of the public school system. And I'd written a gushing fan letter to Waugh. I expect he had millions of them, especially from young people. He was my one hope, so I went to see him. He worked at a publisher's and he knew the editress of the women's page on the *Evening Standard* and she took me on. Then I was seconded from the *Evening Standard* to the *Sunday Herald* to be assistant to the editor – because they needed somebody very quickly. He had clattering false teeth. He was a Manchester man. I had a most extraordinary and interesting job there. I was an errand girl. I was sent out to collect people's articles. I had to correct text. I had to cut articles. I had to do absolutely everything that has to be done on a paper including on a Saturday morning I used to help in the compositors' room. I was a real dogsbody. The tea girl, so to speak.'

This relative affluence was short-lived. Yvonne was sacked after a clash with the editor over a quotation from Shakespeare – 'I was a pretentious little literary snob.' This was August 1922 and she was already in the throes of the final break with her parents that her marriage in that month brought about, her father acting out feminism's paranoia.

'After I had left home, my father made sure that I could not marry under age – and he had given the authorities the names of twelve young men whom I was forbidden to marry. Young men with whom I'd gone out dancing, playing tennis, you know – most of whom I wouldn't have dreamt of marrying. And of course my husband's name was among them. We couldn't do anything about it. I was under age and my father could stop it. In those days fathers didn't have to give a reason at all. The Solicitor-General's spokesman said, "Unless your father is insane" – well, I thought he was, I thought he must be – but that was hardly good enough. There was no way of removing this ban till I was twenty-one.'

The ban was removed in fact when adverse newspaper publicity threatened to escalate. Yvonne was marrying an artist, Edmund Kapp, thirteen years her senior, penniless but with some influential acquaintances in the arts and Fleet Street. A successful exhibition at the Leicester Galleries with an introduction to the catalogue written by Max Beerbohm had begun to make his name known and the story newsworthy. Her parents' retreat was not sufficient to bring them to the wedding. It was many years before a reconciliation was effected.

105

Marriage

Yvonne was nineteen years old when she married in 1922. Theirs was an itinerant life in search of artistic integrity and financial solvency. In spite of their poverty and the precariousness of their material existence, fate and friends in uneven combination offered homes and work at vital moments. If Edmund's career set the pace of their married life – at least in the first year or so before the birth of their daughter – then it was Yvonne's skills as a journalist that brought in the irregular income.

Edmund had a quest. He returned from the war a staff captain with a distinguished record of service. His talents as a linguist as well as an artist were undiminished in spite of traumatic experiences. But he felt desperately that he lacked an artist's proper training. When Yvonne first met him he had just come through a period of 'curious interior crisis . . . a very self-disciplined and agonizing time'. In pursuit of this training they set off for Rome, rucksacks on their backs, and walked 'the whole of the French and Italian Riviera. It was absolutely marvellous. Stopping with people on the way. Max Beerbohm lived on the coast, and Gordon Craig, my daughter's godfather . . . we got as far as Pisa eventually.'

They were given a lift to Rome where they lived for six months in a small hotel and then in the summer took a little house up in the mountains:

'We lived a very, very disciplined life. We didn't even, though we were young, ever go sightseeing. It was quite an austere sort of existence. Every Sunday we went to a concert, but otherwise . . . However, we made a lot of friends. And Edmund started to paint.' When short of money in Rome, 'we went begging into cafés playing our recorders, going round with a hat. We made quite a bit.' They stayed in Capri with Edgar Mowrer, the writer, and his wife where Yvonne found herself 'to my very great delight, pregnant', so they wanted to return to England. In Italy they were without 'a home, roots, anything'.

Joanne, Yvonne and Edmund's daughter, was born in a Hampstead maternity home for soldiers' wives. But her presence did not inhibit their footloose and unorthodox life. Chance acquaintances met at a concert offered them a home – a cottage in Sussex where they took their new baby:

'It was a very primitive cottage I may say. My mother-in-law lent me her sweet maid who came and did do a lot of very early things – nappy-washing and so on. And it was all right as long as I was feeding, but you know the difficulties. Anyhow . . . Edmund got a job drawing judges and advocates in the law courts. A marvellous series and very well paid. It was at this stage that I wrote my first book, *Pastiche*: pieces to accompany Edmund's drawings. When the winter came I was left in the cottage with the baby, breaking the ice of the well to fetch water, every drop of which had to be filtered and sterilized before it could be used. And cooking on calor gas. It was pretty terrible, and I really could hardly stand it. Eventually I just didn't stand it: and I got a friend of ours who lived close and who went to London regularly to drive me to London.'

In London they found a flat in 'Orange Street, off the Haymarket. That's where the baby grew up. She was a little Piccadilly baby. She used to be weighed at the Boots that was there. It was a marvellous studio with a flat upstairs that had a parapet where you could just put a baby's cot. It was at the stage door of the Comedy Theatre with Ciro's Club at the other end. And Constable the publishers.'

But Edmund got restless and went off to Spain so that Yvonne found herself alone again with the baby.

'And I must say I was very miserable. It's frightfully difficult being alone with a small baby. I was twenty-one or two, and everyone else of that age was having a wonderful time, going to the Gargoyle and parties and that sort of thing. Everyone danced in those days. The baby-sitting thing hadn't happened. Occasionally a friend would come in and sit in but I felt fettered by the baby if you want to know. It was less a joy than a responsibility and it wasn't very good . . .

'That was in the spring of 1926 and the baby was nearly two. Then we joined up again in Paris and went to live in Antibes, and I did freelance journalism most of the time. In the autumn, though, Edmund was invited by Nigel Playfair to play the recorder in his production of the "Bourgeois Gentilhomme". So he went off again, you see. I was always being left in places [peals of laughter]. And I minded that very much . . . Edmund was a sweet father, a marvellous father. He would wash the nappies and do anything. But he didn't feel bound by the baby. He could drop us. Anyhow, so he left me in Antibes, in a *pension* there, which was all right as long as he was living there but as soon as he left it was dreadful.'

This time Yvonne was joined by a friend, John Collier the writer, and they had also been adopted, as it were, by a young girl who had 'fallen in love with the family' so stayed to help with the baby:

'It was there that I was interviewed for the job for which Rebecca West had recommended me. You know, to work on *Vogue* . . . She was one of the people to whom I'd been sent as an errand girl when I was on the *Sunday Herald*. When I went to her flat and said I had come for her article, she said, "Oh, come in, come in." And she sat me down on the sofa. She was absolutely charming. She wanted to know all about me and

107

she listened to my ambitions as a writer. Then when we were in the south of France we used to go sometimes to the Juan les Pins casino and we were sitting there with some friends, and people from another table came and joined us and a woman across the table said, "Oh, aren't you Yvonne?" She'd remembered my name. And I said, "Who are you?" [peals of laughter]. Isn't that dreadful? Dreadful! She was living in the same *pension* with us, and we had a very nice time with her.

'Anyhow, I was offered this job – so then in the autumn I left Edmund with the baby and the nanny and went to Paris. And until I'd got enough money I didn't send for them, till Christmas. I had this job as literary editor. It wasn't too bad. It involved all sorts of idiotic things like going to see these fashion house shows. The work was really a matter of putting commas in and taking commas out, because all the people who were really interested in fashion were pretty well illiterate. They couldn't write English and I was quite useful for that. They were absolutely sold on the idea of *haute couture* which didn't interest me at all.'

The job was 'fantastically well paid': £1,000 a year in dollars, tax-free and in Paris. It was 1927 and Yvonne was twenty-four. She lived opposite the Luxembourg Gardens, paid the nanny, took a studio for Edmund and 'we really lived well'.

'The only luxury that I got out of it personally was that I went riding before breakfast [laughs] . . . It was better than doing freelance journalism. I loved being in Paris, and of course we were relieved of money worries for the first time. But here was where the marriage began to crumble.

'He was always in his studio. I don't think he liked being married in those days. I think he would have preferred not to be married although he was a loving person. I don't think he liked having the ties. He painted, he was quite happy, and you know – one can't get away from it – people who went through the First World War were damaged personalities. When we were up in the mountains that summer in Italy on every feast day (which in Italy is, as you know, very often) they used to shoot off some little ancient artillery piece. An old gun they'd got. Edmund was always stunned. He would turn absolutely bloodless, and tremble from head to foot. It was as bad as that.

'He spoke about the war very seldom and not for a long time. He'd had a most terrible experience. He was a brilliant linguist and one of his jobs had been to interrogate German prisoners immediately as they were brought in. And he was sent to a forward post which was then completely deserted. It was no more than a dug-out lined with bully beef. He was supposed to be relieved after three days. But the man who was told to take over was killed on his way up. Then they forgot about him. And he remained there for weeks. And was gassed. When they eventually found him he was deaf, stone deaf, and he had total internal stasis. He'd eaten nothing but tins of bully beef from the sides of this dug-out. He was a complete wreck. This was at the end of 1917. He was in hospital for weeks. And he was never sent back to the front. He'd been in the trenches for over two years. He was in the Sussex regiment. And most of the men who went to France with him were totally, totally wiped out. All that. And then this ghastly experience.'

Yvonne left *Vogue* as suddenly as a few years earlier she had left the *Sunday Herald*, only this time the issue was the appallingly low pay of the clerks and typists:

'I got angry about a number of things that were happening to the lower-paid people. They were very exploited, the typists and clerks. There was a hierarchy and I was at the top of it. Well, I was overpaid really, and these people were dreadfully underpaid. And eventually I said, well, I could be paid twice as much as I'm getting now, but otherwise it's not worth it: double or quit. They said quit, so I did.'

'Back in England Edmund took a cottage just outside Cambridge near some friends of ours, the Bernals. And that's where I began to write the first novel . . . about French people . . . I wrote very slowly. I remember going and reading a first chapter to Rebecca West who thought it was rather good and encouraged me. Some friends of mine had started a publishing firm and said to me, "Why don't you write a novel? We'll give you £50, go away and write." Well now, £50 was a lot of money in those days. You could live on it for six months. So I took my opening chapter and I rented a place in the South of France for a few months very cheaply, and I completed this book. But these young people, these publishers, hadn't got any money of their own. However, one of them had a rich father who was funding the firm. And he insisted on seeing everything on their lists. When I came back and delivered my book, it went into galley proof and was read by the father. It was called *Nobody Asked You* and he sent back the proofs, writing right across them, "I cannot sanction the publication of this book", with his signature. And underneath his name was the title, "Nobody Asked You". So the first thing I did was have this made into a Christmas card and sent it to all my friends wishing them good, clean fun.

'Then I looked through the galleys and do you know he had been so annoyed at certain things, and thought they were so obscene, that he had practically torn the pages with his savage markings. Mind you, it was pretty outspoken, I mean for those days. Anyhow I said to these young people: look, it's all very large and fine but how about giving me some compensation? You've had the type set up, can I have that? And you've got the paper, can I have that? And they agreed. So I had the paper, I had the type. I got a friend of mine, Quentin Bell, to design a cover, I bought a car for five pounds, a lot of stamps and brown paper and so on, and I registered myself as the "Willy Nilly Press". And I published the book myself. I got quite a number of pre-publication orders. And then what do you think happened? On the Sunday after it came out there was a review in the *Observer* by Gerald Gould who devoted two columns to it. He said – unforgettable words – that if he didn't review this book by a remarkable new young writer he might be doing her a grave injustice, on the other hand if he did he might be doing his readers a grave disservice because it was a very shocking book. Well, you couldn't ask for a better review, could you? The next day little men with bag sacks from every bookshop in London were on the doorstep of my house in Brunswick Square. They were taking twelve and fifteen copies at a time and coming back for more. It sold and sold and sold. Within a fortnight it was practically sold out, and I'd made more money than I've ever made in my life on anything I've written since.'

Taking Life Seriously: Politics

Yvonne's publishing adventure was short-lived. She sold *Nobody Asked You* to a wholesaler for the second edition and settled back into writing. At a dinner-party one evening she met Lindsay Drummond, the head of John Lane, the Bodley Head who, obviously intrigued by the tale of the Willy Nilly Press, paid Yvonne £150 a year for the first refusal of any future novels.

The years of writing novels were a sort of watershed in Yvonne's life. She had taken easy advantage of the opening up of higher education and the professions to women that occurred in the 1920s. Easy, that is, compared with the women who had grown to maturity in the years of militant feminism before 1914. Vera Brittain and Virginia Woolf were only two of the best-known literary women who felt the disadvantage of being a woman more keenly than Yvonne. But if chance and women's recently won political identity had lightened Yvonne's path to economic independence and a literary life then the driving forces behind her development as a writer had been personal: rebellion against her parents, marriage and child. Her psychoanalysis was mentioned almost as an aside. Otherwise, after the early 1930s, Yvonne's life-story as she told it, although punctuated with references affectionate, enthusiastic, admiring

110

about others (as diverse as the men in the packing department in the basement of the AEU's headquarters in Peckham, as Harry Pollitt, secretary of the Communist Party, or colleagues and immediate employers), did not reveal the same intimate connection between personal relationships and the development of her professional self.

It was the pressures of external events, the need to give political coherence to an increasingly frightening and chaotic world, which changed Yvonne's priorities as well as her perception of her world. A child of her time, her personal transformation marked the shift from the 'careless' Twenties to the sombre Thirties.

'I began to take life more seriously as a result of outside events; which coincided with my being round about thirty and the beginning of the fascist era in Germany. I hadn't really thought about politics before then, though I'd always been on the left side. Having rows with people in 1926 during the General Strike and that sort of thing . . . my brother actually drove a bus and I couldn't stand that. But I was what you might call rebellious rather than politically conscious. It wasn't until fascism in Germany and the burning of the books that as a liberal, and a Jewish liberal at that, I began to feel really involved.'

From 1933 Yvonne used to put up refugees: 'So I became involved in that way and began to work for refugees and anti-fascist organizations. They were peripheral, not directly political. Because I didn't know enough about politics to know if there was a central way in which you could – what's the word I want – I mean, the proper way for people a little more mature than I was to be politically organized and then deploy one's energies. But I went the other way, you see, doing all these things. And then, before you could say Jack Robinson, there was Spain.'

Before the Spanish Civil War began in 1936 Yvonne went to the Soviet Union: 'I was terribly interested in the Soviet Union. It was fascinating and I had this wonderful time . . . I think it's true to say that people see what they want. What they think they're going to see, they see. What I thought I was going to was a country that had got rid of capitalists and landlords and was getting on with social democracy with everything in favour of the working classes.

'On the way home aboard ship, I travelled with Harry Pollitt who was returning from the Seventh World Congress, which was a very, very important congress, as you know, in which great changes were made from the disastrous policy of "class against class" to the popular front. This, of course, was after the burning of the Reichstag . . . I spent a lot of time talking to Harry Pollitt on the voyage home saying that I would be more useful not being in the Communist Party. He said that was a great

111

mistake ... He said, "You see, the trouble is you'll be discouraged so easily because things go badly in one country or another and unless you are in an international movement you can very easily feel that nothing is ever going to happen."

'When I got back home I decided that he had been right and I joined the Communist Party and lost a lot of friends ... I had really had, do you see, up to then, a sort of playgirl's attitude.'

Yvonne now led the full life of a political activist. One of her first organizing successes was the 'great meeting at the Albert Hall in 1937 in aid of the Basque children ... which collected thousands of pounds'. Paul Robeson arrived unexpectedly and sang. Picasso sent one of his Guernica sketches for auction and Yvonne also wrote a book on the Basque children in England for their funds. A little later, Yvonne began to work for a Jewish refugee organization at Woburn House. She was in charge of the department dealing with refugee dentists and doctors.

'When I took over this office was lined with files up to your neck ... And each file represented a human life. Can you imagine anything so dreadful? So with two shifts of four young refugee workers by day and by night, the papers were sorted out and put in order ... And then you found that out of the thousands of pieces of paper that there were, some individuals had already got to England, some to America. Others had died. Some represented urgent cases that had to be taken up immediately. Doctors and dentists were not allowed to practise in Britain and they were refused entry unless they had a guarantor ...

'I spent practically the whole working week with a couple of secretaries preparing six cases. And on Friday afternoon I would go to the Home Office with those six cases and say, can I have these please? And they were so carefully prepared that I always got them. I had quite good relations with all the Home Office young clerks. And I would not spend my time, unlike the voluntary ladies of the past, in chattering with those who had already arrived here, all of whom wanted to say, "Can't I be an exception and practise?" And some of them wept because they couldn't.

'The refugee organization was of course flooded with applications to come to Britain. I mean people who had the faintest chance of coming out of the Nazi countries. And it's true we did try to get out the people who had the least connections here. Some of them were in concentration camps ... When the war came they were allowed to practise. Three thousand of them were on the department's books altogether.'

Soon after the invasion of Czechoslovakia Yvonne went to work for the Czech Refugee Trust Fund, a government-funded body ('blood money, you might say, to save people who were going to suffer as a result

112

of the sell-out') under the directorship of a retired civil servant, Sir Henry Sunbury. Yvonne became his assistant: 'There were three government-appointed Trustees: a very high-up retired civil servant, a Jewish businessman and a distinguished ex-Trade Union leader.'

Shortly afterwards the war broke out and then, in May 1940, Yvonne was sacked: 'The Home Secretary, Sir John Anderson, sacked me because I was thought to be a Communist . . .' Another member of the staff, who had been in charge of preparing material for the refugees' tribunals, was sacked at the same time. They both went away to the country (Yvonne's daughter was away at school) and wrote a book called *British Policy and the Refugees,* 'because we knew it from the inside.' The book was not published at the time because a Penguin paperback on the subject of refugees by François Lafitte appeared before theirs. There was a paper shortage during the war and afterwards.

'Don't forget: this was the moment when it was thought there was going to be an invasion. It was also thought that anybody who was in sympathy with the Soviet Union would become automatically a traitor to Britain and, because of the Non-Aggression Pact, pro-Nazi, if you please. Our sacking was a signal of the Government's attitudes to the Communists in the coming months . . .'

Working for the Engineers

The two women returned to London when the bombing became bad (in 1941) but they were unable to find jobs. Everywhere she applied Yvonne was short-listed, but never appointed. So she did some voluntary work, including some at the Labour Research Department. From there she was recommended for the post of Research Officer for the Amalgamated Engineering Union (AEU) whose president was Jack Tanner. Within a month of the appointment the Soviet Union was invaded 'and the whole atmosphere changed, and I was able to continue being the Research Officer until after the end of the war. And that was a wonderful job.'

At the AEU Yvonne used to prepare the wage claims for the whole of the engineering industry and write Jack Tanner's speeches for him:

'He had a beautiful voice; strongly cockney, very resonant. There were certain words he stumbled over, and certain words he didn't like, and certain words he did like. I studied him like an actor, so that I could write his speeches in the terms in which he would say them. He got so used to this that the bloody man never read the speeches before he had to deliver them, which used to annoy me terribly. He just took it for granted that I would write the speech that he would want to make. He never asked me

113

anything. I used to beg him before the annual congress, "You read it." He never did.'

The AEU had no women members, and so of course no women on its executive. It took a while for Yvonne herself to be accepted. Because of the manpower shortage women were conscripted into the engineering industry and in 1943 the AEU reluctantly allowed them into the Union. Women attended the annual conference (the National Committee) for the first time in the spring of that year:

'As we drove down to Blackpool, Tanner said, "Look, would you talk to them. Find out what they want to drink. Give them whatever they want. Introduce them.' The AEU never before had a woman in an administrative position on the staff, and they were very thankful for me for once. So I said to the women delegates, "What would you like to drink? Order anything." There I was pouring out these things and one of them got up and said, "Oh, let me do that, I used to be a barmaid!" So she poured the drinks! I told them: whatever you do don't speak of yourselves as skilled workers. You may be skilled but it means something quite special in this Union . . . and don't do this, and don't do that . . . "Skilled" meant you had to be a white card holder, you had to have done your full apprenticeship; served your time, you see. The women were dilutees. They had only come in for the war. They were semi-skilled. They were on the repetitive operations and so on. A toolmaker, for example, was something quite different. And if the women did mention a skill, which they did once or twice, really a kind of rigor went through the men. I mean, they were beside themselves. It was the most macho union.

'The women managed very well. There were a lot of dilutees, also men, young men. They had to accept dilution as men were in the forces. But this contempt for people who hadn't served their time. You only get that among the craftsmen, this extreme craft attitude. Terribly old and terribly traditional. I don't know what it's like now but it was a diehard attitude. I was lucky. I managed to overcome most of the prejudice. I don't think anybody really felt hostile to me. And I did actually attend one or two of their executive meetings.'

Among the most significant achievements of Yvonne's work at the AEU were the wartime Production Enquiries. Many complaints came through from the shopfloor about poor management, and other obstructions to production:

'The very first National Committee for which I wrote Jack Tanner's speech had a lot about incompetent and inefficient management and how war production was not up to what it should be and so on. And the

114

Minister for Production wrote to Tanner and said, "How do you come to this conclusion? We should very much like you to establish your facts." Tanner got in touch with me and said, "Well, what do I do about this?" I said, "That's quite simple. You just get in touch with the members, with your shop stewards. You ask them in every factory." "Oh," he said, "do you?" "Yes," I said, "You do. You send out a questionnaire, that's what you do."

'And in effect, that's what we did . . . I drafted a questionnaire of a hundred questions and it went to a thousand factories, direct to the shop stewards. Then I analysed the returns, three thousand of them in all. The upshot was absolutely fascinating.'

Yvonne was allowed to employ a secretary for this work, and her research skills developed so that for the second Production Enquiry six months later, she was using the punch card and knitting needle method!

'I may say that the first enquiry created quite an uproar. It went only to government departments, but Tanner saw that it also went to certain MPs and so on. Questions were asked in the House. Tanner was terribly pleased that the Union should produce this. It was of national importance. So we did it again six months later. By this time I'd also got two more assistants. After that we did a health and welfare enquiry. Because what was turning up more and more were the inadequacies of physical wellbeing in factories – like air-conditioning, canteens, first-aid, restrooms and so on. This idea of health and wellbeing in the factory was very far from the minds of the Union officials at the time.'

The introduction of women into the Union and the Production Enquiries were only two of the matters in which Yvonne was involved at the AEU. She also helped to organize the Jubilee of the Union, which was transformed into a cultural event, with an exhibition of pictures, a play and a history of the Union. She wrote the pamphlet on post-war reconstruction for the Union as well as the evidence to the Royal Commission on Equal Pay (which was published later as a separate pamphlet by the Labour Research Department: 'And that is my one contribution to feminism, I may say'), and she also assembled the John Burns Library of trade union and working-class movement literature for the AEU which they later gave to the Trades Union Congress.

At the end of the war, however, Yvonne was again at odds with her employers because of her politics:

'Well, then, of course, as we came to the end of the war, Tanner couldn't make the speeches that I wrote, and I wouldn't write the speeches that he wanted to make. He had hit the headlines by demanding the opening of a Second Front, which pleased him mightily . . . He was a very handsome man and he genuinely liked women and respected them, and was awfully nice about the women who came into the Union. He had a naturally good attitude. He was a Labour supporter who had been a bit of a wild boy in his youth. He met Lenin. At the drop of a hat he would tell you what he had said to Lenin. He never told you what Lenin had said to him [giggles]. I got on with him terribly well. I really liked him very much. But we quarrelled. He became more and more right-wing. And I would not write his speeches. In the end we just fell out.'

Yvonne left the AEU in 1947 and went to the Medical Research Council as part of a group 'doing what they call industrial psychology, which is rubbish. But I didn't really care very much – it took me into factories, which included Silvertown and the dock area of the East End of London.' Each factory – chemical, rubber, engineering, sugar – had its own specific hazards, and intimate acquaintance with Silvertown as well as her work with Jack Tanner at the AEU undoubtedly strengthened her research and writing about Eleanor Marx's political work in the East End of London.

'I got to know the district very well indeed. I went into every factory and found out exactly what the situation was. What they had in the way of doctors, nurses, first-aid, and I even went into the little workshops, where they employed only ten people or so who never came under factory inspection. It was fascinating. But of course that material is not mine. It is theirs. It belongs to the Medical Research Council which never published it. It was a marvellous experience. I enjoyed that. But I got into trouble over the report on the silliness of the job satisfaction enquiry at Vauxhall's, so they sacked me.'

The end of her job at the MRC meant a radical change in Yvonne's working life:

'Once I was freed from salaried jobs after many years, instead of going back to writing as I should have done, I made the mistake of agreeing to do a translation from the French and this led from one translation to another. And I got stuck in this . . . like doing crossword puzzles. Translating is not real at all. It's a ridiculous thing to do.'

But in the course of translating (which she did full-time between 1953 and 1960) Yvonne came across Eleanor Marx. 'I was fascinated. And I thought, what a very interesting person this is, I must find out more about her.'

And so her major project was born. It took ten years, survived a serious accident which left Yvonne flat on her back for five months, and the second volume was subsidized by two small Arts Council grants.

116

'I've had heaps of careers. But they were all to do with writing finally – in different spheres. I've never stopped writing. I never thought of doing anything else except writing– I've always been learning about writing. You never stop really. [But] I had to be the family support. It wasn't always by choice that I took paid jobs.'

Yet curiously, for a woman who so identifies herself, her attitude towards most of her writing is often casual, if not neglectful. Yvonne's work is scattered in the archives of the Labour Research Department, the AEU, or the MRC, for instance. (It is oddly reassuring to think that some of the massive literary infrastructure of the Labour Movement has been shaped by a woman such as Yvonne.) Some writings have been published without acknowledgement of authorship. Her fiction she dismisses curtly: 'Oh my novels, Sally,' I was told on a second meeting. 'They were *early* writings – pretty trivial and not very important.' Yvonne is severe on her young self. For her, her life and writing fall into two parts – before and after the Communist Party. Young womanhood was characterized by 'lightmindedness'. 'I joined the Party,' she said, 'not for sentimental reasons. It gave me a seriousness which I hadn't had before.' Her writing, like herself, was not to be taken seriously, until it was harnessed to the cause of socialism.

Listening to Yvonne's story (many of the details of which space and discretion forbid including) I thought how those 'old enemies' evoked by Vera Brittain in *Testament of Youth* (1933) accurately describe Yvonne's early circumstances: 'The Victorian tradition of womanhood, a carefully trained conscience, a sheltered youth, an imperfect education, lost time, blasted years . . .' and I revel in the spirited way in which Yvonne subverted them!

*S*ALLY ALEXANDER *was born in 1943, and was brought up in Berkshire. She went to Ruskin College in 1968 and then took a degree in History at University College, London. She has written on feminist history, is an editor of the* History Workshop Journal, *and a Senior Lecturer in Cultural Studies at the North East London Polytechnic. She has two children and lives in London.*

Molly Keane

talking with Polly Devlin

MOLLY KEANE *was born in 1904 at Ballyrankin in County Kildare, the daughter of a fox-hunting Anglo-Irish gentleman, Robert Skrine, and his wife, who wrote poetry under the pseudonym Moira O'Neill. Although she had three brothers and one sister, she led a secluded and lonely life as a child, educated by a series of governesses and by her mother until she went to boarding school for a short time in her teens. She grew up passionately interested in horses, hunting and houses and these interests formed the background for her earliest novels (written under the pseudonym M. J. Farrell). She first started to write to earn some supplementary pin money, and insists there was no other motivation, but there has never been any feeling of expediency about her ten novels. She also wrote plays, in collaboration with John Perry, many of which were successes in the West End.*

Molly Keane, as M. J. Farrell, wrote, on the whole, of the lives, preoccupations and pastimes of that moneyed, hunting, curiously dislocated class of people in Ireland, the Anglo-Irish, skating over the political angry geographical reality that was Ireland in the first quarter of this century. In some books, notably Two Days in Aragon, *she tackles the enormous, vexed problem of the turbulent relationships existing in Ireland between the Anglo-Irish and the various factions of the 'native' Irish; in others she goes back to the golden days of the Edwardian swansong of the Anglo-Irish. But in all her books she presents – and thus preserves – a detailed and exquisite picture of the last days of the Irish raj; she celebrates, by affectionately chronicling, the beauty and atavistic qualities of the Irish great houses, marooned dreams of tranquillity and decaying splendour standing in their depleted demesnes, lived in by people who refuse to see – or believe in – the fires and diaspora before them. Both Ballyrankin, her parents' house, and Woodrooff, the Perry house, where she spent long formative periods before her marriage, were burned in the Troubles.*

120

In 1932 she met Bobby Keane; they married in 1938 and moved to Belleville in County Waterford where they lived in great happiness with their children Virginia and Sally. Her husband died suddenly in 1946 when only thirty-six and, lonely, desolated, her creative powers injured, she continued to live in Ireland; later she moved to London for five years.

In the 1960s she went back to Ireland, to the pretty hillside cottage in County Waterford where she now lives, but it was not until 1976 that she began to write another novel, Good Behaviour, *which was shortlisted for the Booker Prize for fiction and was made into a BBC television serial. This was followed in 1980 by another novel,* Time after Time, *again filmed (with John Gielgud, who directed her early plays). She is now writing her next novel.*

Her books are witty, sardonic, human comedies, edged by black humour, and like all good comedies sadness and pathos lie close to the glittering surface. But they are now more than novels: they deliver a remarkable and vivid social history, an impeccably observed, occasionally delinquent record, full of relevance and revelation of a way of life and a vanished world that has not otherwise been given its due recognition in the country where it once existed.

P.D. Molly, when did you first start writing?

M.K. When I'd been to school for a short time I got some sort of bug – I don't know what it was – some sort of virus I suppose. But everyone thought (and my mother was determined) that I was getting tuberculosis, so as a cure for that I was put to bed. Now, the only thing I could ever do at school was what they called English Composition. So for an escape and through sheer boredom I began to write a book. I wrote away under the bedclothes, and honestly I must have written about fifty or sixty thousand words or more, and I thought it was pure Shakespeare. Well, not Shakespeare exactly – more Dornford Yates.

P.D. And this was *The Knight of the Cheerful Countenance*?

M.K. Yes. Looking back, perhaps it wasn't as bad as I think. It was probably tremendously pictorial because the only thing I thought about was hunting, and the only thing I wanted was glamour and lovely men.

P.D. A lot of young girls think of glamour and lovely men but they don't sit down and write a novel.

M.K. Yes, but I was on my own, without the lovely men. Well, there was one I fancied, but he wasn't any good for me.

P.D. Do you think it was the influence of your mother that made you write?

M.K. No, not at all, she would have been horrified at the idea of my writing a sort of Romance.

P.D. But she was a writer?

M.K. But she wasn't a serious writer. When she was young she'd been quite a good minor poetess – Moira O'Neill, the Poetess of the Glens – and I don't want to despise her poems because I think some of them are rather magical. She was terribly idle. But we thought they were lovely when we were small.

P.D. So do you think at some level –

M.K. – we were influenced by her? I'm sure I was, but it's so curious because by the time I got to writing I was terribly at odds with her – I'd sort of grown up and I was having great fun with my grown-up cousins and she disapproved of it all. She was frightened for me, just as I would have been frightened if my daughter was, say, in the drugs scene. I think, probably, having led a tremendously secluded life, she was terribly frightened of my knowing people whom she considered fast, which was anyone who had any fun at all.

P.D. Did you ever become friends with her?

M.K. No, alas, no. I mean when I was a child I had no one else to love. I was a terrible lover, and I *adored* her, though I hardly ever saw her; but she did have a sort of rapport with children.

P.D. Did she come round to loving your books?

M.K. No.

P.D. Had she read them?

M.K. I don't know. I never discussed them. Ever.

P.D. But wasn't not knowing unsatisfactory?

M.K. We were at different ends of a civilization. I mean I was frightfully jolly and funny and off to all the doings I could and she thought this was dreadful and she didn't know what was going to happen – I don't know *what* she thought.

P.D. And the relationship between you and your father was a significant one?

M.K. No. None at all. There wasn't any. No, he was completely of a life apart. The only time I think I was ever near to him was when he was dying and my mother had this phobia about doing nothing and not

123

having proper nurses and I looked after him, and I insisted I go and get the old nurse from the village so that she would sit with him all night, and that really turned my mother against me.

P.D. Was he an uncomplaining man?

M.K. Very.

P.D. Was he like the father in *Good Behaviour*?

M.K. No, he wasn't as jolly. He was very well behaved.

P.D. Did you love him?

M.K. No. I admired him because he was such a good horseman. I admired that about him.

P.D. Are you nervous by temperament?

M.K. Yes.

P.D. And shy?

M.K. I think so. Yes, I think I am. I think I'm nervous. I was always disliked as a child. My mother didn't really like me and the aunts were ghastly to me and my father had absolutely nothing to do with me.

P.D. Did you feel isolated . . . unloved?

M.K. Yes, I think I did. As a very young child I sort of depended on my mother and thought she was everything – but I don't think I got much out of her.

P.D. That's a dreadful legacy, isn't it?

M.K. No. I don't know. It's what made me fight myself free. Now Susan, my sister, had always been much more popular. She'd always been gentler and quieter and jolly good at various things and she got on so awfully well.

P.D. Fight yourself free of what?

M.K. Fight myself free of that secluded life – that nunnery of a life, which it really was. Because anything like young men were frightfully disapproved of, and as for anything being done to help us – nothing was done, except the horses of course.

P.D. I remember that story about your mother seeing you lying on the grass showing your knickers.

M.K. Yes, and I must have been only eight or nine.

P.D. And she was genuinely shocked?

M.K. Yes, she was. I remember discussing this with Susan, who really had a much more liberal point of view about it all. And she said, 'You

124

see our mother's generation felt that modesty was a thing that almost had to be beaten into people – that it wasn't naturally born in them. They must be shown and made to be aware that that was a necessary element in life.'

P.D. And in *Two Days in Aragon* there's a moment when Nan and Mrs Fox are discussing sex and they talk about it with a real prurient interest. You make it clear that they didn't perceive anything loving or life-enhancing about sex.

M.K. A disgusting business, yes. And there was so little discussion about it. I remember there was a frightful scandal because we had a sweet old groom who was an ex-steeplechase jockey and he jumped down a stile coming out of the laurels back into the stable yard and he broke his neck and was found dead at the bottom of the stile. And the insurance looked into the whole thing and said he had been in the laurels having a go with the cook and there was a desperate hush about that. And there was another awful scandal, how they couldn't have known all about it I cannot imagine, when a little housemaid had a baby in her bedroom, having done all her work and everything and gone into her bedroom and had the baby and there was an old cook who thought something must be wrong.

P.D. And this was Ballyrankin?

M.K. Yes, and the girl had gone out, how she could have done it, having just had a baby, and she found the baby in a large cardboard box, a dress box addressed to me from some big shop – well strung up and the address in large letters and labels, you know how things were in those days – addressed to me and she was just about to float it down the river. Can you imagine the scandal? How my mother can never have noticed that this girl was just about to give birth.

P.D. I can never understand these stories. At the end of pregnancy it's so *obvious*.

M.K. There's absolutely no mistake, is there? And Cook knew she was, but the cook didn't say to my mother, 'Look, this girl ought to be brought home.' So there's the baby floating down like the Lady of Shallot in a box tied up with string and brown paper and well labelled as Miss Skrine. The poor girl must have been desperate. Oh, those days. To think of them is so extraordinary.

P.D. And were you quite different from your brothers and sister?

M.K. Yes, very different.

P.D. And had they led the same secluded lives?

125

M.K. Well, no . . . They didn't actually because my brothers were in the Army and Navy and that sort of thing that the boys all went into then, and had been to school in England. They all liked my mother, as boys always do, and got on with her.

P.D. You had one sister?

M.K. One sister, Susan, much older. She was four years older, but it made a big difference then; and she'd gone to school in England. And then she'd got tuberculosis.

P.D. Did your sister like your books?

M.K. I think she did. She disapproved and admired both. She thought they were terribly disloyal to the Anglos – the Anglo-Irish.

P.D. Because she was very loyal?

M.K. Oh, tremendously so. Dangerously so. And my mother couldn't think of anything beyond it.

P.D. And was Ireland a foreign country to her, or her country?

M.K. It was my mother's country. It was Anglo-Irish country, except for the poems of the Glens of Antrim. She was a great one for the dialect and I think that she used the dialect to keep her distance.

P.D. Was she an unhappy woman?

M.K. No, she adored my father. She was frightfully happily married to him, and she adored her sons.

P.D. But a show of emotion was not a clever thing to show?

M.K. When we were little she could be affectionate, but when one was older it somehow went altogether because of this tremendous disapproval. I understand now that I was everything that she thought was all wrong.

P.D. But then what happened when *The Knight of the Cheerful Countenance* came out? Did she just ignore it – pretend it hadn't happened?

M.K. I think she shuddered and read it – or read some of it.

P.D. And you continued to stay at home?

M.K. I stayed at home on and off. In those days the funny thing was that if you were asked to stay somewhere you stayed for weeks.

P.D. Had you thought about a career?

M.K. No, it didn't exist. Absolutely not. And the only thing I thought about writing was that it would give me some money so that I could go on having lots of fun and going to horse shows and hunting and enjoying myself with my friends – and actually, what did I get for my first book? About £70, I think.

P.D. But what did you envisage your life to be if you didn't think of a career?

M.K. I just enjoyed life like it was . . . I adored parties. If I thought of anything I should have thought of some sort of dream-happy marriage.

P.D. That's what people did think of?

M.K. Yes, I'm sure they did. And yet they kept awfully quiet about it. One thing I do remember very plainly that children now, girls now, discuss every iota of sex, or lack of sex, with their gentlemen. I do know that I never opened my mouth to my greatest, closest friends about my adventures. I just didn't, and they didn't to me.

P.D. It was taboo?

M.K. No, it was more . . . I don't know how to describe what we were. I think for one thing the language about sex hadn't been invented. I don't remember the word sex occurring . . . ever . . . It just wasn't there. There was a tremendously romantic outlook. I do remember, when I was awfully young, on my very first walk-out I thought I'd practically reached heaven, and where had I got to? Practically nowhere!

P.D. But leading this ambivalent and lonely life in a large house . . .

M.K. But then I had friends outside it . . . I mean I had my hunting and my hunting friends and I had a great friend who lived about four miles away. We were so childish compared to the people of our age today. We were like children of twelve, the sorts of things that amused us. Or just a bit more sophisticated. I mean there was a bottle of sherry and there were the gramophone records, and the hunting was tremendous. When I was young it was the central thing in my life, and any sort of social success depended on being good at it, and success meant a lot to me, really a lot, because it spelt people. It spelt people spoiling me, it spelt people being good to me. Because I had nothing to give back. I was just a lone girl who was fairly amusing and not even frightfully good-looking and I did have a *lovely* time.

P.D. And did the native life affect you?

M.K. Well, we loved all the people.

P.D. And listened to them?

M.K. Yes. Always. It was a kind of fashion then to see who could imitate the Irish peasant, or who could tell a good story about them. That was

127

very popular. I think that was what gave me an enormous memory about dialogue. I can't do dialogue well today, but then it was no trouble to me. I simply could remember what had been said to me, especially anything that hit me as funny. I think everyone longed to be a good entertainer; and I was very good at it, which sounds a vain thing to say, but I know I was. And I got myself into what I thought was exciting society by just being jolly funny – and knowing how to be sharp and funny about people. It must just have been born in me because I didn't learn it from anybody.

P.D. Was your father like that?

M.K. No. He couldn't have been more English and I don't think he was a very clever man. But he was an awfully nice man, and a marvellous horseman, and totally conventional.

P.D. So, you're nineteen, you've written one book, it's been published. Do people know you've written it?

M.K. No!

P.D. Was it hard not to be boastful?

M.K. Oh, no. I was rather secretive about it. I think I told my great chum Daphne. But in the end it leaked out.

P.D. And the name M. J. Farrell? You'd chosen it at random?

M.K. Yes, because it was awfully different from my own name and all that.

P.D. And it is true that you chose it –

M.K. – from a pub, as I rode home . . . Very boring, but yes, I think I did. I wish I was as good as the other Farrell, who was drowned.

P.D. Did you decide then you were going to be a writer?

M.K. My feet nearly left the ground when I heard it was going to be published and I decided that that was the way to get another £70, so I wrote another novel, *Young Entry*, and then Billy [William] Collins, the publisher, stole me away. I thought he was awfully attractive.

P.D. And were you a celebrity?

M.K. No. I was little Miss Nobody. I don't know why Billy Collins went on, but he did go on publishing my books and telling me to write more. No, I was absolutely nothing.

P.D. And when did you use the word 'writer' to describe yourself?

M.K. I never did.

P.D. Have you ever done?

128

M.K. No ... sometimes when I had to sign passports or forms I'd put playwright and author, but that was years later. You see I didn't have to sign forms about income tax or anything else then. I remember I did have a terrible income tax argument, which I managed to win, and so didn't have to pay tax on the £70.

P.D. And did you think, 'I'm going to write a book every two years'?

M.K. Yes.

P.D. No trouble thinking up plots? Getting time?

M.K. Funnily enough I never had much trouble then. I do now of course. I think how hopeless I was – I don't know. It was always tough work for me to write anything except that first book which I thought was so marvellous. I just took time off to write and otherwise enjoyed myself. It wasn't my occupation or my job. I used to come home from having jolly times in Tipperary or wherever and sit down and write a bit for *Blackwood's Magazine* and thought I was getting enormous money – say £30 – for a lot of words. I thought it was marvellous.

P.D. For reviews?

M.K. No, for short stories. Very respectable short stories, sort of hunting and everything. They were done in the book then called *Conversation Pieces*.

P.D. Was writing hard work?

M.K. Always terribly hard work. The grims, absolutely the grims.

P.D. And how did you start your Woodrooff life with the Perrys?

M.K. Oh, that was a big secret. I'd met John's father, William Perry, out hunting and he said, 'You must come and stay at Woodrooff.' And I pretended I was going to stay with a respectable friend and instead took the train to Clonmel, and when I got there it was just seething with young people, like that marvellous daughter of his, Sylvia Masters, and darling Dolly Perry whom I loved.

P.D. So this was an enchantment?

M.K. Oh, *marvellous*. I was never so happy in my life as in those first years at Woodrooff, it was carefree and lovely and the most exciting kind of racing people and everything, and I loved it, had a marvellous time. And I suppose it was there I met Bobby.

P.D. Had your husband read your books before you married?

M.K. Oh yes, very much. But he was never in the least involved in the writing. He used to say, 'I simply won't even look at your books until

129

they're in hardback, because I might be an influence and I might be hopeless.'

P.D. So now you're married, you've come through the war, you're continuing to write and quite suddenly, out of the blue, Bobby died.

M.K. What killed him was a clot after an operation. He was perfectly all right, he was leaving the nursing home the next day. I was having lunch with Gilbert Miller about a play and I thought I'd just go in before I went to lunch. A nurse met me and said, 'Matron wants a word with you, could you wait in the hall.' And Matron came in and said, 'You must be brave, dear, your husband's dead.' It really was unbelievable – I hate to think about it.

P.D. And you'd got two small children? Sally and Virginia?

M.K. Mm. It was a bit much.

P.D. Was your husband's death the cause of the creative block in your writing? Is this a romantic idea or a real one?

M.K. I think it's a combination. I did write a bit after Bobby died. I was in the middle of a play, but I couldn't go on. Then four years later John Gielgud and Binkie Beaumont said, 'Moll, come on, write another play.' Money, you see, got so scarce after Bobby died. So I wrote *Treasure Hunt*. Sybil Thorndike was in it and John Geilgud directed it: it was a great success. I was pretty desolate when I wrote it.

P.D. And had you written during the war years?

M.K. Yes, I'd written *Two Days in Aragon*. I was awfully tormented by the theatre. Binkie Beaumont was always pestering me to do a play for him, and then not doing it.

P.D. What started you writing plays?

M.K. Well, *Spring Meeting*.

P.D. Yes, but how?

M.K. Oh, John Perry saying to me, 'Oh, Molly, you must write a play and I'll get John Gielgud to read it.' And I said I couldn't possibly write a play, and he said, 'Oh, that's all right, just write a play about your own life,' and I suppose *Spring Meeting* is more like my life than anything. Roger Livesey – a very good actor – played the old man, who was very much a portrait of John Perry's father – old Willy. So it *was* my life, I think, very much.

P.D. Well, then, all possibility of anonymity had gone.

M.K. Oh, absolutely, totally gone, everyone from Ireland came to London for the first night.

130

P.D. Did you enjoy it – or were you rather shivering?

M.K. I was frightened, but it was wonderful.

P.D. What a glamorous thing – to have a first night in the West End.

M.K. It was for a girl from the bogs – it really was. And all the old people I really loved, like old Mrs Hall, famous old Master of Hounds, I remember she came wearing a marvellous red dress with a pigskin handbag.

P.D. But you must have been a terrific star.

M.K. In a funny way, you see, I was, because they all adored it, and everybody in the hunting world in England loved it. It was extraordinary. It ran and ran and was sold out night after night, week after week. Of course it was a tiny little theatre, which was perfect – the Ambassadors – sweet little theatre. But it was just absolutely extraordinary.

P.D. And what about the well-known pitfalls of novelists becoming playwrights?

M.K. It was just a fluke, I suppose.

P.D. No, because you did it so many times. Did you read up about plots – points and all that?

M.K. No, honestly. If you told me tomorrow to sit down and said, 'Here's a million pounds to produce a play,' you wouldn't get one that would work. I've written two that were big successes, three that weren't done, and one that was a staggering failure – *Dazzling Prospect*, which came out just at the time of *Look Back in Anger*, though I don't think that was the entire reason for its failure.

P.D. Were you devastated by its failure? By the criticism?

M.K. Yes I was, absolutely. I felt very wounded. I thought, well, I've come to the end of all I can do. I'm obviously no good. Then I really shut up.

P.D. When did you start writing *Good Behaviour*?

M.K. Late in the Seventies. The children were grown up and I was doing nothing and I started writing. It was such a secret. Like my first book written under the bedclothes. I thought, 'Absolutely ridiculous, I know it will be a total failure, but I will have a go.'

P.D. And was it a joy to find yourself writing again?

M.K. No, no.

P.D. Just as painful as ever? And yet you did it. That's called artistic imperative.

131

M.K. No, no, it's just obstinacy, literary obstinacy. No, it's true if someone had said 'this is hopeless' I'd have dropped it at that moment – and when Billy Collins turned it flat down I was really shocked. I had sort of discussed it with him and said wouldn't it be funny to have a fool who doesn't see what was happening. And he said, 'Moll, what a wonderful, marvellous idea, get on with that.' And then flat turn-down. 'It's far too black a comedy, my best readers have said that and I've read it carefully, but if you will make some, or all, of the characters slightly more attractive we'll do it.' And I really had the guts to say, though I terribly wanted the money, to say no. So then I put it away and thought, well, that's finished.

P.D. And the legend of Peggy Ashcroft –

M.K. Not a legend, it's true. It's exactly what happened. She came to stay and got 'flu and was in bed and was frightfully bored and said, 'Molly, haven't you got anything you've written that I could read?' So I said, 'No, there isn't.' And then I said, 'Well, there is this book and I know it's absolutely ghastly and it's been turned down flat.' And, you know, she was absolutely crazy about it, thought it was wonderful.

P.D. And was it a terrific surprise, its great success?

M.K. Yes. I was simply ecstatic over the Booker . . . too extraordinary.

P.D. And you were well and truly re-launched. And you're starting another book?

M.K. Faintly. I must do it. I will do it. I don't know what it will amount to.

P.D. Do you know when you start a book how it's going to end?

M.K. No, I really don't know. If I had a proper education I probably would, but I'm not able to make a scenario. If I do make a scenario it just makes me sick. *Time after Time* was much better constructed than anything I'd done.

P.D. So your plot happens as the book moves along?

M.K. I think so. I mean the characters make the plot to me.

P.D. And are the characters fully fledged before you start or do they develop as you write?

M.K. They're not fully fledged, but they're in my head.

P.D. Are they based on people you know?

M.K. Absolutely, I don't think there is a truly original ghost of an idea in my head. I couldn't use specific characters.

P.D. But Aroon in *Good Behaviour* was a remarkable, original character and a very powerful woman.

M.K. Well, I'm so old . . . I've seen those women of my generation, the
ones who didn't have success, leading barren lives and growing into
directrices, as it were, as they grew older. I often think that snobbery is
as strong as sex for a great many people. They cannot and will not give
up or accept.

P.D. Was it bad manners to be imaginative or emotional then?

M.K. Oh yes, absolutely.

P.D. And was this reticence more agreeable, do you think?

M.K. No. I think it was very harmful. I know when Bobby died in 1938 I
couldn't think of anything except shutting up my grief and not being a
bore about it, even to my best friends.

P.D. And that was harmful?

M.K. Very, I'm sure of it, and very harmful to Sally, because she was
only six when Bobby died and I thought she'd die when I told her. She
absolutely adored him. I can't describe it. I wouldn't describe it. But I
was so terrified that if I talked about him I'd howl and cry and that
would be bad for her. So I did everything I could for her, ponies,
brought her to Switzerland to ski, everything you could think of to
entertain her and take her mind off it. She never mentioned it, she
never spoke of it. Talk about good manners. Immediately after I went
back to Ireland I went to collect her. She'd been staying with her
cousins at Cappoquin House. It was a frightfully frosty garden in
October, we had to go back in to lunch and she was only six and she
said, 'Mummy, mummy, we must stop crying, we mustn't let' – I've
forgotten the butler's name – 'we mustn't let him see us crying.' That
sort of awful good behaviour must be impregnated into people
somehow. Why should she have thought that? And yet it would have
been part of my life. I would have been mopping my tears before I went
back into the house. And another thing she said was, 'Mummy,
mummy, what will you do, you'll never live without a man.'

P.D. Do you think that's the genesis of *Good Behaviour*?

M.K. No. I thought it was such a funny story, *Good Behaviour*. I
thought it was funny – a black comedy.

P.D. But had you thought long about the results of –

M.K. – behaving like that? No, I hadn't.

P.D. It just sprang?

M.K. I don't know about that. It was just generated from knowing so many people like Aroon, not *so* many, but quite a few, and thinking why they were as they were – having the long back-spring knowledge of them growing up with me . . . and what their own lives had been like.

P.D. Do you type?

M.K. I can't type. Pen and paper.

P.D. And do you re-write and re-write?

M.K. I don't terribly because I write so slowly. I do a bit, of course, but I write on one page of an exercise book and then I leave a blank page so that I can correct opposite.

P.D. Do you often have to go back and change motivation?

M.K. No, I don't, because I am so ignorant, you see. I don't know how books are made. I mean give me a book and I'll read it like a story, but I wouldn't ever take it to pieces and say how it is done. I just wouldn't.

P.D. The insights, the descriptions, when you're re-reading them, they're how you think?

M.K. I hardly ever re-read them. I mean it's all a great surprise to me – if you were to give me some old book of mine I'd read it with great surprise as though I had no connection with it at all. I promise you.

P.D. Have you had a happy life?

M.K. Happy and unhappy both. Terribly happy in patches, not happy in patches. I suppose most people's lives are.

P.D. But compared to many Irish women of your class and generation?

M.K. Yes, compared to so many I have had a very amusing and marvellous life – God, yes, I know I have. I wish I could enjoy this kind of success more, but I'm too old for it I think.

P.D. Are you surprised by the shifts and turns in your writing?

M.K. I don't understand anything about my writing. I really don't understand why it's successful and I don't understand why it should fail either. It's all on a level to me.

*P*OLLY DEVLIN *was born in Ireland in the 1940s. In 1982 she began* *to study at the National Film and Television School. Her books include* All of Us There *(Pan) and* The Far Side of the Lough *(Methuen). She is* *now working on a film and a book of short stories.*

Mary Lavin

talking with
Eavan Boland

*M*ARY LAVIN, *since the publication of her first book in 1943, has been one of the most distinct and challenging voices in the Irish literature of this century. She is pre-eminently a formalist. She has understood the anti-Romantic grain of the short story and seems to me to have brought it up with a bleak persistence and power which has eluded some of her celebrated contemporaries.*

Her characters are various. There are strong women, weak and vulnerable women, creative and destructive ones in her stories. There are nurturing men and dependent men. But her themes are constant. They pivot around the afflictions and demands of private conscience; the attempt of the individual, often secret 'I am' to survive the construct of a society – often a repressive society – and the impositions of convention. This theme is handled with particular power in a novella mentioned in this interview – The Becker Wives, published in 1946. It is canvassed again in the story she herself refers to here The Will, published in 1944. Both bring up and weigh out the claims of the individual against those of a social unit. Both perceive the resources of spirit behind often deceptive appearances. It is a continuous melody in her work. Elsewhere she has said, 'Even as a child I was preoccupied with my right to exercise private conscience.'

Mary Lavin was born in Massachusetts in 1911. But she returned to Ireland as a small child and grew up here. In 1942 she married William Walsh and had three daughters. On his death, she became a young widow with a family to raise. Widowhood and the loneliness of women in a hostile environment have been a theme in some of her best work. She has divided her time since the Forties between Dublin and her farm in Bective in Meath. And this too is an image underlying her work. At the moment she lives most of the time in Dublin where she is married to Michael Scott.

It is a mistake, I think, to measure and evaluate Mary Lavin's

achievement against the background of the phenomenology of the Irish short story. This is something which has often been done by critics. But there is really nothing to learn about it by viewing it this way. She has little in common with the spiritual allusions of Sean O'Faolain or the local colour of Frank O'Connor. She is an immensely private artist, writing out of private feeling, often with an obsessive edge to it. The small towns she discusses, the property situations, the erosions of family, are really only the counterpoint against which plays a powerful and unsettling melody of conscience and isolation.

Mary Lavin is one of the few women writers of her generation and one of the few – Kate O'Brien and Elizabeth Bowen lived much of their lives out of Ireland – who remained in the country and wrote of it. 'I could not place my characters in any setting other than Ireland,' she has said. 'When we see Madame Bovary don't we see her in Rouen?' We do indeed, and we see Mary Lavin's characters at least initially against the veils of damp and the soft outlines of the Irish milieu. But they are finally more human than Irish – although, as in all good literature, they are also more human for being Irish. She is a national and international artist and her statement is the more precious for being one of the very few to have emanated from her generation of women in Ireland.

E.B. I wanted to begin by asking you this. In 'Professions for Women' Virginia Woolf speaks of the difficulties in being a woman writer. The woman writer, she says, 'has still many ghosts to fight, many prejudices to overcome'. She's talking, I think, more about interior resistance than exterior pressures. Did you experience these when you started out?

M.L. The answer to that is no; because I never thought I would write. I never intended to write. When I did actually begin, I wasn't conscious of these 'ghosts' you mention. I just wrote. I took up the back of my Ph.D. thesis one day and began to write on it.

E.B. Is that really, literally, how you began?

M.L. Yes it is. One day I went into the offices of my first husband-to-be. He was a solicitor, by the way. I didn't visit him in the office usually. But on this particular occasion I happened to be there when a client of his was there – an old lady who was a great friend of his. She asked me, in a passing kind of way, what I was doing. I told her that I'd just finished my thesis. In fact I was then on my way to collect the typescript of it. She asked me what I'd done it on and I told her the

140

subject was Virginia Woolf. And she said something like, oh, that's strange because I just recently had tea with her. I was really amazed. I walked out of there in a daze. I remember walking down Nassau Street. Suddenly, I realized that Virginia Woolf was alive.

Now, of course, in a literal sense I knew that she wasn't dead. But I hadn't exactly thought of her as being alive in the sense that I was alive. I thought of her as a writer somehow sealed off from life in a glass cabinet. In some strange way I had always thought of great writers – of writers of importance – as having passed over the divide between life and death into a world of the preserved dead; as having left the world of pots and pans and dances and parties. I went straight home, anyway, and began to correct the thesis. Somehow, those words of the old lady kept coming back into my mind. Imagine having tea with Virginia Woolf! And I turned over the typescript and began to write a story.

E.B. You speak there of a very instinctive start to your writing. At some point then it must have begun to deepen and intensify into a more conscious commitment. At what point did that happen?

M.L. That happened when I wrote a story called *The Will*. I used to cycle a lot in those years. When I was cycling round I'd be thinking. I wasn't actually thinking of plots or anything like that. But I would be thinking of experiences of the past, of things my mother might have mentioned to me – that sort of thing. And this was a point in my life where I was finding life itself more interesting. I was learning more about it; and what I didn't know about it I learned through my writing. And it was at that point, really, that writing became my passionate occupation in a way that could never have been true of the early stories. When I wrote this story it gave me an incredible insight into the power of writing. And I realized that this was the same power which had brought into existence the work I had loved and admired from the past.

E.B. *The Will* is a story about property, about the need to possess it and the struggle to be free of it. It has this wonderful central figure called Lally who defies her family and holds on to her own inner world under great pressure. Even with the realization that her mother has rejected her and her family have almost disowned her, she still, although with pain, retains her private, conscientious view of things. What was it, then, about this story, which gave you such a perception at that moment of the power of writing itself?

M.L. I think it was that I realized in this story that this ragged member

141

of the family, Lally, who had made a bad marriage and was rejected by the family – that she was so much more wonderful than them and no one knew it. She was also extremely spiritual. And they were extremely religious. There was a great difference. And I saw the difference.

E.B. In those years, when you were writing stories like *The Will* which were drawing you deeper and deeper into your craft as a writer, you were also a wife and a mother with three young daughters. Was it difficult to combine the roles you had in those early years?

M.L. There just didn't seem to be any difference between cooking a dinner or writing a story. No one thing I did was sharply differentiated from any other. Looking back on it now, I was probably very impetuous and enthusiastic. I'd sweep a floor or I'd wash up. I loved gardening and I spent a lot of time in the garden. The important thing was that, to me, they were all one.

E.B. I associate these years – in the Forties – with you marking out some of your most characteristic themes. I'm thinking especially of a work I particularly admire, *The Becker Wives*. You were living in Dublin then and *The Becker Wives* canvasses some of the themes of urban conformity and destructiveness with which we're more and more familiar in the writing of women. Flora Becker is a marvellous, strained and imaginative girl who marries into a complacent merchant family and is destroyed by her circumstances as they, in turn, are unsettled by her destruction. How did you come to write this?

M.L. To begin with, I actually saw many Becker Wives, so to speak, when I was a child. They were wealthy publicans' wives or the wives of grocers. I might go home after school to have tea with one of their children. We'd eat at one of those big mahogany tables, laden with food. The experience stayed in my mind. I wrote *The Becker Wives* on my own dining-room table, pushing away the dishes after supper, not even bothering to wash up. My mother was living with us at the time. One evening, my mother and husband were beside the fire as I was writing when they suddenly noticed I was crying. Of course they asked me what the matter was. In fact I had just come to the bit where it's evident that Flora is damaged; is, in fact, insane. I had got so deeply into that life that for the moment it seemed just as real as the room in which I sat.

E.B. Anyone who doesn't write stories – and I don't – must have an abiding curiosity about where and how they originate in the life of the short-story writer. Whether it starts as an image or an occasion or a

142

revelation. I'm sure you've been asked this question so many times. But may I ask it again?

M.L. I can't answer that question precisely. But I can say that I think a story is mostly real. It has happened to someone. Maybe it has happened to several people you've known; maybe even to yourself.

E.B. Now, from the process to the method. A short story must evolve in a fairly laborious and complex way. It seems so short that it must give relatively little room for manoeuvre and therefore it requires the closest possible fitting and tucking. How did you manage the actual, physical process of writing?

M.L. I never typed. That's one of the great regrets of my life. If I had typed I wouldn't have amassed such a huge volume of manuscripts, often written at such white heat that I couldn't read it when I went back to it. The first draft often consisted of an outline and I would make a second draft partly from the outline notes. If I knew what I wanted to say, for instance, in the first draft, I would just make a note about it and then go on to something more difficult. What I found really difficult to do was to cope with all this paper. I would get someone to type up the drafts and I found it easier to correct them in that state. In the end, I realized that I was doing an inordinate amount of drafting, possibly more than other writers. I know that now. I don't know that I knew it then! It was really a very wasteful method of working. When I wanted to alter something halfway through a story, or even two-thirds of the way through, rather than patch it, I would start again. I would go right the whole way through it again. I don't mean that I went through it without consulting the other drafts. I went through it with them in front of me.

The advantage was that, after a few drafts, I knew my characters with an incredible intimacy. Through the drafting process itself, I came to know them. And very interesting things would then happen. This, I think, answers the question which people often ask about the short story. Who do you write about? Are they real people? Are they invented people? There is no such thing as invention in the short story. A novel has to have a certain amount of invention; which is probably why I don't like the novel. What became so interesting to me was that, whether the character was one I knew, or whether it was a combination of one or two people who were similar – or indeed myself – I knew that, after numerous drafts and by the end of the story they would have nothing whatsoever to do with the people who inspired them. They had, as it were, assumed a new life. They were newly born people.

143

E.B. The life of nineteenth-century women writers was one which – to me at any rate – often looks restrictive. However free they were as writers, within the art so to speak, they often had to comply with the restrictions of a woman's life in their generation. So they were spinsters or maiden aunts or whatever, even while they were writing wonderful, subversive things. In the twentieth century there were radical changes. Did you, as one of the pioneering women writers in Ireland, feel any of those old constraints?

M.L. I never found being a woman writer restrictive. I think that was because, once I became a serious writer, I was writing out of something very deeply felt, something that was largely autobiographical, although the autobiographical element evaporated as the story progressed. The reason I didn't find it restrictive was because nothing stopped me writing out of that area of feeling. Now, there were superficial restrictions. When I was at college, for instance, the men would be off on walks, in pubs or in their digs, talking about literature, exchanging opinions, discussing contemporary books. Often, I would never have heard of those books; and I didn't get to hear the conversations either. I would be down in the coffee-shop with other girls, talking and laughing. But the talk wasn't of literature. It was of other things and I enjoyed it all to the full. But I was also deprived, if you like, of the wonderful conversations which the male students had. But none of this mattered when I began to write. I didn't need outside information or outside references because I was writing from within, from myself.

E.B. Can you imagine yourself beginning as a woman writer now, in this time, with a new consciousness of women's achievements and history around you?

M.L. I can't imagine my life as being different from what it was. Then again, I do often feel that many young writers, both male and female, write too young now. I published a great deal of which I was extremely critical before I considered myself a writer. In one sense I suppose I was very selfish as a writer. I only wrote what I wanted to write. I like to think that, especially in my middle and later years, anything I wrote was something which I wanted very much to say.

144

*E*AVAN BOLAND *was born in Dublin in 1944, schooled in London and New York and attended Trinity College, Dublin. She is a poet, freelance lecturer and a regular reviewer for the* Irish Times. *She is married with two daughters. Her collections include* The War Horse *(1975),* In Her Own Image *(1980), and* Night Feed *(1982).*

Rosamond Lehmann

talking with
Janet Watts

This article is reprinted courtesy of *Harpers and Queen* magazine

*R*OSAMOND LEHMANN *was born on the day of Queen Victoria's funeral in February 1901. She won great success with the novels and stories she published in the first half of this century, from* Dusty Answer, *her first novel, in 1928, to* The Echoing Grove *(1953), which many readers and critics – and the author herself – believe to be her best.*

Then in 1958 her beloved daughter Sally suddenly died. The catastrophe was to lead Rosamond Lehmann into a new life's work of spiritual and psychic exploration. She writes of this in her autobiographical volume, The Swan in the Evening *(1967), and touches on it in* A Sea-Grape Tree *(1976), her last novel.*

I met Rosamond Lehmann at this time, when I went to interview her for The Guardian. *The meeting left me in a kind of exaltation. A powerful beauty – in her face and presence, her mind and spirit – irradiated our conversation. As I came out into Eaton Square, where she then lived, I remember how the raindrops on the dark trees seemed luminous, alive with light.*

Since then I have talked with Rosamond many times. She has recently suffered illness, pain, and the distress of losing her ability to read and write. Yet there is always gaiety in her. In her company, suffering and sorrows disappear. She enlightens. She transmits joy.

148

J.W. What do you remember of your childhood? It was very comfortable and civilized, wasn't it?

R.L. I was the second of four children. My father was a good deal older than my mother – she was about twenty-five and he about forty when they married. She was a New Englander. My father was a famous oarsman, as well as a man of letters, and he had gone over to Boston to stay with Frank Peabody, an old Cambridge friend, and to coach the Harvard crew. My mother, who was just down from Radcliffe, was tutor to the Peabody girls – people didn't call themselves governesses in America.

My father brought her home to Bourne End, Bucks – it was just a hamlet then, though now it's almost linked to Slough. He'd had this riverside house built, to entertain his friends.

J.W. He was hearty, as well as literary?

R.L. He was very . . . *Greek*: an athlete as well as an intellectual. He was rather idle, and had plenty of money, and he preferred to be with non-academic people. He became a Liberal MP in 1906, when I was nearly five.

I didn't see my parents much. For us children there were nurses, and coming down after tea. It was that sort of Edwardian childhood. The house had big nurseries, a large garden going down to the river. There were four gardeners, two housemaids, a nurse and a nursemaid, two in the kitchen, a butler and a footman and a boot-boy. I was the second daughter. I've seen the letters my mother got from friends after my birth – 'Such a disappointment, another girl' – and I know that my younger sister Beatrix felt rejected by my parents – though she later became my father's favourite. I think she was perhaps the most talented of us all, and after we grew up I was closest to her. My elder sister, Helen, married a cavalry officer, and moved into a different kind of social life – hunting, racing, country house parties – something that's disappeared completely. Later, when my brother John grew up and went to Eton and then Cambridge, we also became very close, for a time.

J.W. And you began writing very early?

R.L. I was always conscious, from as far back as I can remember, that my grandparents had a tremendous musical and literary salon in mid-Victorian times. People like Robert Browning and Wilkie Collins and Charles Dickens had been their close friends, coming to dinner and taking holidays with them; and my great-uncle Rudolf Lehmann had

150

painted all their portraits. They hung in my father's library, and I sat under them and felt they were my ancestors and that I'd inherited all that – yet it was such a grand inheritance, and I wondered how I could possibly live up to it.

My great-grandfather was Robert Chambers of Edinburgh – the one who started Chambers' Journal and Dictionary – and he also wrote a curious heretical pre-Darwinian book called *Vestiges of Creation*, which caused a great stir in orthodox circles. He was asked later why he hadn't published it under his own name, and he said: 'I had eleven reasons.' He had eleven children. He was a great man, I think.

J.W. So you felt that this world of letters was where you too were destined to live?

R.L. Yes – very far back. There was a sense that I was bound to write. I never considered anything else as a possibility for my future. And I remember beginning to write stories almost as soon as I could write. Then when I was seven I began to pour out verse. I couldn't think what I was doing, quite, but I realized I was doing what I was born for. And then instead of being unsure of myself and often in floods of tears and feeling a strange despair, I felt I knew who I was. Everything I wrote was for my father, and shown to him. It was terrible stuff – all about fairies, and nature, and the moon.

J.W. Did it stop when you began growing up?

R.L. It went on. We never went away to school. Both my parents were strongly against girls' schools – they just thought them awful, which at that time perhaps they were. My parents built this pavilion in the garden and we started lessons with a Froebel teacher. Well, Helen started, and I kicked up such a fuss they had to let me go too, at four. In the end there were about twenty-five children, I think.

We just crossed the lawn to the pavilion every morning. I was taught music by a musical lady in the village, and the vicar taught us Latin and Greek, and a French governess taught us excellent French, and somebody came from London once a week to teach us drawing. I suppose it would be thought a wretched education now, but it suited me, because I had the run of my father's library. I could read anything I wanted, and I did. And the thought of leaving home was a nightmare to me.

J.W. What about the thought of going to Cambridge?

R.L. The idea came from my mother, who had been to college, and thought it wrong that girls shouldn't have the same higher education as

151

boys. My sister Helen was already at Girton, and I got a scholarship there; and I think I rather looked forward to it. My father had by then become an invalid, and life at home was rather melancholy.

J.W. Did you enjoy Cambridge?

R.L. I went up to Girton in 1919. It was a strange time in Cambridge. Rather more sophisticated older men were coming back from the war; and there was nothing of the present spirit of coeducation. Dashing young men didn't think Girton girls were worth talking to – if you wanted to be a social success you concealed the fact that you were at Girton. And you had to ask permission to go out with an undergraduate, though in my last year we were allowed to have coffee with them in the morning in the town.

It was all very absurd, really. I never disobeyed any rules, but there was a certain amount of climbing over roofs and getting in late. We were never allowed to be together in any normal way. There were notes dropped, and a few poems published 'To R.L.', which was thrilling, but it didn't seem to have anything to do with reality.

J.W. Were you writing at this time?

R.L. I wrote once or twice for *The Granta*, which my father had started; and I knew that people like Sir Arthur Quiller-Couch had his eye on me – partly because he had a roving eye and I was a pretty girl, but he'd also seen some of my essays and thought them promising. But I began to find my poems very unsophisticated and to feel ashamed of them. My great idea was twofold: to be a writer, and to get married and have a lot of children. A simple vision. I was incredibly naïve. I lived in a sort of dream.

J.W. Happily?

R.W. Not exactly happily. In confusion. Although I see now my letters to my mother showed no sign of it. Just 'Could you possibly send me another pair of silk stockings?' Schoolgirlish letters, mostly about my girlfriends and my lack of the right clothes.

J.W. And after Cambridge?

R.L. I fell desperately in love in my last year with an enchanting boy. That all came to an end after I came down, and I thought my heart was broken. I thought I should never get established in the world. Then I re-met Leslie Runciman, and married him. I don't think I was really in love with him, or he with me, but it was very suitable, and everyone was pleased.

152

They went to live in Newcastle, where Leslie Runciman worked in his family's shipping business.

R.L. We were married in a Methodist chapel, and his grandfather gave us a house. Newcastle was a sort of nightmare to me. Icy cold, hideousness, trams clanking up and down outside my front door. I just couldn't believe it. The Runcimans were teetotal and Methodist. God, when I think of the dinner parties I gave! Northumberland worthies; young men from the office; and not a drop to drink. How could we? But we did.

J.W. And this was where you wrote *Dusty Answer*?

R.L. I started writing because I was so unhappy, I suppose. I remember thinking: 'What is my life? – a mess and a muddle, stuck in Newcastle – I must get out of this maze.' But there wasn't a conscious plan. I think the whole thing came from my unconscious. I suppose I identified myself with Judith, this lonely romantic girl – whom I think a revolting character now, soppy – and I invented the children who lived next door to her, and placed them in the big house adjoining our house at Bourne End. The place was real, but the children were invented – though of course there are fragments in them of children I vaguely remembered.

J.W. Did you begin to feel better, as you wrote?

R.L. Certainly it came with tremendous ease and strength. The whole thing seemed to come out of a part of me which I was tapping for the first time, and that was very exciting. Then I finished it, and got it typed, I suppose; and I showed it to Dadie [George] Rylands, who had come to stay at a house we took for the summer near the Roman wall. He had been the toast of his year at Cambridge, both as a brilliant English scholar and a great actor. He thought highly of it and suggested he sent it to Harold Raymond, who was the director of Chatto & Windus. Three weeks later, a letter came from Harold Raymond, saying Chatto thought it promising enough to publish, though they didn't expect to make a penny out of it.

At about this time, Rosamond Lehmann met and fell in love with Wogan Phillips. He had come to Newcastle to work in the Runciman firm, much as the character Hugh Miller arrives in her second novel, A Note in Music.

J.W. *Dusty Answer* was a shattering success, wasn't it?

R.L. It really was a case of waking up and finding myself famous. Rave reviews. The book also shocked people terribly – some really did see it as the ravings of a nymphomaniac. My poor mother was very worried. Then came this huge article by Alfred Noyes in the *Sunday Times* about 'a work of youthful genius' and 'the sort of novel Keats might have written'; and I found myself labelled as one of these new post-war emancipated women. I was simply horrified. I thought, what have I done? All the reviews and publicity made me feel as if I'd exposed myself nude on the platform of the Albert Hall. I was also quite uninterested in fame, because all I wanted to do was to get divorced and marry Wogan.

She did so in 1928; they had a son and a daughter.

J.W. But neither the public fuss nor your private complications stopped you from writing your second novel, *A Note in Music*?

R.L. I don't think reviews ever really shook me – good or bad. I had a very solid core of self-criticism, that wouldn't let me be either too easily satisfied, or too deeply scarred. And most of the reviews of *Dusty Answer* said, 'This is obviously this young girl's autobiography, and she's not likely to write any more' – and that annoyed and challenged me. I wanted to show them – and myself – I could write something entirely different.

A Note in Music *(1930) had a cool reception, but that did not deter Rosamond Lehmann, either. She published the highly successful* Invitation to the Waltz *and its sequel* The Weather in the Streets *in 1932 and 1936 respectively. During this time, however, her personal life again clouded.*

J.W. How do you look back on this middle period of your life?

R.L. My marriage became pretty stormy. I thought we were going to be happy ever after, but unfortunately we weren't. It was a period of anxiety and sadness; and there was a terrible feeling of approaching doom in the 1930s – certainly from the time of the Spanish Civil War, which Wogan went out to fight in. Yet it was also a very rich life. We rented a little manor house on the Berkshire–Oxfordshire border. I was deeply engrossed with the children, and there was a lot of happiness with friends like Lytton [Strachey] and Carrington, and people staying for weekends; and I suppose I began to be established as a writer. If I looked inside myself I was always rather frightened, thinking: 'This marriage looks as if it's going to collapse.' But outwardly I suppose I was considered a happy young mother with beautiful children. It was hard to make sense of it all.

154

J.W. Yet your career as a writer was developing successfully, and you had close links with the Bloomsbury group, both socially and intellectually. Did you feel you belonged with them?

R.L. Not at all. I never felt I belonged to any group. I never felt I belonged anywhere.

J.W. Did you want to?

R.L. I wanted to be taken seriously as a writer, but I was shy about my work. I was so pulled down by the unhappiness of my marriage.

It ended in 1940.

R.L. I don't know how I got through this time. I must have been stronger than I thought. We left the house, and I took the children back to my mother, who wasn't at all pleased to see me. I was desperately bereft and lonely, trying to keep going for the children. Then I became a reader for my brother when he was editing his magazine *New Writing*: and that's when I met Cecil. And then came years of tremendous happiness – within difficulties, but great happiness.

Rosamond Lehmann lived with her children in a small house in the Berkshire Downs, seeing Cecil Day-Lewis – who was married with children – at weekends.

J.W. This was also a new phase in your writing life?

R.L. I remember that when I first met Cecil, I said, 'My whole life is a failure – I'd better start all over again, and train to be a doctor.' I did actually go and see the head of the Oxford Medical School – he thought I wasn't at all suitable, that I'd never stand it – and when I told Cecil I was thinking of giving up writing, he said, 'You're mad! You're a very good writer! You're a born writer!'

J.W. Was that crucial? Might you have stopped writing without it?

R.L. Oh, no. I don't think it was ever intended that I should stop writing.

During the 1940s she wrote short stories for New Writing *– later published in one volume entitled* The Gypsy's Baby *– and another very successful novel,* The Ballad and the Source *(1944).*

J.W. Was Cecil Day-Lewis a support to you as a writer?

R.L. The funny thing is, I've never looked for outside support for my writing. I was very happy with him; but no, otherwise, he wasn't any support. In fact, I began to feel the vein was running dry. I wanted to give so much to Cecil, to support him so much – as a poet – that my own career became rather secondary.

Cecil Day-Lewis ended the relationship abruptly in 1949.

R.L. I remember two years of absolute despair, and not writing anything at all. But then I sold my house in the country; Hugo [her son] got married; and I came to London and – with enormous difficulty, and all the courage I could command – I began to make a new life. Though I was always in terror I would meet Cecil around some corner. But I didn't. Well, once I did. It was a shock – he looked so altered.

J.W. Yet in spite of this personal pain, you wrote (and published in 1953) what is for many readers your best novel, *The Echoing Grove* – a book of great detachment and composure.

R.L. I do think it's my best. But that time of writing still seems harrowing, though it got me out of the nightmare. And I can't disentangle the roots of that book. The two sisters are partly aspects of myself, I suppose.

J.W. Your writing life has been so enmeshed with your personal life. Do you wish, now, you had produced more books?

R.L. In a way I do wish I had written more, produced more, regularly, like most of my colleagues. But there was always a feeling that if I did that I might write less well. I was rather hurt when J. B. Priestley once said to me, 'You're good, but you're an amateur.' But although I'm tremendously professional about writing, I just can't produce a book a year. I was lucky to have enough money to live on without doing that; and there are so many other things I enjoyed – children, friends, reading, music . . . I always found it very hard to withdraw and think that my writing was the most important thing.

J.W. When you describe the way your novels emerge, you always trace them to 'the unconscious'.

R.L. It does all come out of the unconscious, my unconscious, which is very well stocked – with images, memories, sounds, voices, relationships. There comes a moment when they seem to coalesce and fuse, and suddenly something takes shape, like seeing a whole landscape with figures, or a whole house with all its rooms. You know it's there, the whole thing – you have a vision of it, instantaneous: you see what's to be done. But then you've got to discover it – work at it, heave it up from underground.

J.W. Rebecca West was once asked if any of her books had come particularly easily and she said: 'No – it's always a nauseous process.' Have you found writing a nauseous process?

R.L. Not really. I dread the thought of the effort, but I enjoy it while I'm doing it. I feel I'm doing what I was born to do. And you think, is this a false start or is it really coming up? And then, the excitement of seeing that it really is . . .

J.W. In 1958 your daughter Sally died. It was an appalling catastrophe, but also the beginning of a new life for you. You have described what happened in *The Swan in the Evening*, but can you also speak about it now?

R.L. She died far away, in Java, but three days afterwards I began feeling sure – certain – that she wasn't dead. I was still shattered, in pieces; I didn't know how to express it. But when people came to see me, I stammered, 'But she's not dead.' I knew she was in the room with me.

A fortnight afterwards I had an overwhelming mystical experience. I saw the world transformed – it was illumined, as Traherne says. The whole of the world was semi-dematerialized, vibrating in patterns of energy and colour; and I felt I was part of the creative process of the universe. It was like a great dance, which I was watching; yet I was also part of it, taking part in it. And it wasn't happiness – it was joy. Of course, it didn't last. It lasted about twenty-four hours. But if you've had that, you live by it; you can't ever forget it. It was terrible, trudging on without her – but there was always that to remember. And then – reading, investigating, learning about mediumship, sitting with several remarkable sensitives. Learning to sift, to discriminate.

And then I was directed to Cynthia Sandys, a marvellously gifted clairaudient, now my close friend. She transmitted *Letters From Our Daughters* [edited by Rosamond Lehmann and published in 1971 by the College of Psychic Studies].

I was struck with awe. I felt: My God, I've been asleep, and dreaming, and this is what is real. I've found what I've been looking for all my life.

J.W. Was the change from your old literary life a traumatic one to make?

R.L. No. After I'd finished *The Echoing Grove*, I just knew I should never be able to write that kind of novel again. I don't know why, but I felt I had nothing more to say. I did reviewing and that kind of thing, but I felt the wheel had come full circle.

I had known that spiritual life was important, but I thought it was like a gift for music – something you were born with, that I should never achieve. And yet I had longed to. For dear friends like Lytton and Carrington and Virginia [Woolf], of course, it didn't exist. If they'd been alive, I don't know what they'd have thought of me. Most of my intellectual friends thought I'd gone round the bend, which was very painful.

J.W. Is it a matter of regret to you that this new spiritual life meant the end of your life as a professional writer?

R.L. I didn't feel that, because I felt that what I was learning and experiencing and investigating was far more important. So it didn't matter in the least that my career as a writer was at an end.

J.W. And then – with your novel *A Sea-Grape Tree* – the two lives began to join?

R.L. For many years I had wondered if I could include this element of experience in a novel – thinking it rather impossible, and that to propagandize would be distasteful. I thought that the kind of novels I'd written happen on a level which I'd left behind. Then I did try, in the conversation with Mrs Jardine from 'the beyond' in that novel, and I think I could write one more. Or rather, I don't know if I could, but I no longer think it's impossible.

J.W. Is that because of a change in your view of your novels? Or a change in your view of the level at which a novel can operate?

R.L. The latter. But I don't know if I've got the energy or qualification. I think it would have to be a greater person and a greater writer than I am to do it. But I think that the greatest drama or fiction – if one could produce it – would come out of this level of consciousness, or knowledge, or wisdom.

J.W. Do you have to keep reminding yourself that all this will sound very odd to people outside the world of psychic exploration?

R.L. Yes, I do. My son, and my sisters and my brother never wanted to discuss this part of my life. Only my grand-daughter Anna wanted to hear about it. I used to feel so lonely – though I was standing on a rock of certainty, I couldn't give it to other people. I learned it was best not to talk about it because either you frightened people or they thought you were mad. But I don't think that's so any more. The climate has changed tremendously in the last twenty-five years.

J.W. That's one of the reasons why you feel very hopeful about our world, isn't it?

158

R.L. I do. I do feel that our leaden age of materialism is dying and, though the horrors are polarizing and getting worse, the light is also bursting out all over – though it is hard for us to see it.

J.W. You have a certain self-mockery when you talk about these things – quite a lot of humour about something you also take very seriously.

R.L. Well, I always feel a lot of humour about myself. I have come to feel the comedy view of life is greater than the tragic view. I think life *is* a divine comedy, and – for instance – that *The Tempest* is the greatest of Shakespeare's works: written, presumably, when all the personal agony is over, and can be looked at with detachment and serenity.

J.W. Do you feel you have reached that point yourself?

R.L. Yes. Certainly. I always imagined that one would get more and more unhappy at the end of one's life, as everything closed in. But now I see such enormous vistas of life after life, and expanded levels of consciousness. I don't *hope* they exist – I *know* they exist. I look forward to death, and what comes after.

*J*ANET WATTS *was educated at a Leicestershire comprehensive school and Somerville College, Oxford, where she took a first in English in 1966. She has worked in journalism for the last twenty-one years on* The Times Educational Supplement, *the* Evening Standard, *the* Guardian *and (since 1978) the* Observer, *where she is a feature writer. She lives in London with her son.*

Paule Marshall

talking with
Mary Helen Washington

*P*AULE MARSHALL, *whose parents emigrated from Barbados during the First World War, was born in Brooklyn, New York, in 1929. After graduating Phi Beta Kappa from Brooklyn College, she worked as a magazine researcher, a librarian and eventually as a writer. She has published three novels,* Brown Girl, Brownstones *(1959),* The Chosen Place, The Timeless People *(1971), and* Praisesong for the Widow *(1982), and a book of short stories,* Soul Clap Hands and Sing *(1961). During the 1950s and 1960s, Marshall was associated with American Youth for Democracy and also with Artists for Freedom, a militant Black movement formed after the bombing of a Birmingham church that killed four little Black girls. Although she was a successful writer in the 1960s, Marshall came into her own in the 1970s, the decade of feminism.*

From her mother and the Barbadian–American community in Brooklyn, Paule Marshall inherited an entire cultural and linguistic vocabulary, one that combines idioms and myths from Afro-American, Afro-Caribbean, and African cultures. Marshall's very special relationship with her mother who embodied those cultures has resulted in a unique example of 'mothering the mind' of a creative artist. Marshall says that her strongest and most truthful writing is a celebration of the art she learned from her mother: 'She laid the foundations of my aesthetic, that is the themes and techniques which characterize my work.

'The dynamic of that early struggle had a profound impact on what interests me as a writer. It also influenced me in terms of style. The imaginative and poetic approach to language was as natural as breathing, and I sensed that her power came from her manipulation of language. I couldn't hold forth on my feet but because I had absorbed their [those

This is an abridged version of an article originally published in *Mothering the Mind*, ed. Ruth Perry and Martine Watson Brownley, Holmes & Meier, 1984; it is based on, and supplemented by, an interview with Paule Marshall on 24 October 1981.

Bajan women's] ability to work magic with language, I was trying to duplicate it in standard English, in being as careful and precise as possible and trying to imitate their tough, lyric way of dealing with language. This artistry with language – the marvellous phrases, the strong, artistic quality of Black language, that core of expressiveness which is developed when we Black folk are not allowed other outlets – is expressed in those areas where we're not censored or oppressed, where we can fully express ourselves. It's a solidly African-derived kind of thing.'

In a 1973 essay 'Shaping the World of My Art' and in a recent article ('From the Poets in the Kitchen', *New York Times Book Review*, 9 January 1983), Marshall has explained the ways her creativity was nurtured by her mother and the other women in the Barbadian-American community. These story-telling women, themselves artists, provided a model of woman as artist, thereby giving Marshall the freedom to become one. They left the houses where they worked as servants and gathered in her mother's kitchen after work to talk – about 'this white-man country', about economics, psychology, sociology. These poor peasant women, recent immigrants from Barbados in the 1920s, recounted many of the tales found in her first novel *Brown Girl, Brownstones*. Their angry recollections of poverty and colonial exploitation in Barbados, as well as the racism they encountered in the United States, were the content of their 'exhaustive and vivid discussions'. Paule sat unnoticed in a corner, listening, absorbing the insight and irony they brought to words, and above all, 'their poet's skills': 'All that freewheeling talk together with the sometimes bawdy jokes and the laughter which often swept the kitchen, was, at its deepest level, an affirmation of their own worth; it said that they could not be either demeaned or defeated by the daily trip out to Flatbush. It declared that they had retained and always would a strong sense of their special and unique Black identity.'

'There was this very real situation: my mother and her group of women sitting there in the kitchen after work. These women were extensions of my mother – impressive, powerful – they were the only adults in my world. Men were very scarce and I never got a sense of them sitting around talking with each other. The forces in my world were these women. For them it was a struggle just to be women – they had to 'tie up their bellies' and keep going. They saw those duties as having to work and to take care of a family. They looked to each other for their social lives, not to men. Men and women seldom went out together. Their social lives were among their own sex – an African-based pattern.'

Language for these women of Marshall's youth became both refuge and weapon, a form of self-expression as well as a means to interpret and control their lives: 'In this white-man world you got to take yuh mouth and make a gun' (*Brown Girl, Brownstones*). As these women sat in her mother's kitchen each afternoon, narrating their lives and memories, they not only showed women in the powerful act of story-telling, they formed a peculiar female kind of folklore. They had words for pregnancy: the expectant mother was 'in the way', or 'tumbling big'. A woman who was too free with her sexual favours was known as a 'thoroughfare', or she might be called 'a free-bee', which was Marshall's favourite of the two: 'I like the magic it conjured up of a woman scandalous perhaps but independent, who flitted from one flower to another in a garden of male beauties, sampling their nectar, taking her pleasure at will, the roles reversed.'

'What I did with my mother's voice is to transform it. I was using her approach – her care with telling a story well, finding the telling phrase – I retrieved these things. I am using the voice of the community.'

The dynamic of that early relationship with her mother has profoundly affected the style and themes of Marshall's work. Her own struggle to be in her mother's presence her own person, to break away from her domination, to match her mother's power with words is recreated in *Brown Girl, Brownstones* in Selina's seven-year battle with Silla. As important as this relationship was to Marshall's development as a writer it was, in many ways, problematic and negative:

'The influence was absolutely fundamental and crucial but it came in a negative way. My mother never directly encouraged me to write. What I absorbed from her was more a reaction to her negativity. It was her saying to me when I was in Junior High School after I'd won all the medals, saying to me out of her own defeat and failure, that I was a failure. No, the influence was not positive, it was full of problems, stress, antagonisms.

'My mother was well aware that it was a power struggle, that I was seeking to replace her. She called me a "force-ripe woman"; "two head bulls", she would say, "can't reign in a flock"; or, "Here you've come to read the burial service over me"; "Look how I done brought something in the world to whip me" . . . Because of all my grand ambitions she used to call me "poor great". She wanted me to get a job as a secretary, not to go to college. She wanted to get along in a kind of minimal way and she disapproved of my ambitions. She was always telling me that I looked as if I were living my old days first.'

Writing became for Marshall a way of imitating her mother and of throwing off her domination. She hoped her success as a writer would please her mother so that she would have to retract her verdict of failure.

'My mother's powerful ability to handle language was something I wanted to emulate and to do one better – with the hope that this would please her and she would take back that awful thing about my being a failure.'

Success with words would also signal that eventually she would reign as 'head bull' in the flock.

Marshall insists that the mother-daughter bond, important as it is for revealing character, for allowing women to be the central characters in their lives, the activists, the centres of power, has a significance for Black women far greater than their individual lives. She repeats the theme that recurs throughout Black literature: 'selfhood must be conceived in political terms.'*

'The element of struggle has deeply affected my writing because it reflects my own struggle to be in her presence my own person, and that struggle – that need to break away, to move away from domination, to prove your own worth – is connected to the larger struggle of the Black people. The woman in the story "Brooklyn" throwing off domination to become a political person is an example of how the struggle with my mother influenced the themes in my work.'

In the quest for traditions to illuminate the meanings of the mother-daughter bond, white feminist writers often turn to Western myths – the myth of Demeter and Persephone as an example of generational continuity between women, variations of the Medusa myth as the terrible but powerful mother, mothers and stepmothers in fairy tales who predict an archetypal mother-daughter hostility. That bias towards Western white models ignores African mythology as a source of Black maternal imagery. Without sufficient knowledge of African myths, I cannot trace Marshall's symbols back to their ultimate African sources, but there is enough evidence to suggest that the image of the Afro-American slave mother is one of the sources for the characterization of Silla Boyce. Everything about Silla's portrait suggests the slave mother – her standing on the corner waiting for suburban housewives to offer a day's work; the emphasis on her body as an instrument she uses to protect her children; her working out all day and then returning home to make Barbadian delicacies for her family; her manlike strength. In the one well-known narrative by a slave woman, Linda Brent's *Incidents in the Life of a Slave*

---

*Stephen Butterfield, *Black Autobiography in America*, University of Massachusetts Press, 1974.

Girl, the mother-child bond is central to the entire text. Unlike the male slave narrators, who were often willing to cut familial bonds to escape slavery, Brent will not take an opportunity to escape to the North because she refuses to leave her children in bondage. Like that slave woman, Silla remains behind with the children while Deighton devises a number of escapes from the bondage of his life.

The historical mythology of the slave mother as a way of envisioning and defining motherhood maintains the importance of understanding motherhood in its political context. It challenges the fiction of mother-daughter hostility and the traditional ways of seeing mothers as powerless in the world of men. Clearly, Paule Marshall's mother nurtured her creativity in this tradition. In Marshall's later novels, *The Chosen Place, the Timeless People* and *Praisesong for the Widow*, the mother-daughter relationship is not treated directly; she writes about two women – Merle Kinbona and Avey Johnson – in larger social and political contexts:

'In *Praisesong* the widow moves back into the past because that past provides her with the power to live in the present. In the legend of Abo landing she sees a possible way of dealing with America, with establishing a psychological and spiritual distance from its ethos, its values. But her composure and peace are false. She has to move back to a centre she once had.'

However, the themes generated by that early relationship are still present: the concern with oppressed people engaging their history, facing up to colonial oppression, moving to control their own lives and refusing to be dominated by the materialism of the Western world:

'That whole concern with dealing with history and with third world peoples facing up to colonial oppression – that power dynamic – people moving to control their own lives – the basic pattern is still there but translated into a larger kind of concern.'

*M*ARY HELEN WASHINGTON *is the editor of three anthologies of Black women writers:* Black-eyed Susans: Classics By and About Black Women *(1975);* Midnight Birds: Stories of Contemporary Black Women Writers *(1980); and* Invented Lives: Narratives of Black Women 1860 to 1960 *(1987). She is currently a research fellow and visiting lecturer at the Harvard Divinity School.*

Naomi Mitchison

talking with
Alison Hennegan

'Of course,' said Naomi Mitchison, just two months away from her ninetieth birthday, 'I don't think I shall write much more now.' She gave me an appraising sideways glance to see how I'd take it. I wasn't impressed. *The Conquered*, her first book and her first bestseller, was published in 1923. Since then, for over six decades, she's published more than a book a year: seventy-plus to date, and no sign of stopping yet. And anyway, as I pointed out, she'd said exactly the same thing to me the very first time we met in 1979. (*'Did I?* Yes. Oh well, serve me right!'). Since then she had published several more books, including autobiography, poetry, science fiction and short stories. Moreover, I knew perfectly well that at least three new books were scheduled for publication in 1987, not to mention a Channel 4 project to dramatize two stories from *Memoirs of a Spacewoman*. ('Two very nice young lads have seized on the moral aspects of my various stories, which is perhaps what one would like. And I do *love* collaborating with people. I've always liked that – anyone who's doing something that I can work *with*. When Wyndham Lewis was painting me, I was always asking him questions about painting, trying really to get at what he was on about, making him put it into words.') I also shrewdly, and accurately, suspected that she already had the odd new scheme or two which she would outline during the next few hours. ('Well, I *have* got a few ideas, one or two things somewhere in this rather over-stored cupboard at the back of my mind, but I don't know if they'll . . . I mean, it's a bit like putting in cuttings. I don't know if they'll root.') And then there are the books which are as good as new: reprints of earlier works now finding a fresh audience of younger readers.

Her enormously influential historical novel, *The Corn King and the Spring Queen* (or 'The Prawn King and the String Queen' as W. H. Auden always preferred to call it), reappeared in 1983. In 1985 *The Bull Calves* was reprinted; begun during the darkest days of 1940, set in eighteenth-century Scotland and peopled with the author's own ances-

tors, the book illuminates many of Naomi Mitchison's most enduring convictions and concerns. Within their carefully observed, accurately detailed historical setting, characters wrestle with timeless – and therefore very 'modern' – dilemmas. Chief amongst them is the eternal conflict between the love of cherished individuals and the rival loyalty demanded by larger, less tangibly apprehended claimants. In *The Bull Calves* Family and Clan provide the focus for conflict: in others of her books tribe, party, nation, dogma, faith or gender may force unwelcome choices.

Her work has addressed all the major issues and crises of the past sixty-five years and has done so in a remarkable variety of forms: novels, plays, children's stories, pamphlets, poetry. There's also a dauntingly vast body of journalism to set beside the books. Her presence seems ubiquitous. Her articles appear in Lady Rhondda's staunchly feminist Thirties weekly, *Time and Tide* (where you might expect to find them), and in the sometimes almost soft-porn Forties pocket magazine, *Lilliput* (where you might not). Leaf through the rather formidable Proceedings of the World League for Sexual Reform's Congress (held in London in 1929) and there you'll find her contribution, 'Some Comments on the Use of Contraceptives by Intelligent People'. The essay, just seven pages long and written for a pre-Pill generation, still sparks and fizzes. It's serious and passionate in its aim, lovingly humorous in tone, generous in its self-revelation and startlingly direct in language. Most noticeable of all is the confidence with which it places the specifically female experience of touch, desire, need and fulfilment at its centre. Here, in little, are many of the qualities which gave her early historical novels – *The Conquered, Black Sparta, The Corn King and the Spring Queen* – a not altogether desired 'reputation'. Auden told her, wistfully, that some of her pages were 'hotter' than anything he'd ever read in English or would ever dare to write.

In part, it *was* the ancient settings which made her novels 'safe' in publishers' eyes. As Naomi Mitchison herself was to observe, wryly, all forms of sexual loving become acceptable if the lovers wear togas or wolfskins. Auden, Lowes Dickinson and E. M. Forster were amongst the many gay men who valued and applauded her matter-of-fact and deeply sympathetic depiction of male homosexuality in those novels of the ancient world which she wrote during the 1920s. (More than half a century later, the publishers of *Gay News* were equally grateful for her ready and practical support during their 1978 Old Bailey trial for blasphemy.) Her twentieth century fictional lovers sometimes fared less well. In the early Thirties, *We Have Been Warned* so shocked Jonathan Cape that he refused to consider it without crippling cuts. Even Edward

Garnett, Cape's reader and until then her staunchest admirer, found the book's straightforward descriptions and analyses of female sexuality, contraception, seduction, rape and abortion too much for him. In deference to the two men's wishes, she cut and cut again but finally reached her sticking point. Cape rejected it, as did Victor Gollancz and John Lane at the Bodley Head. Eventually Constable, a staid and unlikely house, published it in 1934. At least one copy of *We Have Been Warned* made its way to Prague where a Czech *emigrée* friend of mine read it in her early teens and decided that Naomi Mitchison was a writer to reckon with. Sometimes, as I said, her presence seems ubiquitous. . . .

The battle with Cape and Garnett left scars and sapped confidence. She returned to historical novels and waited some two decades before venturing once more on one with a modern setting. *We Have Been Warned* is, sadly, not a book which she wants to see reprinted. 'It's got such a lot of *thick* bits, which seem to me like unstirred soup.' All the potato down at the bottom, I suggested helpfully. 'Yes! Exactly! And it's overwritten. But I think there are some good bits in it . . . I've still got the original bits that were cut out and they *were* important. But then, you see, when I next started writing novels it was after the war, and *then* I could have gone all out and what I'd had in *We Have Been Warned* would have been nothing. People had suddenly got used to much more in the way of description of sex in all its many forms. And there would have been no problem about anything I wrote. And now I am – any writer is – hard put to shock the public. Being shocked is very much a thing of one particular epoch. I remember my daughter's writing, in 1944, about her experiences in the A.T.S., including the girls playing at Fathers and Mothers. This was in an article for the *Guardian,* and the *Guardian* typesetters wouldn't touch it. But then, in those days the *Guardian* was very . . . well. . . . For their midday meal the Chapel used to have [she dropped her voice conspiratorially and confided] potato butties with slices of crisps between them. Seems rather curious.'

So vast a body of publications must surely be the work of a full-time writer. But no. The books have always had to wait their turn with a host of other commitments. As in most upper middle class families between the wars, her own six children had nannies and tutors (Auden amongst them) but she involved herself fully with their upbringing and education. There were contradictions galore in that fusion of social privilege and socialist principles: she confronted them with characteristic verve in her 1979 autobiography, *You May Well Ask.* Nannies notwithstanding, much of her writing was done with children tumbling around her desk or with her notebook propped against the handles of the prams she pushed through London parks. If really desperate for peace and quiet she would occasionally buy a ticket for the Circle line and ride around it until she'd drafted a particularly troublesome passage. ('The trouble with the Circle line *now* is that it does tend to be awfully *crowded.*') Yet, looking back, there seems to have been no basic conflict between the demands made by writing and those made by children. 'No, it was all the same. At least, I don't remember conflict. The thing is [lowering her voice confidentially] I'm bloody *tough*, and I've always been able to keep a lot of balls in the air. And only for a year or two was I actually able to have a room of my own just to write in. *Here* I've just got this table,' a table which stands in the window of a crowded, much used drawing room where friends, grandchildren and visitors read, chat, loll and write. 'But I got so used to doing everything in a crowd that I feel quite lost if I'm on my own.'

Presumably, after all those successfully completed books, starting a new one holds no terrors. Or does she still, I wondered, find writing frightening? She gave an enormous smile. 'Oh *yes*! Of *course*,' and added the 'of course' almost dismissively as though the question needn't have been asked because the answer was so self-evident. Beginnings come easier in some places than others – Zambia, for instance, and Wales. Trains help: 'If I can get something *started* somewhere, I can write on the train on the way back.' She has no ideal reader in mind, 'although I used very much to like reading things aloud, but my family can't bear it. But some people used to like it very much. As one reads things aloud, one realizes what's gone wrong . . . Oh dear. There are various people I *used* to read things to. . . .' She withdrew for a moment into silence.

Throughout childhood and adolescence she had rebelled against many of the petty but intractable restrictions of her class and sex: the biggest battles she recounts with vivid intelligence in her autobiographies, *Small Talk* and *All Change Here*. During the Twenties adolescent iconoclasm matured into a steadily increasing commitment to socialism. Her feminism found practical – and sometimes perilous – expression in her work for the North Kensington Clinic which she helped to found. The clinic provided advice and help in birth control and undertook research programmes into contraceptive methods: she was amongst the guinea pigs supervised by the great pioneering feminist doctor, Helena Wright. Less officially the clinic made it possible for working class women to have abortions safely. 'Occasionally we'd be approached by someone who'd got pregnant and was desperately anxious to have it stopped. And so, although of course it was thoroughly illegal, we'd have them done in our own homes. I know Margery Spring Rice did this, and I did, too, and everybody just had to swear secrecy about everything they knew.' Marie

174

Stopes would probably *not* have approved. 'Yes. Poor old Marie Stopes. Really rather an admirable person when she wasn't being mad. She was very jealous of other people, especially if they used contraceptives which she hadn't thought of herself . . . She once gave my mother something for her rheumatism which was extremely good and she said, "Oh, it's something quite simple, I'll tell you sometime." And she never did.'

Naomi Mitchison and her husband, Dick, made the journey towards socialism together. His political career and unremitting work for the Labour Party demanded her constant support until his death in 1970. (Eventually he received a peerage, but you need to be very brave or very rash to call her Lady Mitchison.) The support he offered her was also constant. Both were committed to the ideal of a marriage within which both husband and wife should be free to take lovers, without recrimination or guilt. To make the idea a reality demands constant honesty, hard work and generosity. To a remarkable degree, each succeeded. Those years of sustained mutual effort are recorded with typical openness and warmth in *You May Well Ask*. His belief in her work was also total. Being so, it helped to render hostile criticism impotent. 'One sometimes got cross with critics, but not really. Of course, I was, in a way, very fortunate, especially early on, that I had my husband always very much behind me, and a shoulder to cry on. Especially right at the beginning. My first book [*The Conquered*] was turned down two or three times. I came back in floods of tears. It's very important, then, to have somebody. . . .' She was silent for some moments.

The young Dick Mitchison had been the very first person to whom the fifteen-year-old Naomi confided her scarring dreams and night terrors in which familiar objects took on horrific forms suffused with an ineradicable sense of evil. His calm acceptance of the reality of her fears helped dispel them. A year later, just a few weeks after the outbreak of the First World War, she became engaged to him. In 1916, when she was eighteen years of age, they married. The nightmares were held at bay. Other, more beneficent forms of imagination came into their own and empowered her work. She believes as strongly as ever she did that the imagination is a positive virtue which has its own truth and can reach truths. The belief has not diminished over the years. 'My only difficulty is that I fairly often have not very nice dreams. They're coming back again. Often a terrible lot of bloodshed and a feeling that *some*how I am to blame.' It was a subject she seemed unwilling to pursue. Later that evening, at dinner, conversation turned to ghosts and presences. The other guests and I had swapped anecdotes, exchanged accounts of curious experiences. Naomi had remained silent throughout. 'Have *you* ever had experiences like

175

that, Nou?' asked a grandson. 'Yes,' she said, 'yes, I have.' 'Here?' 'Yes.' 'Seen things or heard things?' 'Seen them.' 'What sort of things?' 'Terrible things.' She refused to be drawn further.

The next morning she took me round the gardens, which are open to the public. (Gardening, unlike raising children, is an activity that really *does* come into conflict with writing. 'I'm sure I took up too much time gardening. And yet one feels that's not entirely for oneself. I planted a lot of things last autumn – and in a way I'm glad to have done it, although so much came down in the gales this spring. All this lot, along here, it's all my planting. And a *lot* of people enjoy it.') As we approached the house again she gave me that characteristic, swift, sideways glance. 'I'm not sure if the house accepts me. It didn't at first, didn't at all. But I *think* it does now.' It should, I pointed out. In almost half a century, she's done a great deal for its estate, labouring to put the heart back into its poor soil. Carradale is the house she never wanted. Urged on by friends, family and Dick, she agreed to buy it in 1937. Gloriously spacious and surrounded by forty-five acres of arable land, two hundred and fifty more of rough pasture, beach and woodland, together with a fishing river, it seemed an ideal holiday house. Children could rampage, guests could walk, relax, paint and write. The setting is idyllic: in Argyll, on the shores of Loch Fyne, facing Arran. 'But you didn't want it, did you?' I said. 'No.' 'Why?' But she didn't answer and we made our way back into the house. In the enormous kitchen, where adult grandchildren and their guests were preparing lunch, she began to talk of the early days at Carradale and of the postwar County Council elections in which she won a convincing Labour victory against the chief Tory candidate. 'He was the Duke of Argyll's factor, so although part of the vote really was for me, part of it was also against the Duke. This is Campbell country.' She paused. 'This was a Campbell house. I'd *certainly* never have bought it if I'd known that at the time.' Again she gave me that sideways look. Campbells: treachery and slaughter. Slowly I made the connection. 'Is *that* what you were referring to when you said last night that you had seen terrible things here?' She nodded. 'Yes, but I think the house is friendly to me now – I *think* so.'

I found myself wondering what it must be like to spend fifty years of your life in a house which only now *perhaps* accepted you. But this is Scotland, where passionately remembered alliances and betrayals make time telescope. And Naomi Mitchison is herself the child of most thoroughly Scottish parents. Her father, John, was a Haldane. As J. S. Haldane he became one of Oxford's most distinguished physiologists. Cloan, a house on the north-western slope of the Ochils, was his family

176

home. His mother continued to live there throughout Naomi's childhood and early womanhood. His siblings lived there, too, including his brother Richard, Lord Chancellor, War Minister during the Great War and Leader of the first official Labour Opposition in the House of Lords during the 1920s. Naomi's youth was spent between the two worlds of Cloan and Oxford, the Scottish gentry and Oxford's intellectual 'aristocracy'. Oxford brought her into contact with leading scholars and her brother's brilliant Etonian friends, amongst them Aldous Huxley and Dick Mitchison. (It brought her into contact, too, with Oxford's less amiable tradition of aristocratic undergraduate thuggery and arrogantly casual destruction, of the sort practised by Julian and Billy Grenfell before their apotheoses as Soldier Poets. She has neither forgotten nor forgiven them for it. Talking with her of the Great War I exclaimed suddenly, 'But you must have *known* the Grenfells!' She clenched her fists and said vehemently, 'We *hated* them! They were the Enemy. They thought nothing of burning a manuscript which represented thirty years of a scholar's work. I *hated* them!' There was something aweful in such passionate emotion still vibrant more than seventy years after the second battle of Ypres in which Julian died. Time telescoped again.) Cloan gave her a sense of her own place in Scottish history and of a past and culture proudly separate from England and Englishness. But whether in Oxford or Cloan, to be a Haldane carried always the same meaning: the obligation to excel.

'I was always *expected* to be good at something. But I think my *writing* was rather a surprise. I remember Auntie Bay saying later on, "You were a rare bird to come from that nest," and she was always terribly interested in what I was doing and took my early writing quite seriously. But when I was a child and saying, stupidly, "I'm going to be a *poet!*" and everybody was laughing at me, one person who always stood by me was Andrew Lang.' The sense of dynastic expectations was imparted most strongly by her grandmother, 'oddly enough, since she was a Haldane by marriage, not by birth. But she felt herself very much a Haldane, and all the intelligence really came from her side. She was deeply religious, but not in a way that forced itself upon people. I remember very well when I was refusing to be married in a church – I was eighteen at the time – and my in-laws were putting a certain amount of pressure on me, she said to me, "My dear, you must follow your own conscience." And she was quite prepared that my conscience should be an anti-Church one.' The family's relations with the Almighty were excellent. 'On New Year's Eve, when other people were no doubt drinking heavily, we all went up to Granniema's bedroom and Uncle

Richard, the Lord Chancellor, would tell the Almighty what the family had been doing that year. And it was very curious, looking back on it: the Almighty, such as it was, was applauding the doings of the family. And Granniema was well into her nineties then. That's something I have, from that side: almost all the *females* lived to be very old. Going right back several generations, the women live well into their nineties.'

The sense of Scottishness, so strong in childhood and early womanhood, receded in early maturity, to return and grow ever more powerful with the commitment to Carradale. *Amongst You Taking Notes*, the diary which she kept for Mass Observation throughout the Second World War, chronicles her increasing understanding of and devotion to Scotland's especial needs and virtues. She has involved herself in Scottish politics at both the local level (those twenty years as a County Councillor for Argyll) and the national one (twenty years on the Highland Advisory Panel). Amongst her hundreds of publications is a recent Fabian pamphlet, *Oil for the Highlands*. 'There was all that working with very committed civil servants who in fact one helped and was helped by, and who trained one to deal with the English Treasury and, often, with the Secretary of State. And all that blew up into Scottishness.' Political allegiances are no easier to work out now than they were in the Thirties. 'It's *so* difficult. I've got friends right across the political spectrum here, for instance. I've got this Communist Party camp here at the moment [in the grounds, where they have been every summer since 1937]. The present Secretary of the Communist Party is one of my lads. I would find it very hard to be friends with a Thatcherite, but I'm sure some of my friends here would vote Conservative. I was staying with some cousins, who are basically Conservative, during the Falkland Islands, and they were *so* shocked – they *couldn't* have been in more agreement with me. Because there *are* those kinds of Conservative who do feel they are there for service of some kind.'

Her own sense of service is redoubtable. Her desk that day was covered with letters demanding help, reassurance, mediation, action. A woman who had left the village some twenty years earlier was preparing to make the lengthy and difficult five-hour journey from Glasgow because there was a problem she felt she could discuss only with the laird. Her laird is Naomi. There were letters from Botswana where she holds the position of Tribal Mother, conferred upon her in the early Sixties by Chief Linchwe. A number spoke of the growing unrest in South Africa, some with foreboding, others with exhilaration. One sought her help in difficult negotiations with the educational authorities of another country. 'There are so *many* people,' she said rather helplessly, gesturing towards

178

the day's correspondence. 'But one's got one's *responsibilities* and I think one would be very wrong not to look after them. I'm very *shocked* with some of the sort of major, best-selling writers who do get right out of the real world and drink and fight and make love, all in order to feed their own egos and – well, *really* – I mean I just think that's *wrong!*' But then, I pointed out, somehow she has always seemed to be able to find the energy to meet both private and public demands. She laughed. 'Well, to some extent, yes.'

In her Haldane heritage, the aristocratic sense of service is strongly linked with the scientific desire for knowledge. Naomi's writing surprised her relations because they had assumed she'd be a scientist like her father and her brother, J. B. S. Haldane, who later became an internationally famous geneticist. In her teens she had worked with her brother on research into Mendelism. Some of their experiments anticipated aspects of the later discovery of chromosome structure. Her consuming interest in scientific research remains. It reveals itself most obviously in her considerable body of science fiction writing, but it also underlies other political and social concerns: her anxiety about the destruction of the rain forests, for instance, or dubious chemical practices imported into third world agriculture. An early, medically controlled experiment with mescalin resulted in an horrific experience which left her with a sense of her world 'tilted at a wrong angle to itself'. It was several distressing years before the world reoriented itself. 'Certainly if I'd known what was going to happen, I'd never have done it.' Yet even the horror was put to good use. Her later account, to doctors and nurses, of the terror she had experienced, her fear of being physically touched, the intolerable pain of certain sounds or colours, influenced nursing methods and interior decoration in some mental hospitals.

Her historical novels, always carefully researched, offer the perfect meeting ground for fact and speculation, as does scientific thought itself. 'In the book that's coming out next January [*Early in Orcadia* 1987] I've gone *much* further than I've *ever* been before! It's very exciting: it's taken a long time. It's about neolithic people and part of my thesis is that there's no reason to suppose that people were really nasty to each other. And I've tried to put forward alternative ideas about what might have happened.' An optimistic world picture to set against 'people red in tooth and claw, like Golding's people'.

Optimism, indeed, is one of the most consistent and striking qualities in her work. In her life, too, it seems. Feeling as I do, already exhausted and despairing, and more than half a century younger than her, I wonder how she manages it. 'Well, I feel it's no good being *pessimistic*. I mean if I

179

really think what's likely to happen . . . well, that's just too terrible. But I must be to some extent optimistic because I've got all these babies coming along: seven great-grandchildren. Mostly three and under. And sometimes I get rather sad to think I'm unlikely to be present at their weddings.' She grins. 'Though you never know. I was much cheered by my Panel doctor in London who said to me just a fortnight ago, "Well, none of the organs of your body seems to me to be more than forty years old".' It did rather sound, I suggested, as though she might be dancing at those great-grandchildren's weddings. She looked speculative. 'The last wedding I danced at – and it was a reel – was in Ireland. That was four years ago.' But then, of course, she was a mere eighty-five.

And in just a few weeks' time she would be off to Zambia, taking with her one of her nineteen grandchildren who had not yet been to Africa. 'Of course, the way things are going at the moment, it might be a bit of a ringside seat by the time we get there,' she said meaningly. 'Naomi,' I asked urgently, 'aren't you *frightened?*' 'Well,' she said, 'the way I look at it is, whatever happens – and I do mean what*ever* happens, it will be very *interesting.*' 'But Naomi,' I said, a little desperately, 'when you were zooming round Vienna in 1934, with secret messages from the Viennese Communists stuffed in your knickers and Nazis stopping you at every corner, weren't you even frightened then?' She considered, then said, 'Well, you see, Alison, *that* was all very interesting, too. And I've always found that when you're *really* interested, there's no room left for fear.'

ALISON HENNEGAN *was born in Surrey in 1948 and read English at Girton College, Cambridge (1967–1970). She was the National Organizer of FRIEND, 1975–1977 and Vice-Chair, Campaign for Homosexual Equality, 1976–1977. She was Literary Editor of* Gay News *(1977–1983) and is Editor of* The Women's Press Bookclub. *She writes as a journalist (mainly for the* New Statesman), *critic and essayist and was a contributor to* Truth, Dare or Promise *(Virago).*

Grace
Paley

talking with
Cora Kaplan

GRACE PALEY *was born in New York City in 1922, the daughter of Russian Jewish immigrants who had arrived at the turn of the century. She grew up in the Bronx. Her parents spoke Russian and Yiddish at home – as well as English. Her formal education ended somewhere in mid-college years. She began to write fiction in the Fifties, extraordinary, vivid tragi-comic stories centring on city life in the neighbourhoods she knew. Her stories appeared in* Esquire, The Atlantic *and* New American Review. *She has published three volumes of short stories, all critically acclaimed,* The Little Disturbances of Man *(1959),* Enormous Changes at the Last Minute *(1974) and* Later the Same Day *(1985), and one volume of poetry,* Leaning Forward *(1986). Grace Paley has a son and a daughter, and has taught literature at Columbia University, Syracuse University, Sarah Lawrence College and City College in New York. She has been actively engaged with left-wing politics much of her life and given a great deal of time and energy to anti-militarist movements and women's movements. She lives both in Vermont and New York City. I talked to her in April 1985 in her New York apartment, in the neighbourhood where some of her stories are set.*

182

C.K. I want to focus our conversation around the relationship between politics and writing in your life and work. Perhaps that means starting with your latest collection of short stories, *Later the Same Day*, because there seem to be more overt 'world politics' in it than in either of the two earlier books.

G.P. Well, when I'm writing I don't think, am I putting politics into it or am I – taking it out. Is it there or isn't it there. I guess I think that *The Little Disturbances of Man* – which came out in '59 – about women alone with kids, is really *very* political, dealing with life and language that hadn't been written about so much. *Later the Same Day* is about more political people. A lot of political writing – even the best that I can think of – is about leaders and big shots, about the class they rose from, how they're moulded and melded, how they destroyed or were destroyed by their country and so on. I don't think I have a gift for writing about leadership, so my general tendency, and my interest anyway is in writing about ordinary political people I think they've been abandoned in many ways, as though they don't exist. The fact that there are a lot of people who are just normally political is a hidden fact in this country. Nobody wants to know it, and they try to pretend that there is only private life, and that people don't even talk politics, which they really do. So you find lots and lots of books – it's as though men and women never have any conversations except about their extremely private life, as though that's the only thing that's interesting. But the ordinary political person is, I think, worth shedding a little bit of light on, because that woman or man is a regular citizen. I mean that's all he is, she is.

C.K. Your stories make it clear that there's a political practice that's part of everyday life.

G.P. Yes. Mothers bringing up sons, which is often a political act of warsome nature, or often today – a feminist act of humanizing the male child, and there's the young and the old, and there's the historical experiences of the old. Newness of the young. Then there's always the world moving in on all these people, and they just seem to know it. No big secret.

C.K. Many of the stories in *Later the Same Day* are about a lost generation of children.

G.P. Well, I don't think they're lost – I've called them in a story 'Friends' the 'beloved generation of our children' – who were I guess all Sixties kids – youngsters really now in their mid-thirties. An unusual number

184

were killed in car accidents (just part of U.S. statistics) or went to war – Vietnam – or drugs. Of course most survived. But I think about them all because I knew them growing up; you really have a very tender feeling for a large person you knew as a two-year-old.

C.K. Many of the stories suggest that these events, what happen to these kids and their parents are not reconcileable, they can't be turned into tales with an implicit moral, they're just part of –

G.P. – Revolutions –

C.K. Yes.

G.P. I agree with you.

C.K. Did you decide, when you started writing, not to write the well-made story?

G.P. Well, I didn't know how to write the well-made stories. I tried, God knows. I just failed miserably, so I just wrote the way I could. I made honest efforts to write a typical novel, but I failed, I just couldn't do it. I can't write longer things – I try to write everything the right size, length and width – and depth, for what it is.

C.K. One of the things I sometimes feel on reading your stories, is that because of how they move in time, they encompass as much as most novels.

G.P. I hope so. I seem unable to just let things go, in a sense. But the novel – it really sort of cuts between time zones so at the end of the story you actually feel you've had many years of someone.

C.K. Yet you've said that you think most novels are too long.

G.P. Well I think it's really true, a lot of writers inflate; they want to write a novel and they do write a very long book, too long for its true size.

C.K. How did you come to your own way of writing?

G.P. It took a long time in the sense that I wrote poetry for a long time, I didn't write stories, but once I sat down to write stories I wrote stories – I mean I wrote the stories in my book.

C.K. You've said that the poems came out of literature, were very 'literary'.

G.P. Right, I think that was true in the beginning. I mean the reason I began to write stories was that the poems up to then had been too literary, it really was a problem. I think writing the stories loosened my poetry and made it easier.

185

C.K. A lot more poetry has snuck into the stories in *Later the Same Day*.

G.P. I have a book of poetry out now [*Leaning Forward*]; I have a graduate student who also had a press and who was interested in poetry, and every now and then I'd read a couple of poems, and she said, 'I want to put out your poems.' So I visualized you know, a collection of ten poems – a little chap book as they say. Well, little by little by little by little –

C.K. A lot of poems. It seems to me that one route to women's history has always been women's fictions, a way of writing to women as well as about them.

G.P. Oh, sure. It's true for Black history too. Though I can't say that I thought I was writing to women or for women or anything. I knew I was writing *about* women, and I felt that might be troublesome.

C.K. Why?

G.P. At the time when I began to write, I thought nobody would be interested, that's all. That's what I mean by trouble. And in my first book I was still so shy that my major public statement would be to second the motion at the P.T.A. I mean that would be as brave as I could get. That would take a lot of courage.

C.K. Your two main women characters that run through your fiction, Virginia and Faith, are single parents for much of the time, and you weren't. How much are their lives yours?

G.P. Not interchangeable. My life and theirs are different. But the characters are like people who could become my friends, very close friends, if I met them. Virginia's street, I lived in that street and neighbourhood for a long time. There were a lot of women alone with kids and I became very, very interested in how they lived. I myself was beginning to develop lots of anxieties about relations between women and men.

C.K. You've said that none of the women are victims, and that seems right. Do you think women take strength from that aspect of the stories?

G.P. Well, I read 'An Interest in Life' in City College about five years ago, and a young Black girl got up and said to me, 'Do you think Ginny is some kind of heroine?' I said, 'No, not specially, I just think she's a pretty brave person, but', I said, 'what do you think?' She said, 'I think she's a dope, wanting to go back to that guy.' So I was taken aback a little bit and I said, 'Well, if you think she's a dope, all I can tell you is I think you're going to have a better life than she has.'

186

C.K. The stories have a lot of unease about men, but they're not anti-men, are they?

G.P. No, and I've always liked the men I've lived with. I mean apart from love.

C.K. The war doesn't figure much in your stories. It's a sort of absent place.

G.P. It's interesting, you're actually right, and yet it certainly is a very important part of my life. I mean there are Jewish stories there, about what happened to the Jews. I feel very seriously Jewish. But you're right, the first book came out in the late Fifties and I was really looking at something else. It seemed that the men had been covering the war. I have things I really should write about because I had a lot of fun living in army camps. My husband didn't (have fun). He went to the Pacific. Okinawa. Both my husbands. Bob was in the Philippines, Japan.

C.K. All three collections talk about how women stay on the block and men go roving around, taking off, coming back when they feel like it. In 'An Interest in Life' Virginia's husband joins the Army –

G.P. Right, but there it's cynical, it's the way men get away from women. That one was written after the Korean War, a war that really went right by him. In fact if there's any bunch of guys who should feel bad, it's the Korean War class. You know the fellows who were in Vietnam feel very injured by the attitude of people towards them, which I think they're wrong about, and then the Second World War guys, everybody knows, a lot of boys. But the Korean War, nobody talks about that at all and a lot of boys died there, the guys who'd just missed the Second World War. I meet these men who are now about fifty-five, sixty years old and they did the Korean War, and they're really not that much younger than me.

C.K. Just as the early books brought women, the neighbourhood and families into fiction in a new way, *Later the Same Day* brings international politics into the stories differently. You've travelled to Chile and to China, for instance. How have your own political activities and experience shaped the writing?

G.P. Wherever you go, if you're a political person, you see the politics of the place. I haven't written too much about travels. We lived in Chile just before the coup, but my husband has done most of the writing on Chile. I haven't really used a lot of these experiences yet. I've written poems about having been in Vietnam in '69. We went to China to see what was happening there, not as part of any government group or

187

anything like that. We went to Chile to see how socialism was working; if it would last. And I was in Nicaragua last June.

C.K. What has come out of the trip to Nicaragua?

G.P. I've done a lot of speaking. Some poems one wants to say to the American people – I said this when I was in England a lot – we would be in Nicaragua today, right now if it was up to this administration, and it's the American people that have prevented it. You know, over 50,000 Americans have been to Nicaragua, have helped out, worked with the Nicaraguans, are building houses with them, are working in their hospitals. That's what's going on and that's this crazy United States. Those efforts, and the organizations of sanctuary that have been set up here, which show some of the fantastic progressive energy – among American religious groups on the left too – need to be publicized in Europe. The superficial view of this country abroad is that nothing is happening here, and that's a view that our media wants to press on Europeans also, but there are pockets of activity all over the country; it's a big country. Tremendous actions taking place everywhere; that's one of the reasons that up to now we haven't really invaded. The government would have been in there in five minutes, but the American people didn't want it. It's important to speak in Britain about this – I love to hear about actions in other countries. It gives you some goddam solidarity and hope!

C.K. What other kinds of things have you been doing politically?

G.P. I've been working with some people on some feminist pieces. As progress is pushed back, as the administration and media gives up on affirmative actions for women and Blacks and other minorities (which is in contradiction to what I said thirty seconds ago) you find there's no money for health clinics, for housing – for kids – it's all going to military expenditure. And when that 'moving back' on women's issues happens it happens in all sectors. Even in our own left movement, you find people saying: 'Oh well, but thank God, we don't have to think about the women today. We were burdened with that last year, but this year we don't have to think about them so much.' So that feminist position, that particular analysis that addresses patriarchy, begins to get lost. You've got to make sure it's still there and solidly present in people's thinking.

You've got to keep your eye on so many things. It's hard. That normal American emphasis on individualism and pride and religion – positions that seem anti-political, are very political really. They come from the ideology and structure of bourgeois capitalism – a wholly

188

private emphasis. The general mode is one of thinking individualistically. It's the only value; it becomes *the* value.

C.K. These latest stories argue against that by integrating the ongoing political concerns of people with their so-called private lives, so that the reader can hear how they are spoken together. Friends and lovers argue about love and politics in the same conversations, without the public topics simply being metaphors for the personal relations. China, civil rights, Chile, U.S. policy, adultery, children and parenting are all threaded through – part of the same fabric of daily exchange. There's also, and I thought this is more true of your recent work, more self-conscious writing about writing. Could you comment on that?

G.P. I don't know where to push that. Almost from the beginning when a child tells you a story, she'll say, 'I want to tell you a story and I'll tell you this.' It's often a very talented story about a story.

C.K. A lot of these stories seem to say: 'It's not what you think it is.'

G.P. Right. I mean, a story is made very often of two stories, until you have one story sort of half-contradicting another or corroborating another, one with the other. Like, the story about China, 'Somewhere Else', it's really two stories, but separately each story would be less interesting, and two stories together really make a third story. And every story is completed by the reader.

C.K. Quite a lot of the politics that your characters are involved in are locally based, in the city. Now that you live in Vermont as well as New York are you still so involved in that?

G.P. Less in New York. A little bit in Vermont. I'm not here enough. When you have a kid, the school's next door, the parks – all the things are part of the city's life. It's hard to do local political work here for me right now; I'm not part of local organizations, but local work is the most interesting work. I miss it a great deal. I've never been happier doing politics than when I did local stuff. Even the peace politics we did was very local – the anti-Vietnam War actions. Out of our neighbourhood organization we really created events that took on a citywide and nationwide strata. We did something called 'Angry Arts' which we initiated and pretty soon the whole city was doing it and then it was organized in Philadelphia and Baltimore. So you can start locally, and what you do can roll over . . . The Women's Pentagon Action – not quite so local – a Northeastern women's action was repeated in the West. Japanese women – Italian women called to talk about methods of organization.

189

C.K. Yes I miss that, living in Britain. That particular kind of community based politics seems harder to get going. When I was a young mother there I was shocked that parents weren't supposed to take such an active interest in the schools. The teachers thought the worst possible case was America where parents had so much say. You were supposed to run jumble sales and sell cakes and that's all.

G.P. Well that's the way things used to be and a lot of the P.T.A.'s fought successfully for a different role. To shift the subject slightly – my granddaughter's first-grade class (she's six years old) asked me to come talk to them – the teacher invited me to speak to the six year olds about women's history – it was women's history week or month something like that. I think I was asked because the week earlier – the teacher told me – she'd been telling the class all about the accomplishments of mankind, how remarkable mankind was etc. My granddaughter worriedly asked, 'But what about womankind? Didn't they do anything?' The teacher laughed. 'Is your mother a feminist?' 'Oh no,' Laura said, 'she's a nurse.' I guess the point I want to make is a small hopeful one. One of the horse's history rides is language. Fifteen years ago maybe ten, in my Fifties, I wouldn't have noticed the word mankind at all. And here in 1986, a six-year-old person heard the word in all its meaning.

C*ORA KAPLAN, born in New York City in 1940, teaches literature, history and feminism at the University of Sussex. Her writing includes* Salt and Bitter and Good: Three Centuries of English and American Women Poets *(1975) and* Sea Changes: Essays on Culture and Feminism *(Verso, 1986). She is on the editorial collective of both* Feminist Review *and* New Formations.

Angela Rodaway

talking with
Carolyn Steedman

I drove to Bristol, and met Angela Rodaway in a restaurant run by a young Black painter Angela had known since her childhood. She was immediately recognizable from the photograph on the cover of A London Childhood, *and I tried to find the Twenties child who is the subject of her book. We talked, and I thought of the idea of the story-taker, one whose function it is to listen and question, to shape the narrative of another's life by her simple assumption that it is there for the telling: to take the story. And I thought of the spaces between writers and readers.*

I had read Angela's account of childhood in working-class Islington and of her Depression-time adolescence as a rare document, one that allows the remembered working-class child to have a psychic and imaginative life, an autobiography that is unconstrained by the conventional devices of the genre which, in general, celebrates powerful mothers, the simple virtues of poverty, and the solidarity of street and community. In A London Childhood *I had found a complex psychology and a sexual development, both of which are usually denied to the children who are the subjects of working-class autobiography. It seemed (and still does seem) a most valuable source of such defiant and subversive evidence. It is valuable too for its precise delineation of 'best friends', the friend in this particular case being the middle-class Sonia, whom Angela Rodaway met when she passed the scholarship exam in 1928 and went to Highbury Hill High School for Girls.*

Together Angela and Sonia roamed around London, once going as far south as Surbiton, to friends of Sonia's family, there meeting the child analyst and paediatrician Donald Winnicott, disguised in the book as 'Donald Waterton' ('Uncle Donald'). It is the early 1930s, Sonia and Angela are about thirteen, and they have both read Winnicott's Clinical Notes on the Disorders of Childhood. *In the poor streets of Islington, things are not what they seem.*

A London Childhood *is in fact a document of these transitions of class,*

these movements between London's poorest streets and the suburban gardens where music is played and books are discussed. Its very point is seen by Angela Rodaway to lie in its last pages, where her younger self, the teenage worker, longs for the time to write, yet is prevented from drawing the dole by the shame and embarrassment at receiving charity that her respectable working-class family has inculcated in her. The book ends at the place where she learns to see drawing unemployment benefit as something 'quite new and strange, adventurous and rather daring, like going to Moscow or Spain.'

We talked; and arranged to meet the next morning at the house where I was staying, to talk again, and to record an interview. During the war, Angela Rodaway did clerical work in various government departments; her son was born in March 1942. After 1945 she worked as a teacher, untrained at first, and then taking part in the Emergency Training Scheme. It was Double Summer Time, and the London streets were full of children, back from evacuation and playing in daylight at ten o'clock at night. Working parents couldn't care for them, and the London County Council organised the time between four and seven with play and twopenny teas.

She left London and moved around the country with her son, working in various schools, some private, some not. She ended up in Bristol, and in 1968 became involved in what was to become the St Paul's Festival, running a drama group. In 1976 the group won the Observer Youth Theatre Competition. They had funding by this time, and took their performance to Jamaica in August of that year. Throughout all this time, with one gap of ten years, she wrote, particularly enjoying the medium of radio. A London Childhood *was published in 1960.*

The writing stopped in 1967, when her son was convicted of stabbing another man in a Bristol library. The year 1976, when he killed himself, marked the end of a decade without writing. She calls herself a survivor, and the reprinting of A London Childhood *by Virago in 1985 'a resurgence'.*

I wanted her childhood to live in her, for her to tell what it means to grow up in the marginalized places of a culture, in poverty, and how that affects a later life: I sought the articulations of class. What I found instead, and came to read when I returned to the book a few days later, were the words that negotiate the space between objects and their meaning. At one point during our three conversations, I read to Angela the part of her book that haunts me. It is the late 1930s, she is poor; she

194

has reached the end of a period of writing, used up all her money, bought a herring for supper with her last pennies:

'I had practically no food in the house, a spoonful of sweet chutney and some rice, nothing more. Some of the grains of rice were black. Mice! I was too hungry to mind very much, but I put my fish on the windowsill outside, and sat down to examine the rice, grain by grain . . . There was a mackerel sky, and the gulls, harbingers of inclement weather, flashed light and dark signals against its moodiness. Grey back against grey cloud. No gull. A turn like the flick of a wrist and a bird was shining white and patting the sky with soothing cloud-tipped wings . . . There was the tender dove-like breast, the slatey wings, the crimson eye, the yellow predatory beak. I sprang up too late. The gull had got my fish . . . Sagging in flight he went over the roof-tops until he dropped his burden on the houses . . . I ate the rice . . . All that night I thought of the fish and how, when the cats and gulls had finished with it, the phosphorescent bones would gleam, in the dark, like moonlight, broken by wind-crazed water, herring boned . . .'*

The words take the fish-bone somewhere else, hunger becomes poetry, in that other place that Donald Winnicott was to call 'a third place of human living, one neither inside the individual nor outside in the world of shared reality,' where the girl lies in her bed, thinking of her budget and a glittering bone. An image: another way of seeing.

I started by asking Angela if she had been conscious of writing within a tradition, and if she had read autobiographies of working-class child-hood in the Fifties:

A.R. I purposely would not have read them. Because I like to do what I feel is best. I'm very conscious as a writer. Marghanita Laski said that *Childhood* missed being literature because there was no actual revelation, no discovery in it. Well, there is. Because when I stand in the dole queue I'm feeling that it's something terribly exciting: I'm doing it with the attitude of the editor who suggested that I actually do it, and not with the cringing attitude – the humble, shamed attitude – that my parents had. I went back proudly and said, 'I've been drawing the dole.' To people who were in the Café Royal in Regent Street. And that was the attitude in which I stood there, and in order to do that, I'd come an awfully long way . . . That's the point towards which I felt the book progressed. I think I am very conscious of what I am doing.

195

C.S. And you revise, do you? You re-draft?

A.R. Yes; I re-draft if I feel it isn't quite taking the form that I want, but I know where it's going. And I know what I'm trying to say, not explicitly but implicitly; because if you want to be explicit there's no point in writing imaginative stuff. You write a thesis instead, if you're going to be explicit, and I think that imaginative writing says a bit beyond what one could say explicitly. So that it's always just ahead; it's always at a point of development in a way that the more conscious stuff is not . . .

C.S. I wonder now how your childhood feels to you. Is it an area still within you that you can draw on, something that still lives in you; or is it a piece of history?

A.R. No, I think it's still part of me. It's rather why, although I've got away from that kind of life, up to a point, I never really lost touch; I continued to be interested. When I go into St Paul's it feels sometimes like going home; and the attitude of those mothers – not that they're angels by any means – but it's very reminiscent of my mother.

C.S. You moved into another world very quickly. Are there still times when you think still that you were formed and shaped in a different way from most of the people you now know?

A.R. I can very quickly get down to absolute basics. It doesn't matter if I have no hot water, and I mean basics of that kind . . . I still enjoy contrivance. Really, I learned that from my mother . . . There is a lot that matters to nearly all the people I know, and I can override it. It doesn't matter to me.

C.S. Do you feel any bitterness about the circumstances of your childhood?

A.R. No . . . During my childhood, I felt inferior all the time, because the people in whom I was interested, and whose interests I shared, I felt were all superior to me. They all had superior facilities, better clothes, different food. But all of that has since become accessible to me so now I don't mind. The feeling started when I went to the other school. I was nearly eleven. Certainly after that first year I felt terribly inferior and unsure, knowing that I wouldn't know how to behave, that I wouldn't be acceptable. But I accepted *that*. Now it seems all wrong that Highbury Corner is ten minutes away by tube from Oxford Circus. It was a totally different world, and I've been surprised going back. I've gone to a different street, or the corner of a street down which we never went, and it's only five minutes away from where we lived. You didn't go for a walk around the streets. You see, until I went to the high school, we were probably slightly superior.

C.S. Respectable?

A.R. Yes. And my mother went to talks run by the Welfare. She used to take the babies there, and they used to organize talks on balanced diet and vitamins. We were taken to parks, which I think a lot of parents were not sufficiently conscientious to do. Even before we went to school, we went out every day. Rain didn't deter her, and we'd go out in pouring rain. I remember a sort of red riding hood. It wasn't red; it was a sort of fawn colour, with a mackintosh hood, with a frilly top, like Red Riding Hood's clothes. It was like a cape, and it was very long, and inside it you could put your hands in your pocket. You could do all sorts of things: it's almost another little world of feeling inside that cape. And I remember going out in that, and it pouring with rain, with my mother . . .

C.S. We've talked a lot about your working with young people, and about teaching, and drama. It's obviously very important to you. Is it a way of reliving your childhood, or making your childhood better, of recompensing yourself?

A.R. Yes, in a way. I know that if it hadn't been for teachers and other people who were prepared to tell me what to do, it would have been very difficult to get anywhere, because you just don't know how things work. I think authority has become conscious of the fact that there are people who simply don't know. And they have classes – I don't know what they call them – but they're more or less about how to beat the system. The kids around St Paul's didn't even know that drama schools existed until they came into the group.

C.S. Is the fact that a lot of the children you've worked with are Black just to do with your living in the bit of Bristol that you do live in? If you'd lived in another city would they have been poor whites?

A.R. They might have been. Except that it was through the Festival – through doing drama in the Festival – that I got to know so many West Indian young people. I feel that there's a lot of hope there . . .

C.S. Did you always want to write?

A.R. I think I consciously wanted to write after I got to the High School. There were all sorts of practical reasons as well. I was quite good at music, thanks to an excellent teacher at Highbury, and at art. I could have opted for art, but writing was the only thing that didn't cost anything.

197

C.S. As women have always found.

A.R. Well, now I paint in water colours, and take four tiny little blocks of water-colour paint and a few brushes, and a tiny bottle of water. And that's my equipment.

C.S. Did you write at home as a child? Where did you get the paper?

A.R. There was usually something to write with. In any case, we had exercise books at school, and I very early learned the trick of taking the middle out and squashing the staples back so that it looked perfect.

C.S. I was trying to think about my writing as a child the other day. We were in much more comfortable circumstances than your family, mainly I think because it was after the war, the Fifties. But I realized the other day that I never could write at home because there literally wasn't anything to write with. On my seventh birthday my grandmother sent me an autograph book as a present, and I remember very clearly writing my first story at home in that, with a tiny little pencil. I'd been writing at school for a whole year. It wasn't that I couldn't write; it was just that there was nothing at home to do it with. So it is unusual, I think, to have had writing material at home. Was your family unusual in that way?

A.R. From what I see of a lot of people now, it probably was. I've gone into houses and said, 'Oh, write this down,' and they haven't even been able to find a pen. But then, because we were at the High School my mother was very keen on our doing homework. Even before I went to the high school she was keen for me to get the scholarship. She coached me in arithmetic at home, and I think perhaps I got my numeracy from my mother and my literacy from my father. She would write shopping lists, and send us out with a written shopping list – that sort of thing.

C.S. It was a very organized kind of household, yours, wasn't it?

A.R. Well, that was largely my mother. She was very methodical. My father was romantic, and my mother – yes; she was methodical. She came from Lambeth. She went to a school called Wantree Walk. That is: Walnut Tree Walk. They say you're only a Cockney if you can say Tottenham Court Road all in one syllable, and Wantree Walk is pretty close. I think a background not as poverty-stricken as ours was. Still quite working-class, but efficient, competent working-class.

C.S. Do you think that if you'd been born ten or twenty years later you'd have had a very different adolescence and young adulthood?

A.R. My sisters *were* born much later, you see. So they were evacuated

198

with the school, and things were much more open altogether. We didn't mention menstruation, or sanitary towels, or anything like that; they had these on their list of clothes. And the whole thing somehow opened out for them. And also they got to stay in other people's houses, which we just never did.

C.S. It was the war that opened everything up?

A.R. Well, it certainly did for them. And when the war ended and they came home, then education opened up . . . So it would have been different if I'd been born later.

C.S. And was writing always something you had to buy time for, by doing awful jobs?

A.R. I don't think the same system existed as it does now, for Social Security. It was the Relieving Officer then. You couldn't do what you can do now. I wasn't so much concerned with earning money to live on during the six months that I worked, I was concerned with earning enough stamps to get the unemployment benefit to give me time to write.

C.S. And did that make writing a pleasure that you bought time with? Do you think of writing as hard work, or pleasure, or as neither of those things?

A.R. As something of an indulgence – still. You know, we were talking about paper. I think it must have been pretty difficult to get. I knew someone who worked with electroencephalographs, and they have long, long sheets of paper, and I used to use that exclusively twenty or so years ago for radio plays . . .

C.S. You were left what we'd call now an unsupported mother during the war. How did you manage? How did you manage writing and being a single parent?

A.R. I used to write everything by hand. There was a nursery in Kingsway, and I took the baby there. We went on the tram. I was working very, very near there. And he had one bottle feed a day. I was breast-feeding, and I used to go in the lunch hour to breast-feed, not at ten, two and six o'clock, but at nine, one and five o'clock, because that fitted in. So I used to go in the lunch hour for a breast-feed. It seems incongruous in a way. I have a feeling that it shouldn't. And the difficulty was that the typewriter was a very old one . . . and it woke the baby when I typed. And this was an awful nuisance. There wasn't anywhere in the flat I could go where I could type.

C.S. Were things easier to manage once he'd gone to school?

199

A.R. Yes, they were a bit. But it's all very well – there's child-care before school, from very early hours, half-past five I think it is around here. But once they go to school, it's nine until half-past three . . . I would have thought that something could be done fairly easily in areas like this. Parents could help. It could be organized, almost in the way that we organized the hours from four to seven immediately after the war. We thought that we'd really got somewhere during the war. I know that Women's Liberation hadn't really started then, but I felt that we'd really got somewhere with regard to child-care, and with regard to women being recognized as important people. And we were dismayed to see it all taken back again.

C.S. When did you do your first radio play?

A.R. In the Sixties. I like radio very much. One of the producers called what I do 'total concept', because I know what I'm doing; I know what sound effects I want, and will work out a score for radiophonics. You've so much scope in radio. There are two things that I really like doing. One was to get the emotional shape of the thing by getting wired up to an EEG machine myself. I lay down, propping up the story, and then very, very quietly – because your reading can interfere with the machine – read it, and respond to it emotionally, and that shows on the EEG. Then when you've got the emotional shape of the thing, if you multiply all the frequencies by a hundred, then you're in the sound range. Then I treated it musically . . .

C.S. Then you stopped doing radio in the Sixties?

A.R. I rather stopped writing altogether for the time being, because it was in '67 that my son stabbed this man. By '65 he'd already become pretty unstable, and things were getting very difficult indeed. He needed a lot of support. Sometimes it was a question of dropping everything and going to find him. And then in '67 when it happened . . . I sort of got the brunt of that. Although a lot of people were very kind and gave me lifts to the prison . . . That's why he finally killed himself; because he knew he wasn't going to get well . . .

C.S. Did he ever blame you in any way?

A.R. Oh, sometimes. And I blame myself as well. If you have a child who even gets measles, you feel you've done something wrong. You feel guilty . . . I didn't want to stop writing. I still felt that I was a writer, and still felt that this was what I was supposed to be doing. And I wasn't doing it . . . I didn't consciously decide that I wasn't able to make a career of anything, but I really think that I knew it would be impossible. I would always have to break off if there was any difficulty. And I more or less gave up when he went to Broadmoor. He was there for seven years, then he came out. Seemed much better, certainly was much easier to live with for a year. But it slowly dawned on me that he wasn't getting anywhere and probably never would. And during the second year, it's possible that he realized that it had been a year . . . and another year was going to go in exactly the same way.

C.S. Do you feel, looking back, that you've had a lot of misfortune? You can see so many ways in which things could have been different . . . the accidents of time and place that you were born in. Especially the time.

A.R. Yes. Well, I feel it has been unfortunate. But, you see, if I hadn't had that, I wouldn't have had the experiences that I have had. And I feel that they're important, to other people, to me. That as a person I have had them . . . I did do quite a lot of work during that time. I helped with battered wives during the time that the drama group was starting. A friend of mine let us have a house in St Paul's, under licence. We didn't have to pay anything except the rates . . . We worked quite a lot, and my son helped with it as well, getting this house in order. The drama group helped with it.

C.S. Did you find out anything about women and how they live that you didn't know before, from that experience? Or did it just confirm the things you already knew?

A.R. What was confirmed was how women will work together when they feel they're all in the same boat. They'll even push their own kids over in bed, so that someone else's kids can come and share the mattress.

C.S. Did what you saw tie up with what you'd learned from your childhood?

A.R. No, because my parents wouldn't have behaved like that. My father would never have behaved like that. He believed in corporal punishment for children, but he would never have touched my mother. And if people around did it, we would not have heard about it: it would have been kept from us. We were protected quite a bit from that sort of thing.

C.S. When we talked about the women's movement last night you said that one thing it had done for you was change your idea of yourself as a woman, especially in relationships with men. I wonder if there was an effect on your writing?

A.R. It eased my consciousness, finding that other people felt in the same

201

way. Before the movement began, I had been arrogant and almost bitter about Women's Liberation (I didn't call it that, but I felt like that). But when it came out, so to speak, that relaxed.

C.S. Why? Why had you felt bitter before? And what relaxed?

A.R. Bitter because I felt up against it. And I had to be bitter, and arrogant, and, yes – almost aggressive sometimes. Because I felt alone. But the mere fact that you can go off and talk about things to people made quite a difference.

C.S. So it was circumstances that made you lonely?

A.R. Yes . . . And also it's terribly difficult to write because there's no stimulation. And you do have to bounce off something if you're going to be creative.

C.S. How do you do it, when you do it now? You said you worked in longhand . . .

A.R. Well, I used to. I have recently come to working on a typewriter. I do get the concept totally. I don't know if this makes sense or not; but you know that on Greek vases they do have the essential situation of the story, so that a woman can be shown embracing her husband, and he's going off on a ship somewhere, and both things are shown at the same time. And I rather get it like that; so that then it has to be organized, either in chronological or some other kind of sequence.

C.S. So you see things as a whole, then as incidents, and then you put them in *time* –

A.R. The important things regarding it have to be brought out.

C.S. And you have to put it into time?

A.R. In a certain order; yes.

C.S. You say at the beginning of your book that time is a dull line to string events along.

A.R. Yes. I still tend not necessarily to do things chronologically. Only if the chronology is important.

C.S. That rather suggests that you're interested in the *how* of things, rather than the *why*. If you ask why, it implies sequence, an interest in what causes something else. But you're describing a feeling, a situation, an essential situation that you're interested in.

A.R. And this ties up with what we were talking about some time ago, as to whether my childhood is still part of me, and this is why I feel yes, it probably still is.

202

C.S. It's on the vase: a little picture.

A.R. Yes, with all the others.

A.R. What I'm doing at the moment is to read fiction by women; and having done that I want to switch, because I want to feel what the difference is. I'm quite sure that there is a difference. If by mistake I've taken something out of the library that is by a man, I know fairly soon, even when there's no very definite indication. I come across something that I suddenly feel is wrong. It isn't just subject matter. I wonder if it's perception. I would like to be able to somehow analyse what it is that women are doing.

C.S. Virginia Woolf said that it was a different kind of sentence, a more diffuse kind of sentence.

A.R. Well, hers probably was.

C.S. But it's not that, is it? It's something about how you describe things in the world. The relationship of those things to the person who's writing about them? I keep thinking of the fishbone in your book, you see. And somehow one would know it was you – a woman – writing that description of you thinking about –

A.R. I go on imagining the fishbone . . . Yes, I certainly wondered what happened to that fish. I wondered if a man would have done it . . . This is something I want to do. Possibly even to confine myself to books about women by men. Again, to see if there is any difference in perception, any difference in the feel of it. It's so subjective, though, that it could be that what I'm doing isn't valid.

C.S. But why is it important to you? Why does it matter?

A.R. It has to do with the whole business of being a woman, of Women's Liberation, of all of that. Because I'm quite convinced, you see, that we are fundamentally different, that the difference is terribly important, is all-important. That if we were not so different, there wouldn't be much point in Women's Liberation. I know a lot of women see it differently from that. They feel that because we're the same that we need liberation to do the same things. I don't. I think we need liberation to do different things. Much has to be discovered.

I objected for a long time, and still object, that the Women's Liberation movement is ageist. Beyond the menopause there's nothing, as far as you can see. And there is in fact a great deal more; but precisely what that is is very difficult to find out. I think older women are just discovering it. I know I am. And it's very hard to pinpoint it, very hard to define it. Half your life is post-climacteric. And that's what I think is important in the Women's Liberation movement. But what there is after the climacteric that is so important is very difficult to describe. It's something that I'm just feeling my way into . . .

*C*AROLYN STEEDMAN *was born in 1947 and grew up in South* London. *She studied history at the University of Sussex and Newnham College, Cambridge from 1965–72. She is the author of* Policing the Victorian Community *(1984),* The Tidy House *(Virago 1983), winner of the 1983 Fawcett Society Book Award,* Landscape for a Good Woman *(Virago 1986). She contributed to* Truth, Dare or Promise *(Virago 1985). She lectures at the University of Warwick, and is an editor of* History Workshop Journal.

Dora Russell

talking with
Cathy Porter

*T*HE ROAD *wound up to a hill, then dipped down into a village, towards a steep cliff path which led to a sheltered beach. On the hill stood the whitewashed house that was Dora Russell's home, off and on, for sixty years and it was there that my two-year-old daughter and I went to visit her in May 1985. Here, on the Cornish coast, she wrote her books and brought up her four children. (Her eldest son, diagnosed as a schizophrenic, still lived with her.)*

For many of those sixty years, her views on women's liberation, socialist revolution and world peace were ignored and suppressed, and it was really only when the first volume of her autobiography The Tamarisk Tree *was published by Virago in 1975 that she was rediscovered as a socialist feminist of immense courage and strength.*

At ninety-one, she and her house were growing old together. The books, pictures and files that surrounded her recalled a life of labour and struggle. The unmodernized kitchen, the very paint on the walls, bore witness to the past. The wind rattled the windows as Dora sat talking.

She was born in 1894 of cultured parents who gave her and her younger sister a good education. On leaving school in 1911, she longed to go on the stage, but instead got a scholarship to Cambridge, where she read modern languages. It was there that she lost her religious faith, joined the 'Heretics' and the anti-war movement, and embarked on a love affair with their most articulate leader, the philosopher Bertrand Russell.

In 1920, they both made their separate ways to the Soviet Union, but 1923 was the start of her involvement in politics. In that year, Margaret Sanger had written a pamphlet about birth control expressly for working-class women. It was declared obscene and seized. Dora organized an appeal. The following year, she and some other socialist women, including Stella Browne, with the support of Bertrand Russell, organized the Workers' Birth Control Group to propagandize within the

Labour, socialist and cooperative movements for birth control to be provided by the state. She and her comrades were hounded by both men and women in the Labour Party for 'dragging sex into politics'.

In 1925, while still involved in the birth control campaign and busy looking after two small children, she wrote (as 'Mrs Bertrand Russell' to please her publishers) Hypatia; or Women and Knowledge, *a history of men's suppression of women's knowledge.*

The carnage of war and the optimism of the Bolshevik Revolution had generated new ideas about the education of children and the possibilities of replacing authority and fear with cooperation and tolerance. Her concern for the education of her own children focused many of these ideas and in 1927 she and Bertrand Russell opened their progressive school, Beacon Hill. (She described the school in The Tamarisk Tree, Virago, 1980.)

When war broke out the school was requisitioned; later Dora worked for the Ministry of Information's Soviet Affairs Division on their weekly newspaper British Ally, *until the intensification of the cold war against Russia forced it in 1950 to close. Anti-sovietism dogged the Labour and peace movements too, and Dora's association with the Soviet Peace Council lost her many friends. But despite political ostracism and unpopularity at home, she continued to visit the Soviet Union and never lost her warm (but never uncritical) appreciation of the Revolution's achievements, her vision of what it might have been had we not been more or less permanently at war with it.*

Perhaps this is the most unpopular of all the unpopular causes she has so bravely defended throughout her life. It is also the subject of the last and, I think most important volume of her autobiography, The Tamarisk Tree, *in which she holds up to the light our own government's sinister part in the early episodes of the cold war. But all her writing is filled with this courage, which is of such inspiration to women peace activists today: 'there's never been anything like this, this ever-rising, mounting, rolling wave of feeling that floods across from country to country, unites women as women, all women, the female sex, half of what goes to create a human being . . . Our one hope is in massive united protest.'*

Dora Russell died in 1986, just a year after this interview was completed.

C.P. What I've always found so moving about your writing, ever since I first read *The Tamarisk Tree*, some ten years ago, is the way you describe your experiences of war, revolution and women's liberation in terms both of political campaigns and of the possibilities within us all for making a better world. What made you a socialist?

D.R. Well, I was never interested in politics at Cambridge, and never joined the Labour Club. In fact I was interested in drama, and wanted to go on the stage. It was at Cambridge of course that I managed to get rid of my religious beliefs, and met Russell. But it was in 1917, when I first visited America – in the place of my father's secretary, who didn't fancy risking the submarines – that I became overnight a pacifist and a socialist. It was there that I saw capitalism in action, and the dominant influence of technology, and I quickly grew convinced that America was likely to become a power seeking world domination. I formed that opinion then, and I've never changed it.

C.P. So revolution was in the air! You've also been remarkably faithful to your first impressions of socialism in the Soviet Union, which you visited shortly afterwards. I was captivated by your account of the Bolsheviks you met, as they struggled to bring forth the new society. What made you go?

D.R. I first visited the Soviet Union in 1920. This was because Bertrand Russell, who had just asked me to marry him, was, like a good many people on the left, very excited by the Soviet Revolution, and wanted me to go to Russia with him to find out what was really happening there. Then right at the last moment he decided to go without me, on a trade union delegation. So I was furious with him for going back on his promise, and decided to go on my own. I travelled to Stockholm, where I contacted the left-wing people, and by this means discovered that one could get into Russia by the north route, via Murmansk. There was going to be a big conference of the Third International, and various delegates were on their way to the Soviet Union, including a British Communist called Madge Newbold. So Madge and I got ourselves Soviet passports, and enough food to last several days, and set out as advised on a steamer round the North Cape to the desolate little northern fishing port of Vardo. There we disembarked, and made for a little house where we'd been instructed to wait for two men who would take care of us. Imagine our horror when we got there and were told they weren't there! Then, as we walked back to the village not knowing what to do next, two men came walking up the street behind us, and they turned out to be the two we were looking for. So they put us on a small fishing smack bound for Murmansk, and when we got there we found everyone celebrating midsummer's day!

C.P. Did the journey prepare you for what you found?

D.R. There was good reason for the Russian authorities' nervousness about foreigners at that point. In Murmansk I actually slept in one of the shanties left by the expeditionary force Churchill had sent against Russia the moment Revolution broke out! He was determined to bring the Revolution down, and he not only sent an army to the north, but send Col. Wedgwood round by Siberia to attack the Russians from that side. (Wedgwood's given a very good account of that, because he found the Russians so different from what he'd expected.) By the summer of 1920, when I was there, the white armies were being beaten back, but the Poles had invaded, and every evening we'd go to the Soviet foreign office for news of the Polish war. But despite all these hardships – the hunger, the smashed factories and mines – you felt a new culture was being born. The very air was charged with it. And people's pride in their Revolution moved one to tears. It was then that I learnt to love the place.

C.P. What did you find the Revolution was doing for women? Was it your first practical experience of feminism?

D.R. Already when I was at school I'd admired the suffragettes, and one of the first questions I asked when I got to the Soviet Union was, 'What's in it for women?' And of course I found that the men there, like the men in the West, had not taken women sufficiently into account. And it was then that I met Alexandra Kollontai. As I said, I'd admired the suffragettes, but Kollontai gave me a much wider vision of what women could do in politics, and it was she who to a large extent shaped my feminism from then on.

C.P. What impressed you so much about Kollontai?

D.R. The Bolsheviks had been campaigning for women's suffrage since long before the Revolution, and Kollontai had herself been active in that campaign, trying always to put forward the working woman's point of view as regards votes for women. And throughout her life it was the position of women and children that mainly concerned her. But she was an important person, too. She was a member of Lenin's cabinet, and of course on one or two occasions she had the courage to differ with Lenin. She was a statesman as well as a feminist, and in my opinion she's never received sufficient acclaim, either as a feminist or as a Bolshevik.

C.P. Did you see any of the practical results of Kollontai's work?

D.R. She and Inessa Armand had been organizing this big conference, the International Conference of Communist Women, to be held in the

210

Bolshoi Theatre in conjunction with the Comintern congress that June. Armand had worked herself to the point of collapse, and was away in the Caucasus, but Kollontai was able to attend, and she took me there. The hall was packed with peasant women, and one by one they came up to the platform to air their problems, and they spoke with that wonderful enthusiasm I've heard so often from women who speak for the first time in public. And what they had to say was so obviously full of admiration for her.

C.P. She was very much an aristocrat, wasn't she? And the women at this and other conferences she organized were peasants, most of them illiterate, most of them new to politics. Yet you say their admiration for her was obvious. It has often puzzled me that she was able to speak so convincingly for women whose background and aspirations were so distant from hers.

D.R. I think you're bound to have leaders. The women at that conference had come from all parts of the Soviet Union, and most of them could neither read nor write, and they naturally looked up to Kollontai as a sort of God-given leader. But what the Marxists entirely forget is that it was precisely these people, the peasants, who were the really big drive behind the Russian Revolution. Not the technological people, the proletariat, but the ordinary people behind them. These were the people who were beginning to be educated, these were the people who were drafted into the army in the First World War, and these were the people who ultimately drove the Germans out in the Great Patriotic War.

C.P. Did you learn anything from Kollontai about her relationship with the Party?

D.R. She took me round a little exhibition she'd organized about motherhood and the bringing up of children, with icon-like pictures of mothers from various countries. And what she told me that did impress me was that the men weren't sufficiently concerned about the use of children's labour – they were saying this wasn't the time, there was a war on, and so on. But she still stood by her demand that more care should be taken of children.

C.P. It fascinates me that you and Bertrand Russell were in the Soviet Union at the same time, and went to many of the same places, yet he was outraged by what he saw, while you were utterly caught up in the spirit of the Revolution.

D.R. You see, Russell was temperamentally a liberal (though he did

211

become a socialist), while my visit to Russia made me much more left-wing than I'd been before, like the French Revolution was to Wordsworth. Then of course there was a difference in the quality of our experiences and the people we met. He met the people who'd lived in exile in the West, and knew all about American technology and factories, and I met the peasants, who had originally adored the Tsar and were religious-minded. It was one thing to meet all the top-level people and hear them talking about developing Russian industry and what the machine was going to mean to Russia's development. It was quite another to meet the comrades, the rank and file, who had just become enthusiastic about the idea of working together to make a new life. And those were the people I met. But I also got a very good impression of the people at the top, who greeted me with great courtesy. They were genuine revolutionaries too, genuine Bolsheviks.

C.P. What did people in Britain think of the Revolution and our government's war of intervention against it? And how did the Russians you met assess the chances of revolution here and elsewhere in Europe?

D.R. In general I think people in Britain were annoyed with the Russians for letting us down in the war. There was this joke, you know, about the Russian 'steamroller', thrown against the Germans in the war, and after the Revolution everyone said the steamroller had gone and only the red flag remained. But people on the left, of course, were tremendously excited about it; the trade unions set up the Council of Action against the intervention, and dockers refused to load the *Jolly George* with munitions for Poland. As for the Russians, they still believed that after all their sufferings and triumphs the German and British workers were *bound* to come to their support and make a world revolution.

C.P. And we were even more badly informed about them! You said you felt uniquely capable of describing Soviet Russia to the West, yet although Russell's views on the Revolution were eagerly sought, your more generous vision wasn't so eagerly accepted. Did you know it would be like that?

D.R. No, I never expected the sort of anti-Soviet nonsense that's gone on ever since. But I said then, and I've always said, it's the greatest tragedy of history that our government didn't recognize the new Soviet government and agree to live peacefully with it.

C.P. You say Russell's anti-Communism was a source of great sorrow to you. Your visit to the Soviet Union must have focused many differences.

D.R. What troubled me to begin with, when I got back and found that I had to go to China with him, was that I couldn't write a book on my experiences of Russia. And yes, we argued a lot about it. We had a terrible argument on the way to China, in the middle of the Red Sea. 'Why d'you keep talking about freedom?' I finally said to him, 'How could there be freedom in the middle of a war? And what's more, it's my belief that the machine system is bound to be run either by dictators or oligarchs. It'll destroy freedom and democracy as we understand it.' And I supported the Bolsheviks.

C.P. You've written about Russell's idealization of the spiritual bond between lovers – which meant you always had to agree with him! But you obviously didn't, right from the beginning.

D.R. He'd kept telling his friends that he didn't think he could possibly marry me, because I didn't agree with him, which must mean I didn't love him! It seemed so odd to me! You see, he did genuinely believe that women's intelligence wasn't as good as men's, and felt he always had to condescend to women when talking to them. He paid me the compliment of saying I was the one woman he didn't feel that with. There was also the fact that Russell was by no means determined, when I went to China with him, on being in love with me. If I'd known at the time about some of the letters he wrote which indicated that I was only on approval, so to speak, I should have felt very differently. But I was blissfully happy and had by then become quite devoted to him. As for the differences – well, we found so many issues in politics on which we were agreed. And when we returned from China in 1921, I began to take up political causes – like my Spanish journalism, the women's cause and the birth control issue – that didn't clash with what he was doing.

C.P. You married, yet you disliked marriage's property basis, with its possessiveness and jealousy. Did you think birth control would free people from that?

D.R. When we campaigned in the Labour Party for abortion law reform, birth control, paid maternity leave and maternity benefit, we roused a storm of controversy. But these subjects, that had till then been covered in shame, now began to be discussed up and down the country. People had so many new choices opened up to them. It also made it possible for women to treat sex the way men do, sleeping with men temporarily, or if they want to.

C.P. I sense a tension there for you. You talk of girls of your generation, far from seeking a mate, actually taking evasive action against sexual

213

involvement. We can take for granted so much of the sexual freedom you had painfully to fight for. It seems that for you work came first, and that love and sexual relationships, to be worth sacrificing work and independence for, had to be of the same consuming life-enhancing importance.

D.R. I never thought there should be love affairs between people unless they were based on genuine love and consent. But then the sexual impulse is such an important thing, and we've completely mismanaged it because we've never really troubled to find out what it really is. That's why the World League for Sexual Reform was so important.

C.P. Tell me about that.

D.R. The first congress was in London, in 1929. On the list of people attending you found practically everyone of a left-wing or forward-looking tendency in England. At the beginning, everyone said: 'Oh, you won't get this started, don't be absurd.' But it was a tremendous success! Hirschfeld, who'd originally started the whole thing at his institute in Berlin, was there, and made a very fine speech. Norman Haire, and Jack Flugel who'd organized the whole thing with me. And two eminent Russians, who gave papers, even though relations between Russia and England were not good at the time. In fact I'd just been to the Soviet Union, and learnt that our birth control campaign [the Workers' Birth Control Group] was being followed with great interest. It was the only such campaign they really respected, they said, because it didn't bring questions of genetics into it, and people being too poor to have children, and so on.

C.P. Your book *The Right to be Happy*, published the same year, is an inspiring exhortation to pleasure and sexual fulfilment. In it you talk of love as the most repressed of emotions. Why aren't we allowed to be happy? Why are love, pleasure and women's sexuality repressed?

D.R. Just because I said women had the right to enjoy sex, they said the book should be banned – which meant of course that it sold six hundred copies in one week! The Victorians said women didn't enjoy sex, but in fact it's the opposite that's true; it's women who actually *need* sex. You see, my whole life, from childhood onwards, has been based on my relation to nature, to things that grow, the natural world and all the living things on this planet. And the reason I've argued against the excessive use of the male intellect, throughout history, is that men have never been sufficiently interested in the natural world. And this has made them cynical and indifferent to creative values. It's always women who take an interest in nature, and men who've been quite ruthless in destroying it and talking about conquering it and building factories. When I wrote that book we honestly did believe that to pursue this matter of sexual reform might not merely make for greater human happiness, but also for peace and understanding.

C.P. When you first married and discussed what would happen if you had children with another man, you insisted that these should be your sole responsibility. You did bear another man's children, and do appear to have been solely responsible for them. Was it not part of your programme for sexual reform to look at ways in which men might share some of that responsibility?

D.R. History shows that men on the whole don't have the same need for parenting, except insofar as they wanted sons to follow on in their profession or continue the glories of war and do all the things their fathers did.

C.P. Surely we should have been able to overcome some of these primitive sexual divisions – which birth control has anyway partly superseded? How can we hope to make better people if men don't learn to look after children?

D.R. I agree that to put the act of parenting on one half of the human race is fair neither to parent nor child. But I think the reason men don't take more interest in their children is that they still tend to regard it as cissy. And after all many people still think you should take children away from their parents as soon as you possibly can and send them to boarding school, to make men of them, precisely in order that they won't get too tied up with women.

C.P. In *Tamarisk Tree, 2*, about the school you set up in 1927, you too wrote that you didn't think parents were the best people to bring up their own children, and that it was a job for experts.

D.R. This was partly due to Freud, and Truby King's ideas on the rearing of babies, a lot of which I now think is mistaken. We thought then that parents could overwhelm a child with their outlook and opinions, and that a child needed to liberate him or herself from the adults who were constantly there. And after all, it isn't every parent who is capable of bringing up their child. Some people are temperamentally suited to looking after children, some aren't.

C.P. Perhaps they shouldn't have them then?

D.R. Yes, that was the point of birth control. We thought that if women

215

were able to obtain the means to limit their families – with the consent of the fathers, of course – then those who liked children could have three or four if they wanted, while those that didn't much care for them needn't have any at all.

C.P. Thoughts about your own children's education seem to have focused many of your ideas – the challenge to traditional views of the family, a disgust with competitiveness and aggression, the revolutionary impact of Freud – into the decision to open your own school.

D.R. We thought first of all that instead of deciding what you wanted to put into a child, you should look at the child and see what he or she is likely to be interested in. We'd come right up to the twentieth century before it occurred to anyone to ask what went on in a child's head! It had to be obedient, its will had to be broken, it was punished, it was just a thing. And that's still true, as far as most grown-ups are concerned. And although Bertie and I were impressed that the Labour Party seemed enthusiastic about education, it always seemed to have to do with appliances and materials, not much to do with content. Of course there were a number of independent schools at that time trying not to be hierarchical, but traditional schools still had caning, and still do, with rigid rows of desks, and everything very regimented, with subservience to the teachers, and for boys, certain kinds of military exercises. We also thought people should be free not to have religious education if they didn't want it. I never thought that Russell would take an enormous part in the work of the school, but I thought that with friends and people interested in the new education we might perhaps do something. So that was how the school opened.

C.P. Are there any schools now running on similar lines to Beacon Hill?

D.R. I suppose we were closest to A. S. Neill's Summerhill. But I think my ideas were closer to Neill's than Bertie's, because Bertie still had a considerable respect – and nothing wrong in that – for intellectual things, and less for artistic and more practical work with the hands.

C.P. You describe Beacon Hill as part of a larger movement – for nursery schools, for freer education, for less authoritarian family relationships. Yet the picture one gets of this wonderful creation of yours is that it was terribly isolated and attacked from all sides.

D.R. Yes, of course, there was immediately this absurd outcry from the press, which said we always walked about with no clothes on and were always talking about sex. We didn't actually do any sex education, in fact, as most of the children were too young, and all we did do in that respect was to answer their questions. And of course the children did go without clothes in summer if they wanted to.

C.P. Yet despite the attacks the school did survive for some sixteen years. Do you think any of its ideals have survived?

D.R. Well, of course, under the present government all the ideals we had of rearing better human beings are disappearing, because this government is determined to kill the basis of our human society by killing the possibility of cooperation between people. We did have some hopes, in the post-war years, that our old dreams of cooperation might be realized. But over the years the profit motive flooded back, values disintegrated. Now, of course, progressive teaching is blamed for bad behaviour and delinquency. But it's the authoritarian people that are to blame, for not allowing children to make more of their own decisions.

C.P. So many of your ideas seem to have been shaped by that first visit to Russia, in 1920, and subsequent visits seem to have confirmed what it might have been had not the West been permanently at war with it. You describe in *Tamarisk Tree* your experience of the cold war's gathering momentum.

D.R. I managed in 1943, through the help of Ellen Wilkinson, to get a job in the reference division of the Ministry of Information. Now the year before that, the Ministry had set up their paper *British Ally*, which was to be the mouthpiece of the twenty-year friendship pact just signed between Eden and Molotov. One day I saw on the noticeboard an advertisement for a vacancy at the Soviet Relations Division, to work as an editor on *British Ally*, and I knew they had hardly anyone there who knew anything about Russia, so I applied and got the job.

C.P. You say that the Russians were terribly excited about the prospects of surviving the war into a new era of peaceful existence, and that the Soviet readership of *British Ally* soared. Were the British contributors equally committed to the alliance with Russia?

D.R. Oh yes! The Russians were absolutely delighted by the idea, and our people were terribly committed, too. But communications were extraordinarily difficult. We appointed an editor, and various people set out by sea for Kuibyshev, where Moscow was being evacuated to, with a mass of photographs, books, films and so on. And their ship was bombed by the Germans off Murmansk, and sunk, and all their luggage was lost. They weren't drowned, but when they finally arrived they had nothing! And it was said that the women typists flew to

217

Kuibyshev in the bomb compartments of the planes. And when they got there the British staff worked in very difficult conditions, and suffered cold and discomfort. For us in London, we considered that the war had brought us a new ally to whom we owed a lot, and we regarded the long hours we worked on *British Ally* as a tribute to that friendship.

C.P. Were the other people on *British Ally* like you, temperamentally pro-Soviet, or was it the spirit of the times and Russian heroism in the war that made everyone pro-Soviet?

D.R. Well, the point is there *was* this enormous enthusiasm for Russia, but they needed people on the paper who had some experience of the place, and I'd been there twice since 1920 and had grown to love the people and their country.

C.P. The fortunes of *British Ally* followed so closely the progress of the cold war against Russia that you must have been exceptionally well placed to follow its post-war origins.

D.R. Immediately the war ended, things changed. During the war we'd been in the university buildings, behind the British Museum. Afterwards, we were moved to some offices, flats they were, near Baker Street, and became much more official. The Ministry of Information turned into the Central Office of Information, and from then on everything to do with us came under the Foreign Office. The atmosphere became more formal. Only a month after the end of the war, eight top scientists invited to Moscow for a conference I was covering were suddenly forbidden to leave the country (in case they got tight and told the Russians of the secret of the bomb). The next year our inner cabinet committed Britain in secret to making its own bomb. And in 1947, the Foreign Office issued a directive that *British Ally* was no longer to be an instrument of friendship, but of war. We had two young men from the Foreign Office appointed as editors who'd just come out of the Navy, and it was their job to instruct us what to do. And I don't mean to be rude to them, but they didn't really know anything about Russia. And more and more new people kept coming in and out of their office, and I kept thinking, I don't really think any of them knows anything about Russia!

C.P. What happened to the original staff under the new policy?

D.R. A lot of them resigned, as they felt unable to work for a paper that was just becoming a vehicle for British foreign policy. I stayed on to defend as best I could the *British Ally*'s original creative purpose. But it

218

didn't last long. The Foreign Office had wanted to continue the paper on the same aggressive lines until the Soviet government itself took steps to close it down, but it didn't, so in the end it was the British that did so, in 1950.

C.P. Just a year after Russia had simultaneously got the secret of the bomb and started the World Peace Council. How was that double message received by your friends on the left?

D.R. Well, most people in the Labour Party said it was just Soviet propaganda, of course, and hypocrisy, but I thought it was a proof of their sincerity. Everyone who has an atom bomb has it in readiness, but you don't have to threaten actually to use it, and they were saying they weren't immediately placing bombers to threaten the West. Whereas what we had done was to place American bombers in East Anglia ready all along to bomb Russia.

C.P. There were already the first stirrings of a peace movement, then. Were there any special initiatives that women were making?

D.R. The Women's International Democratic Federation, set up in 1945 in Paris, was an important anti-Fascist organization, which many members of the previously existing Women's International League for Peace and Freedom were joining. The two feminist women's groups in which I was involved, though, the Six-Point Group and the Married Women's Association, had become quite divided as to whether to campaign on the home front or for world peace, and many of their members were very hostile to any involvement in world politics. I remember in 1949 the Married Women's Association held a garden party in Hampstead, and we took the World Peace Council's petition in and set up a stall where people could sign it. I was then the chairman, and Edith Summerskill, who was our president, saw it and said: 'Either that petition leaves the garden party or I do!' And I was not to be found, so it was she who left!

C.P. So after the campaign launched against the World Peace Council it can't have come as much of a shock to you, in the early meetings of the Campaign for Nuclear Disarmament in 1955, that you and others associated with the WPC were expected to keep their distance?

D.R. No. My impression was then, and always has been, that the Soviet Union continually puts out feelers of friendship, and gets kicked in the teeth – or ignored.

C.P. With your association with the socialist countries keeping you out of print and out of CND, you must have felt very despairing.

D.R. Yes, but it was because of this that we organized, independently of CND, our Women's Caravan for Peace, in which we travelled all the way across Western and Eastern Europe to the Soviet Union and back. Wherever we went we would say: we're coming to make friends with you and to talk about peace, but we're not in any way criticizing your social system. And wherever we went we were welcomed with open arms! But when we got back, of course, we couldn't get anyone to publish our book or show our film about it.

C.P. But a new generation of women peace activists *has* seen your film and read about the Peace Caravan – which must have been the inspiration for many recent Soviet visits organized by people trying on their own initiative to improve the political climate. Do you think we should organize another Women's Peace Caravan?

D.R. No, let them try and come here next time, and everyone will see the obstacles our government puts in their way!

C.P. Do you think the peace movement is going about its East-West bridge-building the right way?

D.R. I think quite honestly that the only proper line to take in talking to people of the socialist countries is the one we took in the Peace Caravan. But unfortunately that's not the line taken by many in the West, because there's always this question of 'human rights', or some other problem. Any contact whatever that says our government, our democracy, is better than yours, is quite wrong, in my view. And while it may be perfectly true that many people in the border countries do want to be free of the Soviet Union, there are also a great many who don't. Moreover, I think it's utterly wrong for people to interfere with the internal policies of other countries – that is the policy of the United Nations.

C.P. But not of the US government! We talk a lot of peaceful coexistence and non-interference, often suggesting rather a static state of affairs like a return to the détente of the Seventies. But your writings contain the vision of something much more lofty and dynamic, which is bound up with your entire lifelong search for completeness, and that is the possibility of a synthesis between East and West. How do you get people to make that imaginative leap?

D.R. I would really like people to try to *understand* Russia – learn about its history, go there and meet its people, and try to understand what if feels like to be isolated and surrounded by enemies armed to the teeth against you.

220

*C*ATHY PORTER *was born in 1947 in Oxford and grew up there. She studied Russian and Czech at University, squatted, taught literacy and wrote* Fathers and Daughters *and* Alexandra Kollontai *(Virago). She has also written books on art of the 1905 Revolution, Moscow in the war, the Civil War and a textbook on women in the Revolution. She lives in London and is active in the local Labour Party.*

Phyllis Shand Allfrey

talking with
Polly Pattullo

*B*EFORE *I went to the West Indies for the first time in 1981, a friend lent me a copy of* The Growth of the Modern West Indies *by Gordon Lewis. I read of colonialism and British neglect, semi-feudal economies and impoverished peasantries, of emerging politicians and fledgling parties. Each island bore the different markings of its people and history and the experience of decolonization was thus different for each. And then I read of 'the transition in Dominica from the rule of the old white plantocracy to that of the town merchants who supplanted them after the First World War, with the scions of the old families living on declining incomes, men who cannot work living on the coloured women who love them, a social process lovingly traced, with nostalgic regret, in Phyllis Allfrey's* The Orchid House.'*

I had heard of neither the author nor the novel. And anyhow The Orchid House *was out of print. On that first trip to the Caribbean I went no closer to Dominica than a brief visit to French Martinique. A few months later, I heard that Virago was republishing* The Orchid House. *When I read it, it did indeed express feelings of 'nostalgic regret', but it also suggested a groundwork for a new political order. It was the voice of a woman who understood the dynamics of her West Indian island.*

Phyllis Shand Allfrey was born in 1908 into an old white Dominican family. When she died in 1986 she left behind poems, short stories, one novel, and another unfinished. But her opportunities for writing had always been limited: financial hardship, political obligations (she became a leading politician in Dominica and a Minister in the short-lived Federation of the West Indies), her husband's illness, the death of a daughter, and, in her last years, her own failing strength all contributed. When I last saw her a year before she died, it was clear that her unfinished novel, In the Cabinet, *would never be completed. She was frail, it was hard to keep going. Always a terrible housekeeper, she would produce the most microscopic of meals – half a frankfurter, a chunk of*

cold yam, the odd biscuit – but would rarely eat herself. 'Get that girl a
drink, man' would be the signal for extracting the rum from the fridge.
She was tired but she was merry – glad of visitors to her broken-down
little house in the shadow of tree-clad cliffs to bring news of the outside
world and talk of books, politics and gossip.

If this then is more the story of Phyllis Shand Allfrey, the writer
snatched from her typewriter, it is necessarily that. And, as such, it is a
compliment.

'I sold my first story when I was thirteen – to *Tiger Tim's Weekly*, a
children's magazine from England. But mainly I wrote poetry. I started
writing at a very early age. I used to sit and write up a tree in my
grandfather's garden. I never went to school. The one girls' school was
the Catholic convent and my father kept his family apart from other
races. My paternal relations never mixed. My maternal relations were
liberal. I was taught at home by an eccentric governess and my lovable
aunt. My father was literary and my mother was just a darling mother.
Literature was very important to me and I devoured my father's books.
When I was in my teens someone gave me a copy of *The Oxford Book of
English Verse* and I read it from cover to cover. I also read Rupert Brooke
– he was popular in those years after the First World War. There was a
dear old man called Dr Thaly from Martinique who lent me books. He
used to come and treat us. He was also a poet but I'm afraid he was very
neglected. Years later, I prefaced my book *The Orchid House* with a
verse from his poem "L'Île Lointaine".'

Such are the earliest literary memories in the dogged and startlingly
singular career of Phyllis Shand Allfrey. They have a particular reso-
nance: of the white ruling class of small-island West Indian society
surviving uneasily but stubbornly amid a maze of racial and class
nuances; of strong links with the European literary tradition; and of the
adult Phyllis Allfrey's pride and passion for her Dominican birthplace.

She was born and brought up in Roseau, the tiny, ramshackle capital
of Dominica with its Frenchified, verandahed homes on the leeward side
of the island where the waves lap fitfully at the sea wall. Then, as now,
there are few white West Indians in Dominica; Phyllis Allfrey is one of
them. She could trace her ancestorship back to Thomas Warner who
landed on St Kitts in 1624 and later became its governor. (As one of her
characters says, 'After the Caribs she is the oldest Anonican,' a reference
to her own long Dominican pedigree.) In the old days, her family were a
kind of 'royal family': her grandfather was Sir Henry Nicholls, a staunch

conservative, doctor and scientist who propagated tropical crops and was a founder-member of the island's Agricultural Society. Her father was Crown Attorney; one of her uncles helped to found Dominica's first trade union.

The days of her girlhood were those when grand white visitors to the Caribbean dropped by in their yachts to pay respects to the island's white gentry. 'We were poor but we had rich friends. There was J. P. Morgan, the US millionaire banker – he came on his yacht and his granddaughter was called Dominica. When I was seventeen I left Dominica with an American family. I was adventurous and I wanted to see the world. It was in the States that I saw my first ever copy of Jean Rhys. [Rhys also came from Dominica but left the island at about the time of Phyllis Allfrey's birth.] It was her book, *Voyage in the Dark*. It was the simplicity and beauty of the prose that I loved. But it was a horrible book, really, for a young girl to read. Jean Rhys felt she was a victim. I tried to tell her that. I only met her once, in London, with her husband. Her style was so pure but she wrote about impure things. I tried to persuade her to come back to Dominica when the film people wanted to make *Wide Sargasso Sea*. That was in the early Seventies. She wrote and said she couldn't travel by air and wouldn't travel in a banana boat because there were no luxuries. So she never came at all. Anyhow there were no houses big enough – we don't have any of those great plantation houses, so they went away.'

For a time, then, the young Phyllis Allfrey left behind the world of her childhood. West Indian experience and, indeed, literature is full of departures and exile: Phyllis Allfrey was no exception.

From the States she arrived in Britain, for a family wedding. 'My sister Celia was getting married at Holy Trinity, Brompton, to a naval officer. At the wedding I met the groom's brother, Robert Allfrey. When I returned to England six months later after being in Belgium and Germany, I went to Sussex to visit my sister's new mother-in-law, and on the platform I saw this tall guy loping around. It was Robert. He was supposed to be in India but he'd never gone. We fell in love – that was the long and short of it. I was nineteen when we married. The Archbishop of the West Indies came and gave me away.

'It was the Depression and there was no work for Robert who had read engineering at Oxford. So we went to the US, to Buffalo. I thought there'd be work there – and we had friends – but it was the Depression there too.

'I wasn't writing novels at that time – I couldn't stick it long enough – but there were always poems and short stories. My poems are the best part of me.' Her poetry is full-blown, lush, often touched with a

227

melancholy for home. 'Wanderer from the Tropics', for example, begins: 'They've trapped you, human fawn, and lashed you tight, And let you from your haven in the sun.' There are poems which lament greyness; more which have a sharp eye for the upright, uptight ex-pat white ladies picking their way through tropical gardens. One ends with Phyllis Allfrey in fighting form: 'Therefore do poets, in their quest for the lovely, Turn their eyes from the white ladies (Save when there rises a queen amongst them Who is brave and light and proud to love) and write poems about us.'

In the late Thirties, the Allfreys returned to London with their two children, a boy and a girl, born, as Phyllis Allfrey has written, 'of snow and apples'. As always, they had little money. 'The year before war started, I answered an advertisement in *The Times* for the post of a part-time secretary . . . The job turned out to be with Naomi Mitchison. I loved her immediately – she was like an Indian squaw. One day, we learnt about a poor woman in Hammersmith who hadn't been able to pay her hire purchase. "I owe only £1," she said. Naomi suggested that we should all go over there and circumvent the removal of the furniture. "We'll sit on it and they won't be able to take it away." We did that but the men said they'd be back. It went on for five days like that. In the end we won and eventually the law was changed. We proved something. Yes, Naomi was a good socialist. I learnt a lot from her. Once she invited us to the Boat Race at her house in Hammersmith – it was a social and socialist occasion. I didn't become a socialist-minded person until I met Naomi. I came from a family which had servants but I had to throw that sort of thinking all aside. I had no race prejudice as a child but, of course, it was all around me.'

In London the Allfreys joined the Labour Party and the Fabian Society. The art of grass-roots politics would stand Phyllis Allfrey in good stead in the years ahead. Employed as a welfare adviser to the London County Council during the war she 'saw then how poor people lived'.

After the war – with the West Indies never far from her consciousness – she worked with the West India Committee in the House of Commons.

'I used to go to the railway stations to meet the West Indian immigrants off the boats in our van. We used to give them warm clothes. Sometimes I meet West Indians now who say how vividly they remember those days.'

There had been a collection of her poems published in 1940 called *In Circles* and, in 1950, a second anthology, *Palm and Oak*, was published privately. This portrays, as she wrote, 'the tropical and nordic strains in my ancestry, hence the title.'

'I entered one of these poems, "While the Young Sleep", in an

228

international poetry competition organized by the Society of Women Writers and Journalists. Among the judges was Vita Sackville-West. The poem won second prize. I was given my award at the Lord Mayor's Show and afterwards this bleached blonde lady came up to me and asked me if I had ever written a novel. She was a literary agent from Curtis Brown. I was overcome.

'I had been trying to write a novel for some time. I had been making notes on it for years. I was homesick. I wanted to write a book about an island – the island is the real hero. It was probably nostalgia. It's a life that's gone now. Some characters are drawn from life, others are made up. I suppose that I appear in it too.

'When I won the prize the boy was at boarding school and Pheena, my daughter, was at Oxford. That freed me. Robert always urged me to write. He took a lot of problems away from me. It's been my conflict to find time to write. I went to Sussex to a wonderful old haunted house, slogged away at it and decided to finish it. The lady literary agent had said I mustn't mind waiting for quite a while for a publisher to make a decision. I chose Constable as my first choice of publishers. Twenty-four hours after I sent it to them, the agent rang to say they'd taken it. I was really amazed.'

The Orchid House was published in 1953. It tells the story of the return of three white sisters to their tropical island birthplace and lovingly unravels a tale of great passion in which the dynamics of race, culture, sex and religion are explored through the eyes of Lally, the old Black nurse. 'Lally, c'est moi,' says Phyllis Allfrey, but it falls to Joan, the middle sister, back from London brimming with political enthusiasms and Fabian politics to assume a morality closest to Phyllis Allfrey's own. Yet it is to Lally that the author gives the lines which provide the best clue to her largely unspoken brand of feminism: 'She would not have it thought that they needed *men* to be supporting or caring for them. Without men they would never be, as it was naked to the eye right from their early days. But with or without men they were Madam's daughters, and that means to say that they could be sufficient unto themselves.'

In contrast, the male characters in *The Orchid House* are shadowy, sickly souls, smitten with mental and physical disease; some the focus of romantic longing, others the incarnation of distorted prejudice and even evil. There is one exception: a strong young Black man who represents the stirrings of a new political order to replace the dying and decadent colonial one. For Phyllis Allfrey was, if nothing else, an idealist; but to accuse her of sentimentality would be wrong – hers was a clear-headed view of Caribbean island life in the 1950s.

229

One year after the publication of *The Orchid House* she returned to Dominica: 'Beauty and disease, beauty and sickness, beauty and horror: that was the island', she wrote in her novel.

'I had a great longing to go home and Robert wanted to see my island. When I came back people wanted us to get involved in politics. I had just started writing again but I had to give all that up. Robert had got a job with the lime juice people (Dominica was the home of Rose's lime juice) and had had to sign a document saying that he would disassociate himself from politics, so I decided I might as well be interested. Politics became more important than writing. I regret that now. I shouldn't have given up writing for politics. If I'd stuck with it I would have accumulated more and got higher up that particular tree.

'In politics, there were so many people who were in distress. It seemed to me important that at that time a middle-of-the-road politics was developed, what would now be called social democrat. Otherwise I believed that there would be a Communist sweep-over . . . I went to organize the people to help them to do something for themselves. But people – my people – were saying bad things about us. Eugenia Charles [now Dominica's Prime Minister] was saying that we were Communists, wicked Communists.

'Oh yes. Politics ruined me as a writer.'

When the Allfreys returned to Dominica there were then no political parties on the island. Full adult suffrage had only been granted to Dominicans in 1951; and in the same year the composition of the legislature was changed to give elected members an inbuilt majority for the first time. Even so, the old-style politics and the dominance of the town-based merchant class survived. Phyllis Allfrey changed all this, and it was her political perceptions that cracked the old order as she began to organize the dispossessed peasantry. With her experience of British Labour Party politics behind her, she founded Dominica's first political party. It was inaugurated from the porch of the Dominica Trade Union hall in Roseau in May 1955. The party's motto, typical of Phyllis Allfrey's politics (once described as a mixture of Fabian socialism and paternalism), was: 'No one is truly free who does not work for the freedom of others.' Hers was a specific brand of Caribbean politics: rejected as she was by her own class and the Black bourgeoisie, she nevertheless remained loyal to her own 'pedigree', her own individual identity as a white West Indian. Hers was not a politics to become part of a radical dynamic. It was too informed by her whiteness, too touched by her romanticism. I was told a story once about her addressing a meeting of the Dominica Labour Party in its early days. 'And now', she announced, 'I want to introduce a princess to you, a princess from England.' It was her teenage daughter, Pheena.

There was still no time for writing, for Phyllis Allfrey was then swept into international politics. In 1958, after decades of discussion and false hopes, the Federation of the West Indies was formed. Phyllis Allfrey stood for election.

'I was in England when the elections were announced and I had to rush to get back for nomination day. I got to Barbados, then to St Lucia where I was given a lift on a Geest banana boat on its way to Dominica. When I came ashore in a straw hat clutching my rucksack containing my precious election leaflets – the first Dominica had ever seen – I heard people saying, "The white woman promised to come and she don't come." I lifted my hat from my face and said in patois, *moi wivai ici*: I have arrived. I felt then that I had already won.

'I campaigned all over the island – walking or riding on a donkey.' She made her way to remote mountainous villages. A fragile, pale-haired woman, she spoke to the people in the French patois which is still widely spoken. 'I and one of my other sisters learnt it from the cook. My father said, "Don't learn it," but I found that patois is a very useful thing. I would never have won the federal elections without it.'

Allfrey and her colleague LeBlanc won at 135 out of 138 polling stations. It was a landslide victory. But as Phyllis Allfrey noted: 'The middle class still discriminated against me. Only one person of my class voted for me.' Nevertheless, she was on her way to Trinidad, the administrative capital of the new-born Federation. Robert went, too, along with their two adopted children from Dominica – a girl, Sonia, and a Carib boy, David.

'It is always difficult to reconcile home and work if one's a very strong-minded woman and I think I am that. I was the one who used to be in the limelight. Robert was always so quiet but, you know, in the background he did so much research and was such a help to me but he never had any recognition.'

In Port of Spain, Phyllis Allfrey was appointed the Minister of Health and Social Affairs – a wide-reaching portfolio. She was also in a double minority: she was the only woman in the Cabinet, and she was white. For her this was not a personal disadvantage but a political strength. Her racial, sexual and social uniqueness was, to her, a symbol that the Federation could assimilate the historic diversity of the English-speaking Caribbean and be the stronger for it. 'In the Cabinet they accepted me as I was. There was such strong backing for me.'

An extract from one of her speeches – this one given to a UNESCO

231

conference in Paris – expresses the essence of Phyllis Allfrey's political ideals: 'Now why, you may ask, does this Anglo-Saxon looking little woman represent three and three-quarter million island peoples who are mainly coloured persons of African and mixed descent. I will tell you. My friends, I was elected by a large majority of coloured people this year, and I represent them in the West Indian House of Representatives, our Parliament. I regard, therefore, that election and my ministerial appointment as a triumph of tolerance over skin-deep differences, and even over historical prejudices. May I add that it is a triumph of tolerance over creed as well as race.

'Now I would not wish anyone in this room . . . to regard me as a British stooge. I have always been from my childhood an anti-Imperialist; in fact, in Committee Room 13 in the House of Commons once, when I sat with other West Indians of varying shades, I even wrote a poem, two lines of which went: "But no frown/hints at the terminating trusteeship or at the adolescence too prolonged" . . .'

That speech also hints at Phyllis Allfrey's need to keep faith with poetry. Her second and unfinished novel *In the Cabinet* which continues Joan's tale from *The Orchid House*, is, in part, the story of Phyllis Allfrey's own political career. Joan says: 'I never dream of making a speech without quoting at least half a verse of poetry. In fact if the poets had a trade union you would find me in its ranks. I won my election partly on poetry. The people in the street understood me well . . .'

But, inevitably, there were conflicts between Mrs Allfrey, Minister for Health and Social Affairs, and Phyllis Allfrey, author and poet: 'Although one of the Ministry's administrative cadets said timidly one day that my minutes were like poems, although I rebelled to the point of striking out "I am directed by the Minister of State" every time I saw those words, I was still a politician and had to submit to incredible banalities of style and expression.'

There is also a certain poignancy about a section of *In the Cabinet* when Joan fingers the Federation files which she had illegally snatched when the Federation collapsed in 1961. Allfrey uses the files to express the part of Joan's life which was separate from her husband and how her pursuit of a political life had momentarily caused a rift between them. 'They [the files] happened before Edward and I became "I and I". The expression I and I is the intimate Dread way of saying We and Us. Those files project my life when I was alone.'

The end of the Federation marked the end of Phyllis Allfrey's life as a high-profile politician. It also brought renewed financial problems. Colleagues in the Cabinet had demanded and won a pension for the

Prime Minister, Phyllis Allfrey's friend and mentor, the Barbadian Grantley Adams, but there was no money for other ministers.

The Allfreys packed for home. Their political and social isolation continued but Phyllis Allfrey also had to deal with a new political dimension, part of the rise of a Black nationalism.

'There was a problem when I got home. The roots of black power had taken root. They were the people who had in the past given me support. Now they looked upon me as a white person – and you know I didn't like that very much.'

Without money, the Allfreys had to find work. There was some teaching available ('All my girls have gone right to the top,' says Phyllis) but, for the most part, they turned to journalism. But once again, this thwarted Mrs Allfrey's opportunities to pursue her own writing.

'Journalism is a different experience to writing for me. It's not romantic enough for me. When I edited Dominica's little newspaper, *The Herald*, it revolved round very petty, small-island politics and after the politics of the Federation, it all seemed rather tame.' But her journalistic work had one particular effect, which was to rebound on Mrs Allfrey. She was expelled from the Dominica Labour Party, which she herself had formed. The Party had taken objection to an editorial she had written in *The Herald* opposing tax levies proposed by the Party. Her years in active politics were over.

But in 1965 the Allfreys started their own weekly newspaper, *The Star*. 'It was an artistic and political weapon. I got my points over with irony. I invented a poet, Rose O. She appeared once or twice a month and I used to satirise the goings on, taking everyone for a ride. *The Star* was also a way in which I could encourage young Dominicans to write – it was their only outlet.' *The Star* survived until the Allfreys, tired and growing frail, packed up the presses.

'That pale pink woman with her pale pink paper,' as she was labelled by the editor of a rival paper, had by then suffered again. In 1977, the Allfreys' daughter was killed in a car crash in Botswana. The pain of Pheena's death enters *In the Cabinet* when the woman says: 'When *she* was killed, I kept beating my breast like a mourning Jewish or Negro mother and calling out soundlessly, "Why was she taken and not us? We've lived tremendous lives against great odds. She was just coming into the fullness of her gifts."' Two years later, Hurricane David struck Dominica: the islanders were unprepared and the Allfreys lost the roof of their tiny, stone-built house and many of their books and archives were sodden or destroyed.

The writing had to stop. But as a white West Indian woman, she made

233

through both literature and politics a specific contribution. As she said once: 'I have made my own society here. I have my own matriarchy.'

Her last speech to the Cabinet of the West Indian Federation shows her own sense of her time and place. 'They may strip us Federal Ministers and Members of honourable dues and even tie me to the stake in rags, but no one can deprive me of the signal and irrevocable honour of having been the first woman Minister in the Federal Government of the West Indies. Let the rains fall on dry lands and holy feathers drop from the sky – the traces of our passage will not be obliterated.' She was buried in the cemetery at Roseau, a Federation flag draped over the coffin.

*P*OLLY PATTULLO *was born in London in 1946 and studied politics at Edinburgh University. She worked briefly in book publishing before becoming a journalist. She was features editor of the* Observer Magazine *until 1986 then joined the* News on Sunday *as head of the features department. She left the* News on Sunday *to write a book with Anna Coote on women and politics, and is the co-author with Lindsay Mackie of* Women and Work, *published in 1977.*

234

Mary Stott

talking with Liz Heron

*M*ARY STOTT *was born in Leicester in 1907, the daughter of journalists. She began her journalistic career in 1925, as a reporter on the* Leicester Mail, *and at nineteen was moved on to the paper's women's page – something which, she has often written, 'was a heartbreak, for I thought my chance of becoming a "real journalist" was finished.'*

After six years there, and two years on the Bolton Evening News, *she went to work for the Cooperative Press in Manchester, editing its women's and children's publications, including* Woman's Outlook, *the magazine of the Cooperative Women's Guild. In her first volume of autobiography she records how she was passed over for the editorship of the* Cooperative News, *because it was considered a man's job. In 1945 the post-war shortage of experienced sub-editors gave her the chance to work for five years on the* Manchester Evening News *as a news sub, a rare position for a woman in those days; but here too her career was curtailed by the prevailing assumptions about women's suitability for senior newspaper jobs.*

Mary Stott is best known for her editorship of the Guardian *women's page, from 1957 to 1972. During this time the page became a forum for debate on a broad range of women's issues, and in the Sixties articles were often the catalyst for the formation of campaigns and pressure groups. Among these were the Pre-School Playgroups Association; the Disablement Incomes Group; the National Council for the Single Woman and her Dependants; the Association for the Improvement of the Maternity Services; the National Housewives' Register (now the National Women's Register) and the National Association for the Welfare of Children in Hospitals.*

A noted campaigner herself, Mary Stott has served on numerous committees; she is a member of the Fawcett Society, the National Council of Women and was a founder member of Women in Media. After retiring, she combined journalism for the Guardian *as a freelance*

236

columnist with broadcasting and other writing, including her books – Forgetting's No Excuse, Organization Woman, Ageing for Beginners *and* Before I Go *– and an increasing amount of public speaking. An OBE, awarded in 1975, confirmed her in her own words, as 'a minor establishment figure'.*

Mary Stott, who has one daughter, was married to the journalist Kenneth Stott, who died in 1967. She describes what she wrote about the experience of widowhood – the last chapter of Forgetting's No Excuse *– as 'probably the most important piece of writing I ever did'. She continues to receive letters from other widows who have read the book, which was first published in 1973, and has become closely involved in self-help for widows, as a patron of the National Association of Widows and a trustee of the Widows' Advisory Trust.*

I interviewed Mary Stott at her flat in Blackheath.

M.S. My mother and father were elementary school teachers when they met. By the time I was four my mother was contributing to one of the newspapers my father was concerned with, probably the *Leicester Mercury* or the *Leicester Morning Post*. My father became a full-time journalist just before the First World War. My mother went on writing women's columns until she died when she was fifty-seven.

I had two older brothers. We all got on well, we were a good, affectionate family. My mother and father were very good friends; what went on in bed was not my business. And you know, the awful thing is that from the time I was seven to the time I was, I think, nineteen, they didn't share a bedroom. I think it was their method of birth control. Isn't that sad? *We* didn't think about sexual relationships, though; there wasn't such a thing. My mother never, never, never gave me any explanation of sex or what would happen, or said to me anything about why I'd started menstruating. They were *terribly* prudish, our foremothers.

I went first to a school at which my father was teaching. It was one of the better local authority schools, but I should think home was more educative to me then than school. You see, in those days we went home for mid-day dinner and, my parents being the sort of people they were, a lot of conversation went on. I got a scholarship to the Wyggeston Grammar School for Girls. I was the only female in Leicestershire who got a first class, first division, in the Oxford school certificate. I don't think I had a top-class brain – I had a reasonable brain and I worked

238

very hard. I remember the year in which I came alive and suddenly thought, 'Oh, it's all rather fun!' Fourteen I was and had a very good form mistress who was also the English mistress. It wasn't a very girlish kind of education. But of course the thing that strikes me as being so sad now is that very few of us went to university. If you couldn't win a scholarship, or at least a grant of some kind, your parents wouldn't be able to afford to send you.

L.H. Were you an avid reader?

M.S. Oh yes, gosh. I walked everywhere reading a book. I was always in trouble for having a book on my knee at mealtimes. The author I read most, because my mother was keen on him, was Rudyard Kipling. I was introduced to Rudyard Kipling from a very early age. *Little Women*, too, and that kind of thing. *A Peep Behind the Scenes, The Wide Wide World*, and so on. Mother used to get the books out of the library for me so I suppose she guided my taste to a great extent. Then, when you began to be a little less childish, books like *The Scarlet Pimpernel*, Baroness Orczy and all that – very romantic-type fiction. That went on for quite a long while before I started reading serious things, *Tess of the D'Urbervilles*, Jane Austen and so on. One would read quite a lot of poetry. We all read Masefield and the great anthologies of English poems. That was one of the staple diets and there was a time, when I was in the sixth form, I used to learn a poem a day. I don't have the same feeling for poetry now, because it's not so lyrical. I expect that's why. And feminist writers, from a very early age, and then there were the novelists Virago are republishing as 'Modern Classics'. I started reading the *Manchester Guardian* when I started work at seventeen. The women's page on the *Guardian* was very influential. Tremendously influential. I'm talking about 1922 onwards . . .

Everybody thinks I invented the women's page in the *Guardian* and it is not so. Madeline Linford was a very remarkable woman, withdrawn, very shy – and she had immense influence through her page. Winifred Holtby and Vera Brittain contributed regularly, and an awful lot of absolutely top-class feminist stuff. I've been asked many times how I became a feminist. I don't know but I think I ingested it from the *Manchester Guardian* and *Time and Tide*. In 1929 I went to the polls with a very high heart. I knew perfectly well I was one of the first women to vote on the same terms as men – we were called 'flapper voters'.

L.H. Did you write stories as a little girl, or keep a diary?

239

M.S. I used to write poetry. I had a little notebook in which I wrote a poem for every month of the year. I wasn't one of these compulsive writers, though I always liked writing letters. I had a pen-friend when I was about eleven and I wrote regularly to one of my cousins. I had a natural impulse to write, but no desire to write creatively.

L.H. Were there any of the women writers that you came across in your youth who particularly influenced your inclination to write?

M.S. No, I don't think any of them. You see I never had any ambition to write novels. I wanted to write plays. I was very keen on the theatre and my father was acting in the local Leicester Drama Society. They had a little magazine and I used to write for it. I did once win a small prize in a competition for a one-act play. I felt proud of myself then.

L.H. You say you don't think of yourself as a writer, but a journalist. A lot of people wouldn't make a distinction, particularly when you're not a hard news reporter.

M.S. What I really wanted to be at first was a drama critic, but I was much more interested in news than features. I always said I would never want to do a women's page; that was the most heartbreaking moment of my life when I was told that's what I had to do. I did want to do hard news. The shortish period when I was going to police courts and inquests and things like that was very pleasing to me. One thing that the women's page did do for me was that I soon got very interested in the subbing and make-up side. *That's* what I would have liked to continue, really.

L.H. You write in *Forgetting's No Excuse* about feeling a vocation to journalism? What was actually at the bottom of that impulse?

M.S. It must have been there all the time. My father didn't want me to be a journalist – he said to me you'll have lots of acquaintances but no friends which hasn't turned out to be true at all, as journalists make very good friends, I've found. And mother was, well, not mad keen. But, it suddenly hit me that this was what I wanted to do. I can't explain. I just know the whole atmosphere of the newspaper, everything about a newspaper suddenly seemed to me that that was where I belonged. You see, I had been in and out of a newspaper office since I was a young child.

L.H. Has writing always been straightforward to you?

M.S. Oh, no. The older I get the worse it gets. I made the news editor at the *Manchester Guardian* laugh once: 'Oh, the hard job's not writing, it's thinking.' Once I know what I want to say, it isn't very hard to say it. But it's thinking it out, that's the difficult bit. It's selection. With all writing, you've got to select the points that make sense. You see, I had a long time as a news sub-editor, and I think that emphasized my feeling that you've got to prune it down and get it taut and clear. I do know when a sentence is cumbersome or repetitive or whatever, and that's no trouble to me. I'm a good sub, I think. I sub myself as well as other people.

L.H. How unusual were you at the beginning of your career? There must have been very few other women journalists around.

M.S. Very few, only one per paper in the provinces, and not always that one. I didn't feel isolated, I always had women friends, thank God, and I don't think I was ever deliberately put down by men colleagues on the grounds of being a woman – apart from when I couldn't be promoted because I was female. But that was not out of blind sex prejudice and certainly not hostility. It was just that editors thought a woman wouldn't have the status, couldn't control the staff and so on. But that is changing. It had begun, of course, especially with the *Guardian* before I retired, but the influx since I retired has been very considerable, both in the newspapers and in the media generally. It's really in the last ten years or so there's been this influx. But of course, they're still a long way from the top of the tree. I think there are several quite influential women in the Street now . . .

L.H. How do you write?

M.S. In longhand. I've always done that, then type it out. That's the way I do a book. When I was at the *Guardian* in Manchester I had a room of my own. I find it hard to concentrate on writing in an open-plan office. When I'm writing here at home I write in the entrance room because it's light, there's a nice big table and the sun comes round, so it's pleasant. Usually this [the little white Pekinese dog] sits on the table.

L.H. Do you ever find excuses not to write?

M.S. Everybody does. Anything rather than getting down to it. The best hope for me is as soon as I've washed up after breakfast and made my bed to start firmly. But I do keep to deadlines. That's the newspaper training – 'on time means on sale'.

L.H. From what you've written it seems that your marriage was very much an equal partnership, and your husband acknowledged that your job was as important as his. But did you ever feel differently from that, that maybe his job mattered more?

241

M.S. Well, in a way. You see, I would quite have liked to go to London, and I did have an offer of a job subbing at the BBC in the 1950s. But he didn't want to go to London. That was that. I wouldn't have dreamed of going. Because I am of my age and time, it would have seemed to me a very destructive thing to do. But I never felt any envy of him, nor any resentment, never.

L.H. How old were you when you became a mother?

M.S. Thirty-five. Vera Brittain said it was better to have your children rather late, psychologically not physically, because you were more mature then and you could look at the whole thing more calmly. I do think there's something in it.

It was during the war, and I had to go on working. Well, I thought I had. I had six weeks off before and six weeks after the birth and when my daughter was a baby I never, never went out in the evening. My parents-in-law had come to live with me, so that Granny Stott looked after Catherine for two, three years, until her health broke down. We had all sorts of different arrangements after that. I daresay people thought I was a bit odd. But I had always intended to go back to work. I looked at my mother, you see. She was a working journalist. She was only part-time, it's true, but never for a moment did I imagine I was going to become a mother at home. In my daughter's early days with her children there were au pairs; she always worked.

L.H. But money does come into it; the cost of childminding.

M.S. My mother-in-law was a working-class woman. She always worked. I think just occasionally one did feel that teachers were a bit resentful of working mums with the best of both worlds: a nice loving husband and children and a job. I do remember from my days of editing the women's page of the *Guardian* that the prejudice against mothers working outside the home very often came from the teachers. That's all gone now, of course; there are far more married women teachers.

L.H. You were married in a registry office. Were there no social pressures to have a church wedding?

M.S. Both my brothers were married in registry offices. We were agnostic in my family. I probably wouldn't have married – we were fairly avant garde – if it hadn't been for displeasing the families. One or two of my friends didn't marry for a long while after they set up home together. It wasn't quite so unusual as people today think. But we were quite convinced that this was what we had to do, that we were going to share our life . . . We thought we were fairly progressive-type people. We never were Communists, but we were both pretty left-wing. It then was the Labour Party for us both. My mother was slightly thrown when I announced that I was joining the ILP and that I wanted to put a Labour Party bill in my bedroom window in 1929. My father said, 'If you don't start on the left, you'll be awful by the time you're old.' But then I don't suppose it mattered so much being lefty and young, because we were all very strongly pacifist. And of course so were the Coop women who were marvellously, marvellously strong in their day. My husband became a Liberal later and I joined the SDP.

L.H. Did you encourage women to write for *Woman's Outlook* [the Women's Cooperative Guild paper which Mary Stott edited for a time]?

M.S. Yes, really it was *Woman's Outlook* that started me writing what we would now call columns. This is what I did when it became a fortnightly. The front page as my editorial, that was my first venture into writing opinion pieces.

L.H. Did women write in? Did they send in articles?

M.S. Oh yes, lots of them; we had the readers' page. I think only now are we beginning to realize how important they were for the movement. I always encouraged a 'to and fro' with the readers; always. That was what it was all about. I have always, and certainly since the Coop days, felt that contact with the readers was absolutely vital. I wanted to feel that they're coming with me. And I think that that was how it felt in the *Guardian* in my time.

You have to let your readers tell you; you have to sense what they want. You're no good as an editor if you're not talking to people. The only way to edit is to listen to people. I saw running the women's page of the *Guardian* as the same kind of job as *Woman's Outlook*. And one hoped to stretch them, the thinking, the concern of the Coop women through the magazine. One hoped to widen their interests. And in the same way in the *Guardian* you had to have a sense of what they were thinking. They write to you, you get letters.

L.H. But *Woman's Outlook* was the publication of a movement, a bit different from a national newspaper.

M.S. They didn't interfere. It was left to us to provide the reading matter that we sensed they would want, a very open relationship. We didn't consult them directly, nor they us. I went to a lot of their conferences. I did feel occasionally that I wasn't *quite* accepted, not because I was

243

middle-class but because I had had a better education than most of them. On the other hand, I did have some marvellous friends who really fully accepted me. But then I think in our times class is much more a question of education than money. I think – it's only my view – that was one of the troubles that the Cooperative movement had, not just the Guild but the movement as a whole. It was a bit too self-consciously working-class and didn't make full use of the opportunities it had to educate its young and bring in more ideas.

L.H. That was one of the important functions of the Cooperative movement, though: education.

M.S. Oh yes, yes. But in spite of this feeling that I was slightly outside I was very happy with them. And indeed I must say that when I went back and was editing *Woman's Outlook* again, I think a lot of that had gone. And I was actually asked to speak from the platform at a congress so I don't feel there was any hostility left.

When I did go to the *Guardian* I'd come to realize sadly, very very sadly, that I was never going to make any progress in the technical side of newspapers. That door had been quite firmly banged in my face and there was no hope it would open. Editing the women's page was the one thing I knew I could do in newspapers. If I'd got to do women's work, the *Manchester Guardian* women's page was the only thing I wanted to do. I mean, the only thing that was quite worthy of me as a feminist, as a real, proper feminist journalist. If it hadn't been that Madeline Linford had made such a creditworthy page in every way, I should never have dreamed of taking on the women's page. That was why I applied for the job and Alastair [Hetherington] saw me and took me on right away.

I did have a marvellous time there. I felt very close to the *Guardian* women's page. But it was – a very good – second-best.

L.H. Do you think if you'd been born a bit later you would have ended up on the executive level of a newspaper?

M.S. I think that's possible. I'm that kind of person by nature. My brother said, 'Just like your mother, you can't stop organizing something.' Well, it hadn't occurred to me, until he said that! Women journalists will never get to the top table, really up top, unless they have some subbing experience. I feel it very strongly. Papers do come out through men's eyes. It's the subs, of course, and there are very few women subs still.

L.H. Were you aware of sexism in language working as a sub?

244

M.S. I wasn't really aware of sexism in language. I couldn't help but be aware of certain sex differences in the approach and handling of things – because they used to give me all the multiple births to do! I had advantages over the men and one of the advantages I've always said was of having been a woman at home with a baby. I was used to coping with ten things at once. If you sub on an evening paper, particularly, the flow of copy is very rapid during the busy time of the day. You have copy descending upon you from the ends of the earth, you've got to keep your head and you've got to watch the deadline. Psychologically, it's not different from being home when the milkman rings at the door and the baby starts to howl, the joint's charring in the oven: all the things that in the home can happen together and you've got to keep your head and keep your mind absolutely clear. It's just like that, I thought.

L.H. When you started as women's page editor, did you have any qualms about being able to continue in this tradition that you admired?

M.S. No, I felt fairly confident. It was the sort of job that all my life's experience had enabled me to do reasonably competently. Suddenly to realize that *you* are the *Guardian*, or the *Manchester Guardian* as it was then, was a big thrill.

L.H. What did you feel were the differences between doing the women's page and doing *Woman's Outlook* in terms of readership?

M.S. You didn't have to explain things quite so carefully to the *Guardian* readers, most of whom were at least as well educated as I and some of them very much better. It was partly a question of the use of language. And, of course, naturally your field of interests was wider. *Woman's Outlook* liked international stories, trade union stories, and there was a lot of writing about women's lives – but it was bigger and broader with the *Guardian*. It was in a way more enjoyable to write for the *Guardian* because if you used a quotation, for instance, you didn't have to explain it.

L.H. Do you think the *Guardian* woman – this rather mythical creature – has changed a lot?

M.S. Of course, she has changed a lot in that the majority of readers when I took over were at home, not even working part-time probably, and now, of course, the majority of them would be working. I should think the proportion of young single women is much higher now, but I can only assume they're different by reading the letters on the page.

245

I suppose, when I took over, I quickly became aware – perhaps more than Madeline Linford had been – of this enormous number of well-educated young women. They were my readership and I suppose they were Madeline's but I had the feeling hers was an older readership than mine. They're still younger now.

I did want it to be very much a feminist sort of page. I didn't have much hassle. Once – it was funny – Catherine Storr, the wife of a well-known psychologist who used to write to me from time to time, did an article about penis envy. It was a very subdued and proper sort of piece but Alastair said to the features editor, 'If I had seen that before it had gone in, it wouldn't have gone in.'

In my time, the proportion of articles by women who were readers of the *Guardian* was very high indeed. The proportion who were purely professional freelance journalists was low. They were very personal experience articles. I think that was the strength of it. The whole point of having a women's page in a newspaper is to get people to voice their views and exchange experiences. I don't see any other justification for a women's page in a modern newspaper except that it is a platform, a place where women and men can say what they're thinking and contribute to it if they wish. That was the whole aim and purpose of my page. That's why out of it grew so many organizations. Women readers had a place where they could talk.

Pat Barr, in the early days of the women's movement, said she thought it was important that women should discuss women's writing together and I said, 'Well, that's the one thing we have always been able to do, isn't it? Where we haven't been all that handicapped . . .' In newspapers, we haven't broken through the barriers on the administrative side, the technical side and the subbing side. But on the writing side, I'd say we've very nearly got there. There isn't any speciality that some woman isn't doing nowadays. The *Guardian* is avant garde to some extent – but once one paper does it, then the breakthrough is made. It's not insuperable.

When I'd been at the *Guardian* a few years, I had a feature every Monday called 'Women Talking' and to that I recruited people like Shirley Williams, Lena Jeger and Margaret Drabble, and so on. That was definitely a mouthpiece for the woman in public life and they were all fairly well known. That was one of my major contributions to the page.

L.H. What were your criteria for accepting articles?

M.S. What I liked! I was a very typical and normal *Guardian* reader and

246

all the chances were if I liked it then the readers would like it too. My whole aim was to listen to what people said. And if I had something go in that was a bit opinionated one day, then there was sure to be something coming in that was a bit opinionated the other way. 'Balance' never seemed to me a problem! It evolved naturally.

L.H. When did you start your first book?

M.S. I did write a whodunnit just after the war, which I didn't manage to sell. I quite enjoyed doing it, but I don't think I have a gift for fiction. I started my first published book just before I retired. I did it exactly as if I were doing a number of articles. All my books are absolutely out of the same pattern. I decide the number of ideas I want to put forward, and divide them up into chapters. I know roughly how long each chapter ought to be. A series of long essays – that's how I perceive it. It's not a very creative kind of thing, it's not like writing fiction. It's not imaginative. I increasingly think as I grow older that I've a fairly analytical kind of mind. I like the tidying of ideas. But I'm constantly pruning my sentences. I have a strong sense of rhythm – the balance of the sentence must feel and sound right to me. I don't show drafts to people – I can't bear anybody to see what I've written.

L.H. Do you find publishing very different from newspapers?

M.S. Totally. I would really rather have always been employed in an office doing a job, with a framework. What I think I would really like would be to have a regular column somewhere, like Katharine Whitehorn, for example. If I'm going to be a writer, that's what I would like: to comment on the passing scene, so to speak.

*L*IZ HERON, *a freelance writer, critic and translator, was born in Glasgow in 1947. She edited* Truth, Dare or Promise: Girls Growing up in the Fifties *(Virago 1985), a collection of autobiographical essays on childhood, and is the author of* Changes of Heart: Reflections on Women's Independence *(Pandora 1986).*

Eudora Welty

talking with
Hermione Lee

*E*UDORA WELTY *was born in 1909 in Jackson, Mississippi, and has spent most of her life there, in the house built by her father. She was a student at Mississippi State College for Women at Columbus, at the University of Wisconsin, and at Columbia Graduate Business School in New York. In the 1930s she got her first full-time job taking Depression photographs in her home state for the Works Progress Administration. Her first story, 'Death of a Traveling Salesman', was published in 1936. Since then she has written five novels, including* Delta Wedding *(1946) and* Losing Battles *(1970), and seven books of short stories, published as* The Collected Stories of Eudora Welty *in 1980. She has been awarded numerous honorary degrees, fellowships and prizes, including the Pulitzer Prize in 1973. Almost all her fiction is about the history, stories, families and places of her native South, but her lucid, eloquent style, and her marvellously tender, humorous and perceptive understanding of people, makes her into much more than a 'regional' writer. In 1972 she published* The Optimist's Daughter, *a novel with some strong autobiographical elements, in which Laurel McKelva, returning to Mississippi in her mid-forties, comes to terms, through her father's death, with her parents' past. In* One Writer's Beginnings, *published in 1984, she discloses a great deal about how her family and her childhood shaped her writing. When I met her on one of her rare visits to London, I began by asking her what led her from a fictional to an autobiographical version of her background.*

E.W. I never in my wildest dreams thought I would write anything autobiographical. Of course, many things in my life were used in the stories, but they were very much transformed. I never expected to write about my mother, or anything like that. The unhappy fact is that usually by the time you're ready to think about your parents they're gone, and can't tell you anything. That happened with both my parents. But I'm awfully glad I did do this book [*One Writer's Beginnings*], because it made me explicitly know what I owed things to.

H.L. Was it a difficult book to write?

E.W. It was difficult mostly because it was a matter of choice. So many things crowded in – maybe to make the same point, and I was trying to use the one detail that would convey it in the most direct way. I think in terms of fiction, and it's awfully hard for me to think in terms of non-fiction, the explanatory. I tried to be selective, just to tell the things that I thought contributed to my being a writer. That's what I'd been asked to do. I threw away lots more stuff than is in there, other things that I thought best left out.

H.L. But there are certain things that obviously keep coming back to haunt you, like your grandmother coming in with her hands cold because she's been out breaking the ice . . .

E.W. Oh – my mother told me that again and again. She would put her own hands in front of her and say, 'Her hands, she had such beautiful white hands, they were all bleeding from the ice on the well!'

H.L. You say in *One Writer's Beginnings* that you had a sheltered life, and that your mother and father were equally supportive of your wanting to become a writer, but in very different ways.

E.W. Very different ways. For a while I thought my father couldn't be supporting me because – oh, he was against fiction, because he thought it wasn't true. He said, it's not the truth about life. And he thought I might be wasting my time, because he thought I was going to write the sort of things that came out in the *Saturday Evening Post*, and if I *didn't* write those things I couldn't earn a living. We never really talked about the kind of things I did want to write. I couldn't have done that, with either one of my parents, with anybody. And how did I know what I *could* do? But he did support me. All he wanted to do was to make sure that I could survive, make my living. And that was good advice. I was rather scornful at the time – 'Live for art', you know.

H.L. He never said, 'Don't do it'?

E.W. No, he never did. But when I was growing up there wasn't much a woman could do to make a living, except teach, or else go into a business office as a stenographer or something low down the scale. I knew I couldn't teach, so I decided to go into business, and he was all for that. He sent me to a business graduate school in Columbia, and that was wonderful, it gave me a year in New York. I went to the theatre every night. Almost no work, it was so easy. Anybody could do it.

H.L. Later on, did you show your mother things that you were writing?

E.W. Yes, but I never could show them to anyone until after I had sent them away, because I was too fearful of having them treated as a school paper – 'I think that's awfully good, dear,' you know. I wanted a professional, objective answer, so I would send them to magazines, and that way I could learn what professional editors thought. If they sent it back I took that as a proper judgement, as indeed it was. If they praised me I was elated, and only after that would I show them to my mother, or friends.

H.L. And did you feel that she understood what you were doing?

E.W. I think she did. I know she tried with all her generous imagination. She was very proud of my work, because she was a *reader*. She loved the written word.

H.L. Many of your stories and novels have very powerful women in them, strong matriarchs.

E.W. Yes, they do. But my mother wasn't really like that, except she was a very powerful schoolteacher. I'm a first-generation Mississippian and though my mother was Southern in her origins and birth – Virginia and West Virginia – she didn't come out of plantation life. Those were the real matriarchies, which sprang out of the South during and after the Civil War years. I don't know that first hand, but I've read it and seen the results down the generations, where the sexes seem to me really divided, with the men galloping around outside and the women running everything.

H.L. You say your mother was a powerful schoolteacher, and you've written about the importance of these women schoolteachers in the South. They come into your fiction a lot.

E.W. Oh, they played such a large part. Because of the poverty in the South, the teachers were dedicated people. They never made any money, they were people who gave their lives to it, like the new women who went into colleges in the Middle West. After the Civil War, when all the schools had been burned and the land was levelled and everything had to start over and there was no money, the churches had to try to raise the money for schools. That's why there are so many church-supported, small private colleges in the South still. It was the immediate need for education, and they were doing it the best way they could. Where my mother came from, in the mountains of West Virginia, there wasn't any money at all in teaching. I remember she told me she was paid 'thirty silver dollars' in salary for the first month she taught there, and she never was paid again. And just like in *Losing Battles*, she had to go across the river to teach. I told the real facts of that in this book [*One Writer's Beginnings*], how she went riding horseback over the mountain, with a little brother on the back to take the horse home, and would row herself across the river, and come back in the evening. And the little brother would meet her and ride home again. If you stayed the night you had to sleep with the family, with two or three children in the bed. They really were marvellous women . . . Of course the men were doing other things, they left the teaching to the women. But people who went to school with them almost never forget them. We had, if you can comprehend this, the fiftieth anniversary of my high school class – Jackson, Miss., Class of '25 – and we all still remembered this Miss Duling who taught us in grade school. And some of our teachers were still alive. They remembered everything about us, and they would say, 'Well, I never thought *you'd* amount to anything.'

H.L. Do you think you had a good education?

E.W. Yes, I had a good basic education, because reading was respected, and writing too. We really had to learn those fundamental things.

H.L. You read a lot at home, from early on?

E.W. Yes, I did. Of course, you learn to read early when you want to. I went to school when I was five and I could read by then. I think that was common in those days.

H.L. Are there people that you read between the ages of say, twelve and sixteen, who still matter to you?

E.W. Oh yes, people like Mark Twain . . . Ring Lardner . . . the Brontës. Books I found in the house, and in the library. I didn't read, you know, Homer and all that lot, like people are supposed to. I always liked fiction. I'm not terribly well-read, I'm sure, I just always read for pleasure. Now, that counts Homer!

H.L. Was it difficult to move away from home? Did you feel a pull between wanting your independence and feeling guilty about the people who loved you?

E.W. Oh yes, I still feel it. It haunts me. I think about how I could have managed it better. And I realized later that both my parents must have felt exactly the same thing when they left home. My mother was especially torn. And distances were so far then. Communications were hard in those days unless you were rich. But daily letters travelled back and forth, and we always knew how each other was.

H.L. Did you know that in the end you were bound to come back to Jackson?

E.W. No, I didn't feel that. I wanted to, and I still do, regard it as a base, which helps me in writing. I feel it's some sort of touchstone. It's what I check up by, in the sense that I know it so well I don't have to wonder about whether I have got it right. Either I have to know everything about a place, so that I don't have to think, or else I must never have seen it before, so that I'm wide awake to everything as a stranger, and can write one thing out of what I see and feel, as I did once with a story about Ireland ['The Bride of the Innisfallen']. I didn't know Ireland and I didn't mean to write a story about it, but it left an indelible impression on my mind.

H.L. Do you think it's especially true that Southern writers in America have to use the place they know as a base?

E.W. I feel that what is maybe kin to the Southerner is the New Englander, who has a sense of place. In urban life, that really isn't possible, in the way that I feel it, as a knowledge of seasons or changes or stability. Of course, the South now is full of people in motion, just like the rest of the country. But when I grew up it was so changeless that it was like a base you could touch and be sure you were accurate about something. But I think New Englanders and Southerners are alike in this, and it's odd how each had their flowering time in literature, New England first, and then the South in Faulkner's day.

H.L. Do you think you get your sense of narrative from the South?

E.W. I do feel that. Because of the pleasure that is taken in it in the South.

H.L. Is that a particularly female thing, do you think?

E.W. No. I think it's really more male. Women are supposed to be waiting on the men and bringing them food while they tell stories. That's the way it was in *Losing Battles*! And my mother's brothers in

255

West Virginia were like that. They would gather and tell stories, and the women just kept bringing food so they'd keep talking and going on, and sometimes the women would scoff and say, 'Oh now, don't tell it that way!' But mother loved it all.

H.L. But it's very often the women who tell the stories in your books.

E.W. Well, maybe what's according to my story wasn't quite true to life . . . I know when I was in William Faulkner's house a couple of times, I heard him and his cronies telling stories, and they were all men. But those would be the stories they would tell at hunting camp or out sailing. Or stories about crazy people in Oxford, Mississippi. Men know more stories, at least they did in those days, because they get out and live in the world more, and their stories are more adventurous and full of action. More to tell.

H.L. But it's women who make up the fabric of gossip, who know what's going on?

E.W. That's true – the gossip, the domestic kind . . . I think women tell their kind of story to women and men tell theirs to men. But when there's a reunion, and everybody comes together for an occasion, then the stories are mingled. Everyone's in one company, they tell them together. It's like a set of voices joining one after the other, sometimes. I made this seem like a chorus in *Losing Battles*, to give the crowd effect.

Story-telling is *part* of life in the South, it's a social activity, always arising in family gatherings. Stories are told not to teach or learn from – everybody knows them already – but to participate in, to enjoy all over again. Their character is the thing. 'Wasn't that exactly like Aunt Maggie?'

H.L. Do any of your stories come out of the photographs you took in the Depression years in Mississippi?

E.W. I am an observer, and I would notice the same thing, I would look for the same kind of thing, whether I was carrying a camera or just watching. But I didn't make up stories from my pictures. The odd thing is that some of the photographs turned out almost to illustrate stories that I wrote later on.

H.L. Did you ever find that it was a disadvantage to be a woman journalist in those days, travelling around Mississippi?

E.W. The only thing that annoyed me was that I was called junior publicity agent, and I was working with somebody called senior publicity agent, who was a man. We did exactly the same work, and of course he got a lot more money. I sort of wondered about that. But I was so happy to get a job that it didn't bother me any then. Otherwise, I never had difficulties. I would go into the poorest parts of the State, in the depths of the Depression, and I would say to people, a lot of them black people, 'Do you mind if I take a picture?' and some of them would say, 'Never had a picture taken in my life.' And I'd say, 'Just stay the way you are.' They'd be in some wonderful pose, a woman on a porch, leaning forward from the hips, like this, her elbows on here and her hands crossed, with this wonderful curve of buttocks and legs, bare-footed on the porch. Beautiful woman. I would say, 'Do you mind if I take your picture like that?' 'No,' she'd say, 'if that's what you want to do, I don't care!' . . . It taught me so much, about coming upon people I didn't know and taking this minute of their lives. But I had to go on to fiction from photographing. That's the only way you can really part the veil between people, not in images but in what comes from inside, in both subject and writer.

H.L. When you started publishing your stories, I believe Katherine Anne Porter was very important to you?

E.W. She was indeed. I suppose Katherine Anne was the first living writer I'd ever seen. I published almost my first story in the *Southern Review*, which was published by Louisiana State University Press and edited by Robert Penn Warren and Cleanth Brooks. Katherine Anne was living in Baton Rouge, and she was married to Albert Erskine, who was also on the *Southern Review*. She wrote me a letter and said that she thought my work was good, and would I like to come and see her. That petrified me. I thought, how *can* I go! It was a long time before I did it. I was really scared to go. But I did, and she was so supportive, as she was to many young writers. If it had not been for *her* work, we couldn't ever have published, because she had such a hard time winning her place as a writer. Indeed it took *me* six years to be published in a national magazine, and that would be about average.

H.L. Do you think that was partly because you were a woman?

E.W. I don't know. I never did think of that. I don't think it was that, I think it was the short story form.

H.L. Do you think the short story, as practised by Katherine Anne Porter, and Flannery O'Connor, and Elizabeth Bowen, and yourself – with a very vivid sense of place, and a lot of close detail, and a strong narrative voice – is a particularly female art form?

E.W. I just don't know. I suppose Mary Lavin would be another

257

example of that kind of writing? But then there's Frank O'Connor and Sean O'Faolain, and they're not female. No, I can't express an opinion about that. But it sounds rather interesting.

H.L. Do you think of yourself as an objective writer?

E.W. That's what I try to be, but I know I'm not. In my work I try to be objective, and I can't really feel a story is finished until I can stand off from it and see it objectively. But in fact I'm sure I'm an absolutely exposed and naked writer. I mean in the way I feel and think about the world. I feel very exposed to it, and I've probably learned from that. But your work has to be objective.

H.L. But are you moved by your own writing?

E.W. I'm afraid I am! That is, there has to be some criterion of whether or not you brought it off. It has to meet that emotional test. You feel that only you yourself can judge it. Something tells me when I have not been objective enough, and I've got a story now that I won't let go for that reason. I know that it's not controlled enough.

H.L. Is there a moment when you know, when you can say to yourself, 'I've got it'?

E.W. Yes. Or so I say.

H.L. And then you're completely confident?

E.W. Well – as near as you can be. I have a friend who's a writer – I won't tell you his name because he might not want me to, I mean it's his story, not mine. He kept all the versions of a story he'd written in a drawer, till he'd written about thirteen versions, and then he opened the drawer much later, and found that number seven was it. I think that's a wonderful lesson.

H.L. Do you revise a great deal?

E.W. Yes, I do.

H.L. And do you work quite slowly?

E.W. I revise very slowly, and I like to revise. I like to write the first draft quickly, to do it in one sitting if it were only possible, and I would like to write the last version all in one sitting. That's hard to do! But revision, I don't care how long it takes. I love it.

H.L. Do you think a writer's life is a lonely life?

E.W. No. I feel in touch. I like doing things, you know, privately. But I like to write with a window that looks out on to the street. I don't feel that I'm in a cell. Some people like that feeling – to be a monk or a nun

258

or something. But I like to be part of my world. No, writing is solitary. But I don't feel lonely.

*H*ERMIONE LEE *teaches English at the University of York and reviews books for the* Observer. *Her published works include* The Mulberry Tree: Selected Writings of Elizabeth Bowen *(Virago, 1986) and introductions to* Bowen's Court *(Virago, 1984) and Willa Cather's* Sapphira and the Slave Girl *and* One of Ours *(Virago, 1987), as well as books on Elizabeth Bowen, Virginia Woolf and Philip Roth, and two anthologies of short stories by women,* The Secret Self 1 & 2.

Rebecca West

talking with
Marina Warner

WHEN REBECCA WEST *first appeared in London as a working writer, in 1912, she dazzled her audience by the precocious ambition of her voice and its barbed brilliance. H. G. Wells wrote to her towards the end of their painful relationship: 'I loved your clear open hard-hitting generous mind first of all and I still love it most of all, because it is most of all you.'*

Rebecca West was born Cicily Isabel Fairfield in County Kerry, Eire, in December 1892. At the age of twenty she changed her name to the heroine of Ibsen's play Rosmersholm, *who is characterized by a burning passionate will. As 'Rebecca West' she began in journalism and literary criticism, especially in radical journals like* The Freewoman *and* The Clarion, *and continued to write throughout the traumatic years when she was alone bringing up her only child, Anthony Panther West, born to her and H. G. Wells in 1913. She published her first novel,* The Return of the Soldier, *in 1922, followed by* The Judge, *also 1922,* Harriet Hume, a London Fantasy, *1929, and in 1928 her collected criticism,* The Strange Necessity. *More essays followed:* Ending in Earnest: a Literary Log *(1931) in which, notably, she acclaimed the genius of D. H. Lawrence. Two years later, she published her biographical masterwork,* St Augustine.

In the late Thirties, she travelled widely with her husband Henry Andrews in the Balkans and from these experiences she built her formidable analysis of European conflict leading up to the Second World War, Black Lamb and Grey Falcon *(1941). The marked political and historical character of this work, with its emphasis on first-hand observation, led naturally to the post-war books,* The Meaning of Treason *(1947) and* A Train of Powder *(1955). Her account of the Nuremberg*

This article is an abridged version of an interview originally published in *The Paris Review* and in *Writers at Work*, © 1984 The Paris Review, Inc., and Viking Penguin, Inc.

Trials is a matchless investigation into the nature of Nazism and the character of freedom. However unrelenting her dissection of the personalities and the clashes of betrayal and loyalty, Rebecca West never loses in these works an extraordinary capacity for empathy with all the people involved – the accused, the witnesses, the judges or the lawyers, the authorities.

In Black Lamb and Grey Falcon, *she wrote: 'There is nothing rarer than a man who can be trusted never to throw away happiness.' Her loosely autobiographical novel,* The Fountain Overflows *(1957) and her political thriller* The Birds Fall Down *(1966) are testimony to Rebecca West's curiosity, energy and grip on what she has termed the 'will-to-live'.*

Rebecca West often interrupted her replies to talk of the quarrel with Anthony; later, she asked for some of her references to its effect on her to be edited out.

Yet, in 1980, when this interview took place, her relish for life was undiminished by age. She enjoyed food and knew a good deal about it; she had a taste for splendid kaftans and big jewels. Her fingers were set off by several beautiful rings, and she wore the two pairs of spectacles she needed on flamboyant chains. Her flat in Hyde Park Gate was filled with drawings and paintings, by friends, like Wyndham Lewis who drew her portrait, or Carel Weight, whom she admired. She had an exquisite Vuillard. Though a radical who preferred the adversary role in almost all areas of debate, there was something majestically authoritative about her. She looked enthroned, rather than seated, and her energetic, clever voice had kept some of the vowel sounds of the Edwardian period and some of its turns of phrase ('I can't see someone,' meaning I can't tolerate). She spoke words of foreign derivation in the accent of the parent language: 'memoirs' still sounded French on her tongue. All this added to her splendour; she was tonic to be with, and though one wished that life had treated her more gently, it was plain that her mettle required excitement, that she could never have become quiet or tame.

M.W. In your novel, *The Fountain Overflows*, you describe the poverty of the educated class very beautifully. Was that your background?

R.W. Oh, yes. I'll tell you what the position was. We had lots of pleasant furniture that had belonged to my father's family, none that had belonged to my mother's family, because they didn't die – the whole family all went on to their eighties, nineties – but we had furniture and we had masses of books, and we had a very good piano my mother played on. We were poor because my father's father died when he and his three brothers were schoolboys. Their mother was a member of the Plymouth Brethren and a religious fanatic with a conscience that should have been held down and, you know, been eunuchized or castrated. She refused to keep on, to accept any longer, an annuity, which she was given by the Royal Family. And nobody knew why she was given it, and she found out the reason and she didn't approve of it, and she refused it, and they were poor forever after. The maddening thing was nobody ever knows why she said to Queen Victoria, 'I cannot accept this allowance.' It was hard on my father, who was in the army, because you needed money to be an officer. He was a ballistics expert. He did quite well in various things.

M.W. He was a professional soldier?

R.W. No. Not all his life. He left the army after he got his captaincy. He went out to America and he ran a mine and wrote a certain amount, mostly on political science. He wrote well. He had a great mechanical mind and he drew very well. He did all sorts of things, and he'd had a fairly good training at Woolwich, a military academy. We were the children of his second marriage and he could no longer make much money. He went out to Africa and just got ill there. He came back and died in Liverpool when I was twelve or thirteen.

M.W. Was he a remote and admirable figure, as the father is in *The Fountain Overflows*?

R.W. Oh, he wasn't so cracked as the father and he didn't sell furniture that didn't belong to him and all that sort of thing. That was rather a remembrance of another strange character.

M.W. You've written very movingly, in several of your books, on how cruel natural death is, how it is the greatest hardship as opposed to some of the more violent deaths that you've also written about. Was it a very traumatic experience for you, as a child, when you lost your father?

R.W. Oh, yes, it was terrible ... The whole of life was extremely uncomfortable for us at that time. We had really got into terrible financial straits, not through anybody's fault. My mother had had to work very hard, and though she was a very good pianist, she was out of the running by then, and when she realized that my father was old and wasn't going to be able to go on with things, she very nobly went and learnt typewriting. Do you know people are always writing in the papers and saying that typists started in the last war, but they've been going on since the eighties and the nineties and 1900. Well, my mother did some typing for American evangelists called Torry and Alexander and she took over their music. They toured in England and my mother whacked the 'Glory Song', – a famous hymn, you still hear it whistled in the streets – out on the grand piano on the platform. It was a very noble thing to do. She wasn't well and she wasn't young, and then we came up to Scotland.

M.W. In your home, was the atmosphere for women very emancipated, because you were left alone?

R.W. Oh, yes. We were left alone. We had an uncle, who was very preoccupied. He was President of the Royal Academy of Music, Sir Alexander McKenzie, and he didn't really think anything of any woman but his wife. He was very thoughtless about his own daughter, who was an actress who acted very well in the early Chekhov plays. He treated her very inconsiderately and made her come back and nurse her mother and leave her husband in Paris, and the husband, after six years, lost heart and went off with someone else. We were very feminist altogether and it was a very inspiring thing.

M.W. But you yourself broke with the suffragette movement.

R.W. I was too young and unimportant for that to mean much. I admired them enormously, but all that business about venereal disease, which was supposed to be round every corner, seemed to me excessive.

M.W. You have written that there is a great difference between a male sensibility and a female sensibility, and you have a marvellous phrase for it in *Black Lamb and Grey Falcon*.

R.W. Idiots and lunatics. It's a perfectly good division. [The Greek root of 'idiot' means private person; men 'see the world as if by moonlight, which shows the outlines of every object but not the details indicative of their nature.'] It seems to me in any assembly where you get people, who are male and female, in a crisis, the women are apt to get up and, with a big wave of the hand, say: 'It's all very well talking about the defences of the country, but there are 36,000 houses in whatever – wherever they're living – that have no bathrooms. Surely it's more important to have clean children for the future.' Silly stuff, when the enemy's at the gate. But men are just as silly. Even when there are no enemies at the gate, they won't attend to the bathrooms, because they say defence is more important. It's mental deficiency in both cases.

M.W. But do you think it's innate or do you think it's produced by culture?

R.W. Oh, I really can't tell you that. It's awfully hard. You can't imagine what maleness and femaleness would be if you got back to them in pure laboratory state, can you? I suspect the political imbecility is very great on both sides.

I've never gone anywhere where the men have come up to my infantile expectations. I always have gone through life constantly being surprised by the extreme, marvellous qualities of a small minority of men. But I can't see the rest of them. They seem awful rubbish.

M.W. In many of the political things that you've written, it would be impossible to tell that you were a woman, except that here and there you sometimes produce a comparison to do with a child or something, which may betray a certain feminine stance, but, in fact, you have overcome completely this division between idiot and lunatic. You're not an 'idiot' at all. You don't only think of the personal angle.

R.W. I think that probably comes of isolation, that I grew up just as I was without much interference from social images except at my school.

M.W. What were they at school?

R.W. We had large classes, which was an ineffable benefit, because the teachers really hadn't time to muck about with our characters. You see, the people who wanted to learn, sat and learnt, and the people you didn't, didn't learn, but there was no time, you know, for bringing out the best in us, thank God.

M.W. What did your mother expect you to be? What images did she set up for you?

R.W. There was a great idea that I should be an actress because a woman called Rosina Fillipi had seen me act in a play and she thought I was terribly good as a comedian, as a sort of low comedy character, and she said, 'If you come to the Royal Academy of Dramatic Art, I will look after you and you can get a job.' I'm the only person I ever heard of who wanted to go on the stage not because I was stagestruck but it just seemed to be the thing to do. I loved the theatre. I still love it, but I had no stagestruck feeling. I felt how nice if people would give me a part. I went to the Royal Academy of Art, where there was a man called Kenneth Barnes, who ran it, who had got his job because he was the brother of the Vanbrughs, Irene and Violet Vanbrugh, if that means anything to you. He couldn't understand what Rosina Fillipi

267

had seen in me and he made me very uncomfortable. I didn't stay out the course.

M.W. But you chose the name of a dramatic character – Rebecca West.

R.W. Yes. Not really for any profound reason. It was just to get a pseudonym.

M.W. It really wasn't profound? You don't think unconsciously it was?

R.W. People have always been putting me down in any role that was convenient but it would not, I think, naturally have been my own idea. I've aroused hostility in an extraordinary lot of people. I've never known why. I don't think I'm formidable.

M.W. I think that your hallmark is that you have always disliked people who wanted approval. You like the heterodox.

R.W. I should like to be approved of. Oh, yes. I blench. I hate being disapproved of. I've had rather a lot of it.

M.W. And yet, in your writing, there is quite a strong strain of impatience with people who do things because society approves of it.

R.W. Oh, yes. I think I see what you mean. Oh, that's Scotch, I think, yes, Scotch, because . . . oh, yes, and it's also a bit of my mother and my father. My father was educated by Elisée and Eli Reclus, two famous French brothers, early geographers; my cracked grandmother, the religious maniac who refused the family fortune, had hired them because they were refugees in England; she thought that, as young Frenchmen in England, they must be Protestants who had escaped from the wicked Catholics' persecution. They were actually anarchists and they'd escaped, run away from France, because they'd seized the town hall – I can't remember which town it was – in the course of an *émeute* against Louis Napoleon. They were very sweet. They said, when they found out the mistake, 'Oh, well, we must be careful about teaching the children.' They taught them awfully well. My father was a very, very, well-educated man and so were all his brothers.

M.W. What did you read at home as a child? Who were the early formative influences?

R.W. Oh, pretty well everything. We read a terrific lot of Shakespeare, which my mother knew by heart and so did my father . . . and a lot of George Borrow. Funny thing to read, but . . . really early Victorian England was quite familiar to me because of that. Oh, lots . . . I can't think. My mother and my sister, Winifred, who was much the cleverest of us, she read frightfully good poetry. She taught me a lot of poetry, which I've all forgotten now but, you know, if I see the first line, I can go on.

M.W. Would you acknowledge Conrad or anyone else as an influence on you?

R.W. Well, I longed, when I was young, to write as well as Mark Twain. It's beautiful stuff and I always liked him. If I wanted to write anything that attacked anybody, I used to have a look at his attack on Christian Science, which is beautifully written. He was a man of very great shrewdness. The earliest article on the Nazis, on Nazism, a sort of first foretaste, a prophetic view of the war, was an article by Mark Twain in *Harper's* in, I should think, the Nineties. He went to listen to the parliament in Vienna and he describes an awful row and what the point of view of Luger, the Lord Mayor, was and the man called George Schwartz, I think, who started the first Nazi paper, and what it must all lead to. It's beautifully done. It's the very first notice that I've ever found of the Austrian Nazi Party, that started it all.

M.W. But do you feel, with your strong sense of justice and of pity, that our wars have remained as terrible, or do you feel that we have learned?

R.W. I don't know what *you've* learnt. I'll tell you I think the Second World War was much more comfortable because in the First World War women's position was so terrible, because there you were, not in danger. Men were going out and getting killed for you and you'd much prefer they weren't. My father was always very tender about armies, having been a soldier. The awful feeling for a small professional army was that they were recruited from poor people who went out and got killed. That was, do you know, very disagreeable. There was a genuine humanitarian feeling of guilt about that in the first war. It was very curious, you see. There I sat on my balcony in Leigh-on-Sea and heard guns going in France. It was a most peculiar war. It was really better, in the Second World War, when the people at home got bombed. I found it a relief. You were taking your chance and you might be killed and you weren't in that pampered sort of unnatural state. I find the whole idea of a professional army very disgusting still. Lacking a normal life they turn into scoundrels. As Wellington said, they're despised for being scoundrels and it's not their fault and they die like flies and have the worst discomforts.

M.W. And yet a conscripted army, as fought in Vietnam . . . you laugh?

R.W. Well, I can't help thinking that the whole of the Vietnam War was

269

the blackest comedy that ever was, because it showed the way you can't teach humanity anything. We'd all learnt in the rest of the world that you can't now go round and put out your hand and, across seas, exercise power; but the poor Americans had not learned that and they tried to do it. The remoteness of America from German attack had made them feel confident. They didn't really believe that anything could reach out and kill them. Americans are quite unconscious now that we look on them as just as much beaten as we are. They're quite unconscious of that. They always have talked of Vietnam as if by getting out they were surrendering the prospect of victory, as if they were being noble by renouncing the possibility of victory. But they couldn't have had a victory. They couldn't possibly have won.

M.W. Did you want to write about trials?

R.W. Not at all. I had done it once or twice, when I was very hard up, when I was young, just to get some money, and so I learnt how to do them, and then I used to sit and listen to William Joyce [Lord Haw-Haw, hanged in 1945] when he was broadcasting. Then I arranged to go to his trial because I was interested in him. A man called Theo Matthew, who was Director of Public Prosecutions, though not a prosecuting sort of person, said: 'I wish you'd report a lot of these trials because otherwise they will go unnoticed because there is so little newsprint.' He said: 'Really, if you will consider it as war work, it would be extremely valuable.' So I did that for one book (*The Meaning of Treason*, 1947) and then I did it for another (*A Train of Powder*, 1955). Most of the people in Intelligence didn't agree with my views. I don't know whether it had any effect on them at all. Someone asked me recently how did I think Intelligence had found out John Vassall? [British spy, jailed in 1963]. It seemed to me such a silly question. He had it tattooed on his forehead. I never know how people don't find out spies.

M.W. Are you interested in espionage still?

R.W. I won't say I'm interested in spies but they do turn up in my life in quite funny ways. There was a man called Sidney Reilly, who was a famous spy, a double agent. My mother-in-law was very upset because my husband married me instead of the daughter of a civil servant. My husband's mother thought she was a nice Catholic girl, who'd be so nice for my husband, and it always tickled me because it gradually emerged that this girl was the mistress of this *very* famous and very disreputable spy. It was a wonderful thing to have in your pocket

270

against your mother-in-law. My mother-in-law was an enormous huge woman, and extremely pathetic.

M.W. What can you remember as being a moment of great happiness?

R.W. Extremely few. I had a very unhappy time with H. G. Wells, because I was a victim of a sort of sadist situation. Partly people disapproved of H. G. so much less than they did of me, and they were very horrible to me, and it was very hard. It was particularly hard later, people being horrid to me because I was living with H. G., when I was trying as hard as I could to leave him. It was really absurd and now I think it's rather funny, but it wasn't funny at the time. Then I had a short time of happiness on my own and a time of happiness with my marriage [she married Henry Andrews in 1930], but then my husband got ill, very ill. He had meningitis, this thing that's always struck at people near me, when he was young and then he got cerebral arteriosclerosis, and after years it came down on him. He was in a very unhappy state of illness for a good many years before he died, but we had a great many good years together. I was very happy.

M.W. Have any of the men you've known helped you?

R.W. The men near you always hinder you because they always want you to do the traditional female things and they take a lot of time. My mother helped me to work because she always talked to me as if I were grown-up.

M.W. Are there any advantages at all in being a woman and a writer?

R.W. None, whatsoever. You could have a good time as a woman, but you'd have a much better time as a man. If in the course of some process, people turn up a card with a man's name on it and then a card with a woman's, they feel much softer towards the man, even though he might be a convicted criminal. They'd treat the man's card with greater tenderness.

M.W. You don't think there's been an improvement?

R.W. Not very much.

M.W. *The Birds Fall Down* and *Return of the Soldier* have both been adapted for stage/film. Have you ever written for the stage yourself?

R.W. I've had so little time to write. Also theatrical people can't be bothered with me. I wrote a play in the Twenties which I think had lovely stuff in it, *Goodbye Nicholas*, and fourteen copies were lost by managers – fourteen, that's really true – and I just gave up. One of them, who lost three, was a man called Barry Jackson, who was at the

Birmingham Repertory Theatre; after we'd had terrific apologies and that kind of thing, about a year later he met me in the bar of some theatre and said, 'Rebecca, why have you never written a play?' They are like that.

I would like to write old-fashioned plays like de Musset's. I think they're lovely. I think de Musset's essay on Rachel and Malibran is one of the lovelist things in the world. It's lovely about acting and romanticism. It's beautifully written and it's quite wonderful.

M.W. You said once that all your intelligence is in your hands.

R.W. Yes, a lot, I think. Isn't yours? My memory is certainly in my hands. I can remember things only if I have a pencil and I can write with it and I can play with it.

M.W. You use a pencil, do you, when you write?

R.W. When anything important has to be written, yes. I think your hand concentrates for you. I don't know why it should be so.

M.W. You never typed?

R.W. I did, but not now. I can't see in front and behind a typewriter now with cataract-operated eyes. If you have the spectacles for the front thing, you can't see the back, and I can't do with bifocals. I just get like a distracted hen. I can't do it. Hens must wear bifocals, if one looks closely. It explains it all. It's so difficult dealing with ribbons too. I can only write by hand now. I used to do a rough draft longhand and then another on the typewriter. I'm a very quick typist. When I had mumps I was shut up in a bedroom, because both my sisters had to sit examinations. When I came out, I could type.

M.W. Do you do many drafts?

R.W. I fiddle away a lot at them. Particularly if it's a fairly elaborate thing. I've never been able to do just one draft. That seems a wonderful thing. Do you know anyone who can?

M.W. I think D. H. Lawrence did.

R.W. You could often tell.

M.W. How many hours a day do you write?

R.W. I don't manage much. When I write uninterrupted, I *can* write all day, straight through.

M.W. Did you find any of your books especially easy to write?

R.W. No. It's a nauseous process. They're none of them easy.

M.W. Have you ever abandoned a book before it was finished?

R.W. I've abandoned work because I've not had time. I've had a worrisome family thinking up monkey tricks to prevent me finishing books, and I had a terrible time when I was young and in the country, because I had no money, and no reference books, and I couldn't get up to London and to the London Library where I had a subscription.

M.W. There is a great diversity in your work. Did you find it difficult to combine criticism and journalism and history and fiction?

R.W. I did really. My life has been dictated to and broken up by forces beyond my control. I couldn't control the two wars! The second war had a lot of personal consequences for me, both before and after. But I had enough money at that time, because I had a large herd of cows and a milk contract. I had to take some part in looking after the cows, but the dear things worked for me industriously. At one time I had to write articles because I had to put up a lot of money for family reasons. Everyone has to pay for their families every now and then.

M.W. Who are the writers you admire?

R.W. I'm a heretic about Tolstoy. I really don't see *War and Peace* as a great novel because it seems constantly to be trying to prove that nobody who was in the war knew what was going on. Well, I don't know whoever thought they would . . . that if you put somebody down in the wildest sort of mess they understand what's happening. The point's very much better done, I think, by Joseph de Maistre. He wrote a very interesting essay in the late 18th century, saying how more and more people would not be able to know what was happening to them in wartime because it was all too complicated. Not E. M. Forster though the Indian one [*A Passage to India*] is very funny because it's all about people making a fuss about nothing, which isn't really enough . . . T. S. Eliot was a poseur. Somerset Maugham couldn't write for toffee, bless his heart.

M.W. I believe you admire A. L. Barker.

R.W. Enormously, but I'm the only person who does, so far as I can make out. I think she's the best novelist now writing. She really tells you what people do, the extraordinary things that people think, how extraordinary circumstances are, and how unexpected the effect of various incidents. Oh, she's almost better than anybody, I think. She's much better than Iris Murdoch, I think. But then Iris Murdoch I like enormously except when she begins to clown and be funny, because I don't think she ever is very funny.

M.W. How do you feel about Doris Lessing?

273

R.W. I wish I knew her. I think she's a marvellous writer. There's a peculiar book about European refugees in Africa, but it fascinates. It's beautifully done, the play side of philosophy. They were talking about all their ideas and it was as if the children were trying to go into a shop and buy things not with coins but with butterscotch or toffee apples. It's very curious. Yes, she's the only person who absolutely gets the mood of today right, I think. An absolutely wonderful writer.

M.W. English writing hasn't really produced the kind of giants it produced in the Twenties. The stagnation of English writing since then is extraordinary. Joyce, Virginia Woolf, Wells, Shaw: all these people were writing, and who have we got to compare now?

R.W. I find Tom Stoppard just as amusing as I ever found Shaw. Very amusing, both as a playwright and as himself. But I'm not now an admirer of Shaw. It was a poor mind, I think. I liked his wife so much better . . .

M.W. Did you meet Yeats?

R.W. Yes. He wasn't a bit impressive and he wasn't my sort of person at all. He boomed at you like a foghorn. What he liked was solemnity and, if you were big enough, heavy enough and strong enough, he loved you. He loved great big women. He would have been mad about Vanessa Redgrave.

M.W. Is your Irish birth important to you?

R.W. Frightfully, yes. I loved my family. I have a great affiliation to relations of mine called Denny. The present man is an architect, Sir Anthony Denny. He's exactly like Holbein's drawing of his ancestor, Anthony Denny, which I think is a great testimonial. Anthony Denny lives up in the Cotswolds and he and his wife are most glamorous people in a very quiet way. They have two charming sons, one of them paints very well, and they adopted a child, a Vietnamese child. Tony went out to see his brother, who had fever there and he was walking along a quay and one of the refugee babies, who was sitting about, suddenly ran up to him and clasped him round the knees and looked up in his face. So he just said: I'll have this one – and took him home. It was the most lovely reason. The Dennys did nice things like that. And then my father used to speak about this cousin in Ireland, in the west of Ireland, called Dickie Shoot. Dickie Shoot beggared himself by helping people.

M.W. Do you think it has become easier for women to follow their vocations?

R.W. I don't know. It's very hard. I've always found I've had too many family duties to enable me to write enough. I would have written much better and I would have written much more. Oh, men, whatever they may say, don't really have any barrier between them and their craft, and certainly I had.

Rebecca West died in 1984.

*M*ARINA WARNER *was born in London in 1946 and educated in Cairo, Brussels, at an English convent and Oxford, where she read French and Italian.* She is the author of Alone of All Her Sex: The Myth and Cult of the Virgin Mary (*Weidenfeld 1976*), Joan of Arc: The Image of Female Heroism (*Weidenfeld 1981*) *and* Monuments and Maidens (*Weidenfeld 1985*). *She has also published two novels, short stories and criticism.*